Mental Health in a Multi-E

This new edition of *Mental Health in a Multi-Ethnic Society* is an authoritative, comprehensive guide on issues around race, culture and mental health service provision. It has been updated to reflect the changes in the UK over the last ten years and features entirely new chapters by over twenty authors, expanding the range of topics by including issues of particular concern for women, family therapy, and mental health of refugees and asylum seekers.

Divided into four parts the book covers:

- Issues around mental health service provision for black and minority ethnic (BME) communities including refugees and asylum seekers.
- Critical accounts of how these issues may be confronted, with examples of projects that attempt to do just that.
- Programmes and innovative services that appear to meet some of the needs of BME communities.
- A critical but constructive account of lessons to be drawn from earlier sections and discussion of the way ahead.

With chapters on training, service user involvement, policy development and service provision, *Mental Health in a Multi-Ethnic Society* will appeal to academics, professionals, trainers and managers, as well as providing up-to-date information for a general readership.

Suman Fernando has been a consultant psychiatrist and an academic in the mental health field for over twenty-five years. He is Honorary Senior Lecturer at the European Centre for the Study of

Migration & Social Care and honorary Professor in the Department of Applied Social Sciences at London Metropolitan University.

Frank Keating is Senior Lecturer in Health and Social Care at Royal Holloway University of London where he is Programme Director for the MSc in Social Work. His main research focuses on the inequalities in mental health for African and Caribbean communities in the UK.

Mental Health in a Multi-Ethnic Society

A Multidisciplinary Handbook
Second Edition

Edited by Suman Fernando
and Frank Keating

Routledge
Taylor & Francis Group

LONDON AND NEW YORK

First published 2009 by Routledge
27 Church Road, Hove, East Sussex BN3 2FA

Simultaneously published in the USA and Canada
by Routledge
270 Madison Avenue, New York, NY 10016

Routledge is an imprint of the Taylor & Francis Group, an Informa business

Typeset in Times by Garfield Morgan, Swansea, West Glamorgan
Printed and bound in Great Britain by TJ International Ltd, Padstow,
Cornwall
Paperback cover design by Design Deluxe, Bath

British Library Cataloguing in Publication Data
A catalogue record for this book is available from the British Library

Library of Congress Cataloging-in-Publication Data
Mental health in a multi-ethnic society : a multidisciplinary handbook /
edited by Suman Fernando & Frank Keating. – 2nd ed.
    p. ; cm.
 Includes bibliographical references and index.
 ISBN 978-0-415-41486-9 (hardback) – ISBN 978-0-415-41487-6 (pbk.)
 1. Minorities–Mental health services–Great Britain. 2. Social
psychiatry–Great Britain. 3. Community mental health services–Great
Britain. I. Fernando, Suman. II. Keating, Frank.
 [DNLM: 1. Mental Disorders–ethnology–Great Britain. 2. Community
Mental Health Services–Great Britain. 3. Community Psychiatry–Great
Britain. 4. Ethnic Groups–Great Britain. WM 140 M54893 2008]
 RC451.5.A2M465 2008
 362.2089–dc22
                                                         2007049882

ISBN 978-0-415-41486-9 (hbk)
ISBN 978-0-415-41487-6 (pbk)

To all those who strive for equality and justice in mental health services

Contents

List of illustrations

Figures

Boxes

Notes on contributors

Tanzeem Ahmed has worked in the voluntary sector for twenty years, holding several posts around policy and research, and campaigning for recognition of mental health issues in Asian communities in UK. She is Director of Olmec, which is a charity focusing on community empowerment.

Aileen Alleyne is a psychodynamic psychotherapist and author of several book chapters and articles exploring themes on black/ white dynamics, shame and black identity wounding. She works as a clinical supervisor and researcher in private practice, and is a visiting lecturer at several training institutes.

Shun Au has been active in mental health service development in the voluntary and statutory sectors for nearly twenty years. He is Founding Chairman of the Chinese Mental Health Association, UK, and is a non-executive director of Hillingdon Primary Care NHS Trust.

Qadir Bakhsh was formerly head of the Race Equality Unit in the London Borough of Waltham Forest and has published on social and public policy areas regarding equality and diversity issues. He is an adviser to the Qalb Centre.

Joanna Bennett has been involved in mental health education, training and research for over eighteen years. She is Visiting Professor in the School of Health and Social Sciences at Middlesex University and has held two Visiting Professorships at the University of the West Indies, Jamaica. Until recently, she was Senior Research Fellow at the Sainsbury Centre for Mental Health/Kings College London.

Angela Burnett has been involved for many years in training and advising on health services for refugees and torture survivors. She is a general practitioner at the Sanctuary Practice and at the Medical Foundation for the Care of Victims of Torture.

Yasmin Choudhry has been active in the voluntary sector for many years, initiating and developing various programmes involving service users, their families, and the Asian community at large. She is Director of the Qalb Centre and manages several projects within Qalb.

Jagroop Kaur Dhillon has a background in sociology and psychology. She works for Olmec (a charity focusing on community empowerment) in the capacity of Projects Manager, her main responsibilities being around education and employability.

Raina Fateh trained as a medical doctor in Bangladesh and obtained a masters degree in Family Therapy from the University of East London and the Tavistock Centre. She is employed as a senior systemic psychotherapist at the Marlborough Cultural Therapy Centre.

Suman Fernando (editor) was a consultant psychiatrist for many years before becoming an academic. Also, he was a member of the Mental Health Act Commission where he chaired its National Standing Committee on Race and Culture. He is Honorary Senior Lecturer at the European Centre for the Study of Migration and Social Care (MASC) at the University of Kent at Canterbury and Visiting Professor in the Department of Applied Social Studies at London Metropolitan University.

Peter Ferns has a particular interest in mental health, learning disabilities, advocacy, equality issues, social work education and service quality issues. He works as an independent training consultant, based on a wide experience of working in social services, health, probation services and voluntary sector organisations.

Sandra Griffiths has worked at management and consultancy levels in mental health services for over twelve years. Currently she is employed by East London and City Mental Health Trust as the Service Development Manager for the Mellow programme.

Rakhee Haque is currently completing a PhD in psychology, researching self-harm in Bangladeshi young women. She is employed as a systemic psychotherapist at the Marlborough Cultural Therapy Centre.

Chinyere Inyama has been involved for many years in representing people appealing against 'sectioning' under the Mental Health Act. He is an assessor of the Law Society Mental Health Review Tribunal Panel of specialist mental health lawyers. He sits as a President of the Mental Health Review Tribunal and also as Deputy Coroner for Essex and Thurrock.

Yasmin Jennings has a background in history and social policy. In the past, she has worked at Olmec (a charity focusing on community empowerment), where she led programmes around equalities, diversity and education.

Robert Jones has two decades of experience in the field of race and mental health, as someone who has had direct experience of the mental health system, as a human rights activist and campaigner, as a trainer and as a freelance consultant. Currently, he is Head of Equality and Diversity at East London and City Mental Health Trust.

Jayasree Kalathil has worked as a researcher and activist in mental health both in India and in the UK. Until recently she was working on the Race Equality Education and Training Project at the Sainsbury Centre for Mental Health, London.

Alpa Kapasi has worked within the field of equalities and anti-discrimination at a strategic level for over nineteen years and was a Race Equality Lead in the London area until recently. She works as an independent management consultant.

Frank Keating (editor) comes from a background of social work and social studies. He was involved in a major review of mental health services for African and Caribbean communities called *Breaking the Circles of Fear*. Formerly Lecturer in Mental Health at the Tizard Centre, University of Kent at Canterbury, he is Senior Lecturer in Health and Social Care and Programme Director of the MSc in Social Work in the Department of Health and Social Care at Royal Holloway University of London.

Nutan Kotecha has been involved in legal and family law and worked at an Asian women's refuge for four years. Later, she co-ordinated the service user-led monitoring network at the Sainsbury Centre for Mental Health, London. Currently, she works as an independent consultant.

Rabia Malik was until recently Senior Lecturer in Psychosocial Studies at the University of East London. Currently she is Cultural Services Co-coordinator and a senior systemic psychotherapist at the Marlborough Cultural Therapy Centre.

Nimisha Patel is a clinical psychologist. She is Head of Clinical Psychology at the Medical Foundation for the Care of Victims of Torture, and Senior Lecturer on the Doctoral Degree Programme for Clinical Psychology at the University of East London.

Jeanette Stanley has been involved with various community organisations for many years. She is founder member of the Women's Action Forum and a Justice of the Peace. She is Director of the African and Caribbean Mental Health Service.

Rebecca Tang has been involved in community research and is completing a doctorate study in health psychology. She works as service development manager at the Chinese Mental Health Association.

Premila Trivedi is an Asian long-term user of mental health services. She was a founder member of the Black user group SIMBA at the Maudsley Hospital. She works part-time as a service user trainer in the training department of a large mental health trust in London.

Acknowledgements

The book as a whole owes much to many mental health service users, professionals and workers in the voluntary sector for formal and informal discussions with the editors over the past ten years. Chapter 4 is based on a paper published in a review of London's mental health and we are grateful to the King's Fund for permission to use it. Dawn Edge, Research Fellow at the University of Manchester, kindly provided helpful comments on early drafts of this chapter. The authors of Chapter 5 are grateful to the Sainsbury Centre for Mental Health for allowing them to use material from research carried out while employed at the centre. The authors of Chapter 13 thank Ann Miller Inga Britt Krause and Eia Asen at the Marlborough Family Service, Karina Hedley and Peter Carter at Central and North West London Mental Health Trust, and their colleagues, Cecilia Ko, Marigold Lee, Manu Rehman, Nuran Islam, Shaheena Khan, Farra Khan and Houssam Ebrahim with whom they shared the journey in establishing the Marlborough Cultural Therapy Centre. The authors of Chapter 14 wish to acknowledge the help of Leon Lee, Chief Executive Officer of the Chinese Mental Health Association (CMHA), and the staff of CMHA for help in preparing the chapter. Hartley Hanley, Chair of the Windrush Millennium Centre, and Dawn Bryan, Senior Administrator, African and Caribbean Mental Health Services, helped with Chapter 16.

Introduction

British society has moved on in many ways since the first edition of this book appeared in 1995. Basic issues in the mental health field for black and minority ethnic (BME) communities – essentially inequalities where BME communities are at a disadvantage – have not really changed very much fundamentally and in the experience of people who use services or are forced to do so. But the context in which these issues may be considered is different in many ways. For one thing, detailed information about BME communities is now available; but, more importantly, the politics of 'race' and the ways in which racism is expressed in society are now different compared to the situation in 1995. In the mental health field itself, the issues affecting BME communities may not have changed that much, but there are many more professionals from BME communities working in the mental health services; consequently, the approaches to redressing inequalities have become more complicated.

Data

In both 1991 and 2001 census respondents were asked to select (from a list) the ethnic group they considered themselves to belong to. In 2001 the list of options was increased: in particular, they could tick the box marked 'Mixed' for the first time, specifying the type of mixture – 'White and Black Caribbean', 'White and Black African', 'White and Asian' or 'any other mixed background'. However, it should be noted that the question under the heading 'What is your ethnic group?' asked about *cultural background* not 'race', although it is generally assumed that people who describe themselves as 'mixed' in the census registration fall into the category of 'mixed-race'. The confusion between what is 'culture' and what is 'race' is a consistent problem in many settings and one discussed early on (Chapter 1) in this book.

The census (2001a) shows the size of the BME population as 4.6 million, or 7.9 per cent of the total population of the United Kingdom (UK). In Great Britain (England, Wales and Scotland) this represented a rise of 53 per cent compared to the figures in the 1991 census (when ethnic data were not collected in Northern Ireland). Half of the 4.6 million identified themselves as Asians of Indian, Pakistani, Bangladeshi or other Asian origin; a quarter identified themselves as Black, that is Black Caribbean, Black African or Other Black; and 15 per cent identified themselves as 'Mixed' – a third of this group identified themselves as being from White and Black Caribbean backgrounds. A survey in the late 1990s for the Policy Studies Institute (PSI) (Berthoud and Beishon, 1997) had found that half of black British-born Caribbean men and one-third of women who were married or cohabiting had white partners; for Indians and Asian people from Africa ('African-Asian' according to PSI nomenclature) 19 per cent of British-born men and 10 per cent of women had white partners. So it is not surprising that the mixed-race group is estimated as growing at a rate of 4.9 per cent a year and likely to become the largest BME group by 2020 (Grimston, 2007).

Although the census figures are important, it is not clear to what extent they present a full picture of Britain's BME population. The census is unlikely to have included several groups of recent immigrants who fall within the category 'BME', namely (a) refugees and asylum seekers or people who have migrated to live in Britain but have not registered under these categories; (b) people who have overstayed their visas and/or feel uncertain of their (legal) right to be in the UK; and (c) women who have been trafficked into the country for the sex trade – essentially sex-slaves (Skrivánková, 2006). All these people live in unsettled ways, often 'illegally' as far as the State is concerned (in the case of sex-slaves under the control of criminal gangs), and are unlikely to show up in population statistics. It is worth noting that these are the very BME people who face extreme hardship, exclusion and often high levels of hostility to their presence in the country from the so-called 'host community' (that includes settled BME communities). Also it is worth noting that these newcomers, compared to BME people who form settled communities, have diverse and complex problems, such as poor command of English, insecurity of status, overt exploitation in the UK and a history of persecution abroad.

Socio-political context

In the 1980s and into the 1990s 'race and culture' issues in the mental health field were reported in ways that gave an impression – though seldom voiced – that racism might be involved. The discourse then shifted in the mid- and late-1990s into one of 'diversity', implying a 'cultural' emphasis. But this was rudely interrupted when the report on the inquiry by Macpherson into police inaction following a racist murder in London (Home Department, 1999) highlighted institutional racism in all public bodies. But since the riots in Bradford in the summer of 2001 (see Editorial, 2001; Independent Review Team, 2001) and the destruction of the twin towers in New York that autumn, the discourse has again shifted away from 'race' (and the need to address racism) to 'diversity' as the reason why BME communities 'lack confidence in mental health services' (Department of Health, 1999a: 17), while in society at large the focus is now on promoting 'community cohesion' rather than counteracting discrimination – and the pressure is on BME communities to be good (sic) citizens (Cantle, 2005). So, understanding their cultures, enabling people in these communities to become good citizens, enhancing their capacities to help themselves and so on are seen as the way forward. And the definition of who is required to change – who is seen as the 'other', the outsider – has shifted to some extent from people identified purely on racial grounds of skin colour, to individuals and groups seen as alien because of their religion (or what people think is their religion), particularly Muslims, although here too physical appearance is taken as the mark of their 'religion'.

An important point to note is that the changes described above in the position of BME communities and the identification of the 'other' have occurred in a context where civil liberties are being systematically eroded (Kennedy, 2004; H. Porter, 2007) – so much so that an eminent lawyer writes: 'We are seeing a serious retreat from civil liberties, mimicking what is taking place in the United States' (Kennedy, 2004: 184). This tendency is seen in the attitude of government to mental health legislation too. In spite of being opposed by every professional group involved in mental health, including the Royal College of Psychiatrists *and* Mind (the

National Association for Mental Health, which speaks for service users), the government has brought in mental health legislation which widens the scope of 'sectioning' (compulsory detention) – something that will undoubtedly exacerbate the inequalities currently experienced by BME service users.

Mental health field

The statutory system for delivering services has changed over the past fifteen years; many large mental hospitals have closed and a variety of community services, early intervention teams and crisis teams have developed in many areas. At a basic theoretical level, thinking around meanings of terms like 'culture' and 'multiculturalism' has developed during the past ten years. This is sometimes reflected in training of mental health professionals – or should be. The training of psychiatrists may not have changed very much over the past ten years in spite of psychiatrists from BME communities being a little more prominent in administrative posts; training still remains strongly linked to narrow medical approaches to (mental) health and 'illness'. However, training of other professionals in the mental health field, such as social workers and psychologists, is now very different from that fifteen years ago, especially in relation to addressing issues of 'race' and culture. In the 1990s there were relatively few projects in the voluntary sector that could be seen as focusing on mental health of BME communities; today there are many more. Indeed the projects described in the 1995 edition of this book have mostly disappeared, for a variety of reasons, and this edition describes new ones.

Compared to 1995, there is an obvious change in the ethnic structure of the workforce in mental health and indeed in health services generally. For whatever reasons, today people from BME communities are a much more visible presence as professionals in mental health services than they were in the early 1990s. More generally too in the political arena, black visibility is evident – mainly because the Labour government (which came into power in 1997) has appointed BME peers to the Upper House. BME people, admittedly more often of Asian or African origin rather than black Caribbean origin, are a common sight as consultant psychiatrists – and some have risen to the top of their profession. Both versions of a government plan to change the nature of mental health care, generally called *Delivering Race Equality* or DRE (Department of

Health, 2003, 2005b), were fronted by BME people, although not necessarily carrying the confidence of BME communities. But in spite of the high BME visibility in mental health services and BME people seemingly having power and influence, *the mental health system continues to be experienced as racist by BME service users.* This apparent paradox resembles a situation commented upon by some of the leaders of the 1960s Black Power movement in the US.

In a 1992 re-issue of the book *Black Power* (Ture and Hamilton, 1992), originally published in 1967 (Carmichael and Hamilton, 1967), Stokely Carmichael – now calling himself Kwame Ture – adds an afterword on what lessons can be learned from the struggles of the 1960s: the US is a different place today compared to 1967. There are black mayors with power but they seem unwilling and/or unable to use their power to improve conditions of the masses. There is a desegregated education system but more blacks in prison than there are in high school. Blacks are visible but seem powerless – at least in the sense that Black Power envisaged. Ture sees this 'powerless visibility' (1992: 190) as neocolonialism – the modern form of colonialism where western domination is effected through trade laws, military interventions (to install 'democracy'), targeted aid, targeted assassinations and so on. In another afterword to the book, Charles Hamilton contends that getting black people into high office was a strategy adopted by 1960s Black Power (although never its main aim), but because of this the movement was 'vulnerable to abuse by those in its own ranks' (Ture and Hamilton, 1992: 214). Using the black ticket to get into office became the end rather than the means. The mistake was to allow black power to be equated with black visibility by enabling black people to seize 'the opportunity to advance themselves solely on the basis of race' (Ture and Hamilton, 1992: 212). And so sometimes black people in high places have become a barrier to moving forward – just as having local natives running the British Empire was a barrier to independence. Another way of looking at it is that visibility has become a tokenism that blocks real change, and impedes the struggle against racism.

The US civil rights struggle and its aftermath may not be exactly replicated in the British race scene in mental health but there are some similarities and so some lessons to be drawn. The struggle to get justice for BME service users may not always be promoted by merely getting BME people into positions of power. Perhaps getting statutory systems to change, getting justice for BME service users, is more about changing systems than about changing people who run services, especially if they are trained to do so in a traditional style. Therefore what may be crucial is for the BME service user voice to be empowered. In fact, the voice of service users from BME communities is at last making an impact at least within BME communities if not on the Department of Health and government circles. The space we have given to the BME service user voice in this book is a minor indication of this.

The book

This second edition of *Mental Health in a Multi-Ethnic Society*, compared to the first, covers a wider range of topics: by focusing on problems of particular concern for women and on family approaches in therapy; by addressing the important field of mental health of refugees and asylum seekers; through entirely new chapters in the field of training; and by including two chapters that provide a direct voice for BME service users. Although this second edition is a complete revision of the first, it remains essentially a *Multidisciplinary Handbook* geared to address the training needs of mental health professionals while providing up-to-date information about the BME mental health scene for a general readership.

The title of the book refers to a 'multi-ethnic' society, a term which encompasses both 'race' and 'culture'. Each contributor to the book has tried to steer a way through somewhat variable understandings of these concepts and of the idea of ethnicity. As a result, some use a capital 'B' or 'W' in designating people's race based on skin colour, while others do not do so. Also contributors may differ in their perceptions of what services are meant to do. Hence, some may refer to 'clients' while others refer to 'users' of services, and seldom if ever to 'patients'. The editors have not attempted to introduce uniformity in use of terms across the chapters but have tried to ensure that the use of words is consistent within each chapter.

This book is structured in four parts: Part 1 ('Current scene') presents the situation in mental health as it affects BME communities from a variety of viewpoints. Part 2 ('Confronting issues') covers some ways in which there have been attempts to make changes so that services serve BME communities as well as others sensitively and equitably. Part 3 ('Making it happen') provides descriptions of service models that appear to be successful in both satisfying current needs of BME communities and being sustainable in the socio-political context of modern British society. The chapters here are written by those who actually run the services concerned. Part 4 ('Lessons for the future') consists of just one chapter written by the editors after reading the initial eighteen chapters.

Part 1 ('Current scene') begins with a chapter by Suman Fernando entitled 'Meaning and realities'. Here he discusses the terminology with respect to race, culture and ethnicity, making reference to the changing face of racism where 'cultural difference' or religious affiliation may be a signifier of the racial 'other'. He then goes on to consider concepts of mental health in the context of human beings trying to understand the nature of the human condition; and to discuss the meanings attached to therapy as a concern of service provision.

The legal framework underpinning mental health work in relation to race and culture is presented in Chapter 2 by Chinyere Inyama, a solicitor who has worked closely with BME clients caught up in the mental health system. This chapter presents the legal background in which issues around 'racial equality' in mental health service provision may be considered – legislation on human rights and race relations in particular. The prolonged process undertaken by the government to bring about changes in mental health legislation is discussed. And the complicated issues around the failure by the government to carry out a proper evaluation of the impact of these changes on 'race equality' are presented.

In Chapter 3, Suman Fernando covers briefly the historical background of psychiatry *vis-à-vis* 'race' and culture, and then goes on to describe and discuss issues around inequalities, discriminatory practices and social exclusion that affect black people in a variety of systems – education, criminal justice and mental health. This chapter shows how complicated the politics of race and mental health have become now that there are many people from BME communities in positions of visibility at management levels sometimes with authority and even possible power – if only they are able/willing to use it.

Chapter 4 is about the position of BME women in the mental health scene. It is based on a report originally compiled by Nutan Kotecha for the King's Fund Centre, but expanded and updated. This chapter points out how gender blindness and negative views of minority cultures are contributing to BME women's mental health needs being severely neglected across the spectrum of research, policy development, service provision and practice. It provides powerful arguments for insisting that more attention be given to BME women's issues both in research and in service provision.

Time and time again in government reports we get the statement that proper training is important – but that begs the question as to what is 'proper'. In Chapter 5, Joanna Bennett, Jayasree Kalathil and Frank Keating provide a historical overview of race equality training (RET) in the UK, drawing from a scoping exercise to map RET in the UK carried out while the authors were working at the Sainsbury Centre for Mental Health in London.

Part 2 ('Confronting issues') begins with Chapter 6 in which Alpa Kapasi, who until recently was in a leadership position within the government's DRE plan (see above), shares her ideas on how management and policy-making can, if properly thought through, bring about changes in statutory mental health services – something that recent government plans have achieved. Chapter 7, written by a team led by Tanzeem Ahmed, who has been in the forefront of the BME voluntary sector for many years, highlights the important contribution of BME voluntary sector agencies in responding to the mental health needs of these communities. More importantly, it illustrates how the voluntary sector can lead innovation and work creatively to improve mental health and emotional well-being. In Chapter 8, Peter Ferns, a leading trainer and producer of literature on training in the field of mental health, describes the challenges in devising and implementing training for professionals in the BME mental health field – something he has done many times, most recently in a major project within DRE. Nimisha Patel has been working with refugees and asylum seekers for many years. In Chapter 9 she provides an overview of the challenges that psychology services and professionals generally in the mental health services face when called on to address the varied needs of these groups of people in the UK. She shows how a compartmentalised approach, where health, social care and political issues are considered separately, does a grave disservice to them.

Premila Trivedi has been voicing the views of service users for many years and more recently has been actively involved in practical projects in alliance with professionals and managers of mental health services. Therefore, she is in a unique position to analyse the challenges that service users face when they try to bring about changes in services, known as 'service user involvement'. In Chapter

10, she shows how rhetoric seldom represents what actually happens on the ground and presents suggestions for ways in which issues around service user involvement may be tackled. Changing attitudes among professionals is an important aspect of this and in Chapter 11 Sandra Griffiths writes about the work of Mellow, a project within the National Health Service to promote mental health in African and Caribbean men by engaging with mental health practitioners in a dialogue aimed at changing their attitudes about racism, culture and mental health.

Part 3 ('Making it happen') is about successful interventions and innovations. Aileen Alleyne has been engaged in studying particular aspects of racism for a PhD thesis and in Chapter 12 she brings to us some unique insights on how 'hidden' racism is tackled in one-to-one work in a psychotherapeutic context. Rabia Malik and others from the Marlborough Cultural Therapy Centre describe in Chapter 13 how they have established a family therapy service designated specifically for BME communities. In Chapter 14, Shun Au and Rebecca Tang describe the provision of mental health services specifically geared to the needs of the Chinese community in the UK. Chapter 15 by Yasmin Choudhry and Qadir Bakhsh is about the Qalb Centre – a place where Asian people with mental health problems get services that they value. Jeanette Stanley in Chapter 16 traces the development of a service for African and Caribbean people in Manchester which has clearly established itself as a model for others to follow. Another unique service of a very different kind is described in Chapter 17 by Angela Burnett, a general practitioner: this is a primary health care practice with a holistic approach set up to meet the diverse needs of refugees and asylum seekers. In Chapter 18, Robert Jones shows that the model of a successful service led by black service users is very different from the sort of 'user involvement' that many mental health trusts claim to have within their purview.

Part 4 ('Lessons for the future') is composed of one chapter, Chapter 19, entitled 'The way ahead'. Here Suman Fernando and Frank Keating, the editors, try to capture the most salient points made in the book and try to look ahead to see the directions which service provision may take. This is not a blueprint for the future nor is it a definitive statement of what should or should not happen. The authors of this chapter are only too aware that service provision must be seen in the social and political context of British society and they try to envisage what this context will look like *vis-à-vis* Britain's BME communities and the effects of this on mental health service provision. They try to analyse the reasons why changes in statutory services have been so difficult to achieve, and suggest some ways of getting over some of the barriers to change. Finally they draw the book together with conclusions on how we should approach the future.

Part 1

Current scene

Mental health is something we all aspire to, and the provision of services for people with mental health problems is undoubtedly an obligation of society. The preferred style in most of the industrially developed world is for care to be provided in the community on an informal (voluntary) basis, although hospital care including locked units, where people's ordinary human rights are curtailed, is all too common. In such a situation, society is beset by problems of equity and fairness, especially evident with respect to issues around cultural diversity and 'race'.

This part of the book sets the stage for the rest of the book. It provides a background to mental health service provision as it affects black and minority ethnic communities in British society by examining the socio-political-legal context in which services are provided, culturally determined differences in the understanding of health and illness, the nature of the inequalities that are all too evident, the special position of women and the history of training to bring about race equality.

Chapter 1

Meanings and realities

Suman Fernando

The discourse within mental health circles in Britain has changed considerably over the past fifteen years; 'health' is talked about instead of 'illness' and even 'symptoms', 'service users' instead of 'patients' and 'interventions' instead of 'treatment'. Currently there is talk about 'spirituality' in mental health care (e.g. Cornah, 2006; Sperry, 2001; Swinton, 2001) and 'recovery' in place of 'care' (see Department of Health, 2001; Lester and Gask, 2006; Pitt *et al.*, 2007). That is the talk. Yet in practice, mental health services in the statutory sector (within the National Health Service) are dominated by the traditional bio-medical approach characteristic of western psychiatry, whether in community care settings, outpatient clinics or inpatient units. Admittedly, though, this may not be the case in a few instances and in services in the voluntary sector, i.e. non-governmental organisations.

In this chapter I shall explore first the use of some terms within the race and culture discourse, such as 'race', racism, culture and ethnicity. Next I will discuss the diverse ways in which the concept 'mental health' is understood, and then go on to explore what mental health care is all about – or should be.

Terminology of 'race' and culture

The classification of human beings into 'races' based on certain visible physical characteristics, particularly skin colour, has a long history in Western Europe (see Dobzhansky, 1971; Molnar, 1983). Today the idea of a 'racial type' and 'race' (based on physical appearance) is no longer useful in human biology (J.S. Jones, 1981) and has been largely discredited – as discussed by me elsewhere as 'myths and realities of race' (Fernando, 2002: 19–25). Yet, 'race' as a social reality persists mainly because of racism – a doctrine or dogma based on a belief in 'race' that fashions or determines behaviour, ways of thinking, assumptions we make and so on (see Banton and Harwood, 1975; Husband, 1982). For practical purposes racism should be distinguished from race prejudice – a feeling or attitude of mind, expressed as 'an antipathy based upon a faulty and inflexible generalisation' (Allport, 1954: 9). As Wellman (1977) argues in *Portraits of White Racism*, once race prejudice is embedded within the structures of society, individual prejudice is no longer the problem – 'prejudiced people are not the only racists' (1977: 1). The notion of 'institutional racism' first appeared in a book on 'Black Power' by Stokely Carmichael and Charles Hamilton (1967). The Macpherson Report (Home Department, 1999), dealing with the failure of the London (Metropolitan) police to properly investigate a racist murder, opts for the following definition:

> The collective failure of an organisation to provide an appropriate and professional service to people because of their colour, culture or ethnic origin. It can be seen or detected in processes, attitudes and behaviour that amount to discrimination through unwitting prejudice, ignorance, thoughtlessness and racist stereotyping that disadvantages minority ethnic people.
>
> (1999: 28)

Many of the racist stereotypes of black people originate in the era of colonialism and slavery. Their history and power in European culture have been tabulated and illustrated by Gilman (1985) and Pieterse (1992). The strength of stereotypes in a racist discourse was enunciated in Frantz Fanon's *Black Skin, White Masks* (Fanon, 1952) and Edward Said's *Orientalism* (Said, 1978). And, as Jean-Paul Sartre (1948) said of Jews in the past, black people often believe the stereotypes that others have of them – or, at least, behave as if they do, thereby sometimes helping to maintain their own oppression. However, it should be noted that racist images can change from time to time and from place to place, reflecting the changing face of racism. And instead of racism being openly applied in racial language it may be applied in cultural language or the language of religion. Thus, instead of stating – or implying – that 'other races' are inferior, possess some unsavoury characteristic or pose a threat to social cohesion, the reference is to 'other' cultures, religions, ethnic groups or kinds of people, thought of in the same way as 'races', that is groups that are unchanging and easily recognisable usually by physical appearance. Racism against Jews, namely anti-Semitism, is in fact hostility towards (what is perceived as) a racial group although defined in terms of religion; religious practice and belief do not come into it. More recently, especially since the attack on New York in September 2001, Islam (a religion) has been used to signify the racial 'other' in a similar way, with victimisation being justified on the grounds of preventing 'terrorism'. This type of racism has been termed 'Islamophobia' (Casciani, 2004; Halliday, 1999; Seabrook, 2004). This shift is seen in the statistics for 'stop and search' by British police under the Terrorism Act (2000). It is well known that BME groups are much more likely than other groups to be subject to this police activity (see Chapter 3). The rate of being subject to stop and search for black (African and Caribbean) people increased by 30 per cent between 2001 and 2002, but the increase for (brown-skinned) Asian people was even higher at 41 per cent (R. Cowan, 2004; Metropolitan Police Authority, 2004). The ethnic disproportionality figures for stop and search in London between April and August 2007 were 2.1 for Asian:White and 1.6 for Black:White (Metropolitan Police Authority, 2007).

Mixed race

The historical issue of 'race mixing' has been a prominent part of the discourse of European racism. The idea that such 'mixing' would be a threat to the integrity of the 'white race' and lead to loss of white supremacy led to pejorative terms such as 'miscegenation' and theories of maladjustment and marginality of people who did not 'belong' to one 'race' or another (Furedi, 2001). The place of 'mixed race' as an ethnic identity is difficult to unravel but potentially important. The statistics on 'mixed race' derived from the census (2001b), based on a question about 'culture' (an example of the confusion between culture and 'race' noted below), were discussed in the Introduction (see pp. 1–2). Although the concept of 'mixed race' has been criticised because its use reifies 'race' (Parker and Song, 2001) – in other words, we are all racially 'mixed' in a biological sense – as a social category, 'mixed race' seems here to stay (Smith, 2007). How it pans out depends very much on how society itself deals with ideas about 'race', nation and culture in the future. Research among British children by Suki Ali (2003) shows that the understanding of 'race', racism, culture and ethnicity in terms of how children build their identities may be complex and flexible. In her studies of children with multi-ethnic parentage in London and Kent:

> Children of both black and white mothers, in all locations and across classes, identified themselves as 'mixed-race'. Children of both black and white mothers also identified as black. None of the children from Malaysian, Polynesian, Chinese or Turkish backgrounds identified *solely* with that part of their heritage. . . . What seems to be most important is the way in which parents (mothers) communicate with children about their identities. In this process, location and parental history, and parental connections to 'diaspora' or an imagined 'home', play a crucial part for the negotiation of ethnic identification.
>
> (Ali, 2003: 174, italics in original)

Culture and ethnicity

Traditionally (for example in anthropological literature) 'culture' refers to non-material aspects of everything that a person holds in common with other individuals forming a social group (such as child-rearing habits, family systems, and ethical values or attitudes common to a group), described by Leighton and Hughes as 'shared patterns of belief, feeling and adaptation which people carry in their minds' (1961: 447) – and in general pass on from generation to generation. But in today's world, culture has a much looser meaning, as expounded in the book *The Location of Culture* by Homi Bhabha (1994).

In general, culture refers to 'conceptual structures' – a flexible system of values and worldviews that people live by, define their identities by and negotiate their lives by (Fernando, 2002) – a sort of road-map for living, relating to one another and so on. In a more practical sense, cultures are 'systems of knowledge and practice that provide individuals with conceptual tools for self-understanding and rhetorical possibilities for self-preservation and social positioning' (Kirmayer, 2006: 163). In other words, 'culture' is located in – emanates from – real lives of real people; it comes out of the struggles and connections with one another, the wishes and dreams of ordinary people against a background of heritage, what we inherit culturally, a sort of cultural DNA. So naturally there is a variety of experiences with greater or lesser degrees of similarity across cultures. And, no culture is static. 'Cultural groups' can be recognised by the degree to which individuals are similar, but we have to be careful not to stereotype.

In practice we tend to regard a variety of items as indicative of a person's culture – markers of culture, although these too are variable. They include main language or mother tongue, religious affiliation (or nominal religion), background in terms of heritage, values, loyalties, certain practices (say about food), dress codes, kinship tics, 'cultural' habits such as marriage preferences, world-views and so on.

Ethnicity is a subjective impression of how people see themselves. It is an ambiguous term in that one's ethnicity may be different according to context and change from time to time. In practical shorthand, the term 'ethnic' is taken to mean (at least in the UK) a mixture of cultural background and racial designation as experienced by a person, a family or group of people – the significance of each (i.e. 'culture' and 'race') being variable, depending on context. If racism is felt strongly, people from various backgrounds and cultures may see themselves largely in racial terms (e.g. as 'black people') but also (or alternatively) identify themselves in 'cultural' terms of history, religion or parental birthplace (e.g. as 'Muslims' or 'Caribbean' or 'Asian'). The current tendency in the UK is to refer to 'black and minority ethnic communities' or BME communities, leaving open the issue of what exactly an ethnic community comprises. But this means that recent immigrants, especially refugees and asylum seekers, often get left out of the BME category and may be called 'migrants' (as different from BME) – a category of exclusion in many parts of Europe.

Multicultural/multi-ethnic society

In the sense of the meaning of 'culture' that I have outlined, a multicultural society is one where there is a plurality of cultural forms and influences – a diversity of cultures. A multi-ethnic society is then a multicultural society that includes people seen as belonging to several 'races'. In the UK, we have developed a form of 'multiculturalism' which goes back to 1966 when the then Home Secretary, Roy Jenkins, voiced the overall aim of social policy to promote integration of immigrants from non-western cultural backgrounds as 'equal opportunity accompanied by cultural diversity in an atmosphere of mutual tolerance' (Poulter, 1990: 2).

The idea being put about recently in Britain is that multiculturalism has led to 'self-segregation' and to an 'isolationism', especially among Muslims; the head of the Commission for Racial Equality, Trevor Phillips, has talked about 'sleepwalking our way to segregation' (Leppard, 2006: 2). However, research does not bear this out: Ludi Simpson (2004) found evidence in Britain of *increasing* dispersal of ethnic minority groups, even in Bradford, where the so-called 'riots' of 2001 were blamed on segregation of Muslim communities (see Independent Review Team, 2001), in spite of real barriers resulting from racism and activities of the extreme right, reviewed at the time in an eminent British newspaper (*Observer*, Editorial, 2001).

One reason, apart from obvious political agendas of right-wing groups, for this attack on British multiculturalism stems from the conflation of (or confusion between) 'race' and 'culture', coupled with the use of the ambiguous term ethnicity. National statistics about ethnic groups are interpreted both as differences in 'culture' *and* differences in 'race' – you take your pick. Racists (whether consciously so or not) have a field day, and others get drawn in, perhaps in the way Amartya Sen (2006) records in his recent book *Identity and Violence*. When people are identified in 'ethnic' terms (both 'cultural' and 'racial'), we tend to impose 'culture' on people because of the way they look ('racially') instead of allowing people to find their own position in the stream of changing and varied cultural forms. Then, people resent this feeling of being assigned to having just one overarching 'culture' (one's ethnic group), essentially *given* this because of the way one looks (racially). 'Multiculturalism' gets blamed instead of the real culprit, racism expressed through cultural language.

Another problem that arises when 'culture' and 'race' are conflated is that 'culture', and hence multiculturalism, is seen as concerning non-white people alone. So, cultural diversity remains a minority issue and multicultural society a place where minority (i.e. 'Black and Asian') issues are given primacy. To complicate this discourse, racism undermines multiculturalism by introducing the idea (not necessarily expressed openly) that cultures are on a hierarchy of sophistication, some being less 'developed' than others, and so feeding on the negative aspects of discourse in the international scene where 'under-developed' or 'developing' countries (and their 'cultures') are seen as 'primitive' and needing to be changed for the better. So, effective multiculturalism must have an anti-racist dimension or else there would not be equity within the (multicultural) society. But a multicultural society must include the opportunity for white people to belong, to have a 'culture' or, more correctly, several 'cultures'.

Conclusions

The concepts 'race', culture and ethnicity tend to get mixed up in our discourse and in our thinking, but they have different emphases. Although race is a scientific myth, it persists as a social entity for historical, social and psychological reasons – in fact for all the reasons that result in racism. And skin colour remains the most popular basis for distinguishing one race from another in a British – possibly West European – context. When a group of people are perceived as belonging to a racial group, the assumption is of a common ancestry with implication of biological similarity. So when a society is referred to as being 'multiracial', that means it contains people whose ancestries vary; but, more importantly, that these ancestries are related to their heritage, their biological make-up – their 'blood'.

What is mental health?

Mental health is a nebulous concept at the best of times. In a broad sense it is 'a rubric, a label which covers different perspectives and concerns such as the absence of incapacitating symptoms, integration of psychological functioning, effective conduct of personal and social life, feelings of ethical and spiritual well-being, and so on' (Kakar, 1984: 3). How this concept is best interpreted in the provision of mental health services in a multicultural context is complicated. Clearly we need to look carefully at differences in the way mental health is seen in the diverse (cultural) traditions that comprise British society – in broad terms, Asian, African, Caribbean, and European. But there are important reservations to this approach. Similarities (between cultural traditions) should never be under-estimated and generalisations (about cultural traditions) have dangers: they may be taken up as stereotypes of people who are seen as 'belonging' to one or other cultural group because of the way they 'look'; or be used to reduce a specified culture to one or two

	Western tradition	Eastern tradition
Mind and body	Distinct entities	Indivisible whole
Analysis	Reductionist	Holistic
Tools for study	Objective	Subjective
Spirituality	Add-on	Integral

Figure 1.1 Culture and mind

basic tenets – in most instances misleading if not downright errone-
ous. Notwithstanding these problems, I do not see any other way of
exploring cultural diversity in this instance except by comparisons
between 'western' and 'eastern'. However, by doing so, I am not
implying that east and west are any more than traditions from the
past – current states of mind rather than geographical regions
(Kakar, 1984).

One way of simplifying a complex field is to see cultures (in
relation to mental health) as being on a sort of continuum but (for
ease of discussion) divided into 'eastern tradition' and 'western
tradition' (Figure 1.1). At one extreme (as represented in traditional western psychiatry and western psychology), what is seen as
'mind' and what is seen as 'body' are conceptualised in rather
concrete ways as entities, usually by reducing them to simpler
entities (the 'reductionist approach'), and examined objectively
with special tools (akin to medical tests); at the other extreme,
human life is conceptualised as an indivisible 'whole' that includes
not just 'mind' and 'body' as one but also the spiritual and other
dimensions of human life. I think the term 'spiritual' in this setting
refers to a sense of inter-connectedness between various aspects of
life and even entities not generally considered (in western thinking)
as being 'alive' (see Fernando, 2003).

The search for knowledge, the seeking after an understanding of
the human condition, the yearning for knowing the 'truth', all this
characterises human societies the world over. But ways in which
societies and individuals have gone about this search are diverse –
representing the diversity of 'cultures' themselves. Generally speaking, in non-western cultures knowledge about the human condition
does not naturally divide up into the fields of study (each divided
further) designated by 'psychology', 'religion', 'philosophy', etc., as
it does in western thinking. Rather this search is holistic. Studying
the 'minds' of human beings as separate from their bodies and

spirits (as western psychology does) and interpreting human problems concerning thinking, beliefs, emotions and feelings, etc. in 'illness' terms (as psychiatry does) may be very confusing to someone with a holistic worldview. Similarly a holistic approach may be confusing to people steeped in divided-up or 'reductionist' thinking.

In simple shorthand, eastern traditions see health as a harmonious balance between various forces in the person and the social context, while western traditions see health as an individualised sense of well-being. So, the Chinese way of thinking sees all illness as an imbalance of *yin* and *yang* (two complementary poles of life energy), to be corrected by attempts to re-establish 'balance' (Aakster, 1986); the Indian tradition emphasises the harmony between the person and their group as indicative of health (Kakar, 1984); and the concept of health in African culture is more social than biological (Lambo, 1969).

The dominant theme in western culture, reflected in psychiatry and western psychology, is that problems identified (by the person concerned or a 'specialist') as being concerned with thinking, emotional reaction, feelings, fears, anxieties, depressions, etc. are conceptualised in terms of illness, dealt with – 'treated' – with a variety of interventions aimed at 'cure' or alleviation of 'symptoms' (of illness). Even family problems and social behaviour (as in 'psychopathy') and hatred and jealousy (as in 'pathological jealousy') are sometimes fitted into the illness model. Clearly, this western way of conceptualising such a wide range of human problems is alien to Asian and African cultural worldviews, although admittedly some problems identified by specific bodily changes may be seen as illness, although even then 'illness' is conceptualised as disharmonies within a total (holistic) self. Figure 1.2 illustrates how, speaking very generally, balance and harmony, both within oneself and within the family or community, are important aspects of eastern thinking about mental health, while, in the west, self-sufficiency, efficiency and individual autonomy, with problems being located in specific places (in body or mind), are the overall model of life.

Anyone trained within western schools of thought (for example in the disciplines of psychiatry and western psychology) will naturally see self-sufficiency, personal autonomy, efficiency and self-esteem as the correct basis for discussions about mental health – and this applies to people from BME communities as much as 'white' people. In other words, there is an unwitting credence given to western ideas – this is institutional racism.

Eastern tradition	Western tradition
Integration and harmony	Self-sufficiency
between person and environment	
between families	
within societies	
in relation to spiritual values	
Social integration	Personal autonomy
Balanced functioning	Efficiency
Protection and caring	Self-esteem

Figure 1.2 Ideals of mental health

The importance of understanding the variety of 'ideals' (as above) for anyone involved in service provision centres on how this understanding can be applied in practice. In my view, the 'ideals' noted above are seldom if ever held by any one person or cultural group in an uncontaminated form. As with all cultural forms (see pp. 16–19) the concept of ideal 'mental health' is 'hybrid', or a mixture of elements from the (above) ideals. So, in practical terms, what is required is to make out what sort of mixture is the reality in the case of each person or group. This may be the primary expertise necessary for professional practice in a multicultural setting. Clearly, then, the aim of service provision is to provide means for this particular ideal to be realised.

Care and therapy – control or liberation?

Current mental health systems in the statutory sector are usually dominated by a model of identifying, at best, 'problems' or, at worst, pure 'illness' and then devising 'interventions' or 'therapies' aimed at alleviating (or resolving) problems or eradicating (at least some aspects of) illness. However, designating human problems in terms of 'illness' or people requiring 'help' has become very mixed up with social control of people (see Fernando, 2002). So the everyday work of psychiatrists, social workers and others in compulsory detention and forced medication is a natural part of our mental health system codified in the Mental Health Act.

Treatment, self-help and need

In the western tradition of providing treatment or care for people with mental health problems, the therapist learns the treatment and

Eastern tradition	Western tradition
Acceptance	Control
Body–mind–spirit unity	Body–mind separate
Contemplation	Problem solving
Harmony	Personal autonomy
Understanding by awareness	Understanding by analysis

Figure 1.3 Liberation/therapy East and West

applies it – and does so within the overall 'medical model' of dealing with problems as individual 'illness' or 'disorder'. In a cultural setting where such problems are seen as (say) spiritual experiences or ethical dilemmas, the process for dealing with them – or coping with the distress caused by them – is not 'therapy' in a western sense. It is more like liberation (from distress); techniques used for achieving this are interactive alliances between people and (perhaps) forces in nature, rather than interventions ('therapies') that are objectified and separable from the person or persons involved. In my view, current moves to emphasise 'recovery' rather than 'care' (Department of Health, 2001; Lester and Gask, 2006) merely reinforce the western ways of thinking – what does one recover from if not illness?

A transcultural approach to mental health work should try to balance concepts of liberation (from problems or suffering) and therapy (aimed at recovery or health). The latter (western) approach focuses on control (of, for example, symptoms) or understanding by analysis (in, for example, psychotherapy). In cultures which emphasise harmony, balance and integration within the individual (and between the individual and others), acceptance (of problems or 'symptoms') is more important than control, and understanding by contemplation or an interchange of feelings supersedes the need for intellectual analysis of feelings (Figure 1.3).

The degree to which a particular intervention is something done *for* someone else and the degree to which it enables a person to help themselves is never clear, but cultural differences may play a significant part in determining it. Indeed, cultural differences in the quality of interventions by professionals can be evaluated in terms of a therapy–self-help dimension, looked at from the service user's point of view. For example, if depression is seen as a spiritual matter to be handled with meditation or prayer, the 'remedy' is not so much 'therapy' as 'self-help'. If hallucinations are seen as a form of communication which is welcome to (or at least not resisted by) the person experiencing them, neither therapy nor self-help may be appropriate but perhaps the person concerned may need understanding and acceptance – a sort of therapy or self-help for society perhaps. To a person whose main reason for seeking help is to 'get rid of' some unwanted feeling such as early morning depressions, it is 'therapy' that is needed. And the therapy may be physical medicines or something called 'therapy' given by talking – psychotherapy or counselling (see below).

Another important dimension along which the concept of therapy differs cross-culturally is that of the 'magical' element in it – and indeed the degree to which 'magic' plays a part in the success of the therapy. To many clients, whether in western or other settings, therapies coming out of psychiatry and western psychology are often a magical process emanating from a near-mystical field called 'science' with its own special language and understanding of human beings. In some cultural settings, an intervention (such as fortune telling) for a mental health problem may be seen as a matter of evaluating interactions around and within persons involved – very matter-of-fact, not 'magical' at all (Pugh, 1983).

In the changing scene today, the move is towards organising services to meet the needs of those who use them. What is favoured is an epidemiological system of needs assessment (Stevens and Raftery, 1992), possibly because the sort of information (sic) required (e.g. rates of diagnosed 'illness') is easily available (though of doubtful validity since the meaning of 'illness' itself is debatable) and the process is likely to be backed by powerful forces allied to 'epidemiology'. This approach makes little or no allowance for the fact that the *ways* in which needs are being met are often inappropriate for many BME communities. Anecdotal reports of such an approach indicate that BME organisations are sometimes consulted but seldom influence the final decisions, for a variety of reasons, one being that 'epidemiological' findings are presented as 'scientific' facts, thereby undermining viewpoints that are negated as mere conjecture.

Western psychotherapy and counselling

'Talking therapies' today as practised and taught in the UK are firmly grounded in theories of mind, the psyche–soma split, and the ideology of identifying pathology and correcting it. When people from BME communities who are strongly embedded in their cultures of origin – i.e. non-western worldviews – 'receive' these therapies, many find it confusing and most find it problematic. Some therapists try to modify their approaches in ways that are meant to be 'culturally sensitive', and a vast literature has grown in both the US (e.g. Aponte *et al.*, 1995; Pedersen *et al.*, 1981; Roland, 1996) and the UK (e.g. Lago, 1996; Palmer, 2002) on how this 'cultural sensitivity' may be achieved. The most popular approach in Britain is called 'transcultural counselling' (d'Ardenne and Mahtani, 1999; Eleftheriadou, 1994). Essentially, what these approaches attempt to do is to enable therapists to recognise the limitations of traditional western psychotherapy, develop ways of working that try to take on board these limitations, and understand the cultural backgrounds of their clients in order to meet at least some of their culturally determined expectations. In this type of therapy provided as a part of a mental health service, more than in any other, the nature of the training undergone by the therapist and indeed many personal qualities of the therapist are both crucial aspects of the quality of the service itself. The dissatisfaction with traditional psychiatry that dominates the statutory mental health services sometimes leads people from BME communities to suppose that 'talking therapies' are the answer. Yet anecdotal evidence suggests that BME communities are on the whole disappointed with psychotherapy and counselling provided at generic centres, whether private, voluntary or statutory. However, I know from talking to people working at ethnic-specific counselling centres which aim to provide counselling for specific ethnic groups – nearly always in the voluntary sector and run by people from BME communities – that clients attending such centres often express a high degree of client satisfaction (see Fernando, 2005). Chapters in Part 3 of this book describe some of these centres.

Summary

Although the mental health discourse itself has changed over the past fifteen years, mental health systems in the statutory sector continue to be dominated by western psychology and psychiatry with a theory and practice based on an outdated scientific paradigm and ways of thinking derived from nineteenth- and early twentieth-century Europe. British society, like many other societies, is characterised by a diversity of cultural forms where influences from many cultural traditions come together. In such a multicultural setting, cultural forms overlap, undergo hybridity and seldom remain 'pure'. Therefore, the boundaries of cultural groups in such a multicultural society are never clear-cut and seldom static. Although the classification of the human being into different 'races' is no longer held to be scientifically or ethically valid, 'race-thinking' continues and racism is a social reality in most societies. In a British context, racism is expressed most frequently in a subtle form as institutional racism. The discourse on culture and 'race' that pervades discussion around issues in mental health is often confused by use of the term 'ethnicity', with its meaning drawn from both 'culture' and 'race'. The resulting inherent ambiguity of the concept of ethnicity contributes to a conflation of 'race' and 'culture' in current mental health discourse.

The concept of 'mental health' is culturally determined. But since cultures are not static, the resulting mixture of differences and similarities across cultural groups is complex. Issues reflecting injustices in the provision of mental health services have been known for many years and these are generally attributed to both cultural misunderstandings and racism. Attempts to address these at a national level are caught up in the intricacies of race politics, more recently involving BME people themselves. What goes for 'therapy', 'care' and a needs assessment model for delivering services must be understood in the context of power structures in society and the way 'mental health' is generally interpreted in the context of a (western) definition of illness. Unless these are addressed, injustices and inequalities will continue. There is no easy resolution. Fundamental changes in service provision in both style and content are necessary, but in the meantime professionals need to work closely with service users, their families and the wider community both to adapt current practices and to develop innovations. Since the statutory mental health services in the UK look to medication and other physical treatments for much of their therapeutic input, BME communities often look to 'talking therapies', psychotherapy and counselling, as a preferred option. There is little evidence that their needs are met as far as the statutory sector is concerned, but this does not seem to be so in the case of services provided by the voluntary sector, such as those described in Part 3 of this book.

Chapter 2

Race relations, mental health and human rights – the legal framework

Chinyere Inyama

This chapter aims to provide an outline of British race relations, mental health and human rights legislation – the framework within which mental health services are provided.

Race relations legislation

Prohibition of discrimination on any grounds, including racial grounds, has always been seen as vital to the protection of human rights. In this way protection from discrimination developed alongside the human rights movement. Article 14 of the European Convention on Human Rights and Fundamental Freedoms 1950 provides a broad protection from discrimination in the enjoyment of the other convention rights on any ground, including race, colour, language, religion, political or other opinion, national or social origin, association with a minority, property, birth or other status. The interface between race relations legislation and Article 14 will be covered later in this chapter.

During the early 1960s, racism and racial inequality were inescapable facts of life in the UK. Perhaps this was inevitable given the growth of chattel slavery and colonialism alongside European economic expansion. In any event, signs outside properties reading 'no dogs, no children, no coloured, no Irish' (Powncy, 2002: 4) and Enoch Powell's 'rivers of blood' speech (http://www.vdare.com/misc/powell_speech.htm) in 1968 are indicators of the state of race relations in the UK at that time.

The first attempt to improve race relations via statute was the Race Relations Act 1965. This Act related to discrimination in hotels, public houses, restaurants, theatres, public transport and any place maintained by a public authority. The Race Relations Act of 1968 built upon this and outlawed discrimination in other areas. The Race Relations Act of 1976 prohibited discrimination on the grounds of race in training and education, the provision of goods, facilities and services, housing, employment and other specified activities including public appointments made by ministers and government departments. This Act established the Commission for Racial Equality (CRE) and gave it a statutory duty to work towards the elimination of discrimination, to promote equality of opportunity and good relations between persons of different racial groups generally, and to keep under review the working of the 1976 Act. The 1976 Act also placed a statutory duty on local authorities and on specified local educational bodies to promote racial equality.

The Race Relations Acts of 1965, 1968 and 1976 helped to change behaviour and attitudes, especially in the field of employment. However, there was a limit as to how far the 1976 Act could apply to public authorities exercising their functions. The courts have developed a narrow interpretation, through case law, of which public functions were covered by the Act as goods, facilities and services. For example:

- It was decided that in respect of public authorities, the Act only applied where the act done was at least similar to an act that could be done by a private person (R v Entry Clearance Officer, Bombay, ex parte Amin [1983] 2 AC 818).
- It was decided that the Act did not extend to immigration control functions (Savjani v Inland Revenue Commissioners [1981] 1 QB 458 and R v Entry Clearance Officer, Bombay, ex parte Amin [1983] 2 AC 818).
- It was decided that whilst a police constable provides a service when giving directions to a member of the public, the same constable would not be providing a service when making an arrest, exercising stop and search policies or otherwise enforcing the law (Farah v Commissioner of Police for the Metropolis [1998] 2 QB 1965).
- It was decided that private organisations carrying out public functions, such as transporting prisoners or assisting in immigration control, were excluded from the scope of the Act.

There was a growing body of evidence to suggest that there were inequalities on racial grounds in the way in which public authorities developed and implemented policies and the means by which they provided their services to those from ethnic minorities. This was fully exposed by the Macpherson Inquiry into the racist murder of Stephen Lawrence in 1993 (Home Department, 1999). The Inquiry report defined institutional racism as:

> the collective failure of an organisation to provide an appropriate and professional service to people because of their colour, culture or ethnic origin. It can be seen or detected in processes, attitudes and behaviour which amount to discrimination through unwitting prejudice, ignorance, thoughtlessness and racist stereotyping which disadvantage ethnic minority people.
>
> (Home Department, 1999: 28)

And, significantly, the report found that 'institutional racism . . . exists both in the Metropolitan Police Service and in other Police Services and other institutions countrywide' (1999: 29). Meanwhile mental health services too have been accused of being institutionally racist – see, for example, the report into the death of 'Rocky' Bennett (Norfolk, Suffolk and Cambridgeshire Strategic Health Authority, 2003).

One of the important recommendations (number 11) in the Macpherson report was to adopt the suggestion by the CRE that 'the full force of the Race Relations legislation should apply to all police officers, and that Chief Officers of Police should be made vicariously liable for the actions and omissions of their officers relevant to that legislation' (1999: 328). The report made it clear that it did not believe that such problems of discrimination in services were confined to the police but that equality of access was an issue all public institutions needed to face: 'If racism is to be eliminated from our society there must be a co-ordinated effort to prevent its growth. This needs to go well beyond the Police Services' (1999: 324). The Home Secretary adopted recommendation number 11 in its entirety and extended the 1976 Race Relations Act to cover not only the police, but all public services such as the Civil Service, the Immigration Service and the National Health Service (NHS). Accordingly, the Race Relations (Amendment) Bill 2000 came into force on 2 April 2001. During the passage of the Bill through parliament, the Human Rights Act 1998 came into force on 2 October 2000, bringing the protection from racial discrimination in the enjoyment of convention rights in the European Convention of Human Rights 1950 (Article 14) into domestic law.

The Race Relations (Amendment) Act 2000 strengthens the 1976 Race Relations Act. It stresses the special responsibility of public bodies as employers, policy makers and service providers to deliver race equality. Section 1 of the 2000 Act inserts a new Section 19B into the 1976 Act, outlawing racial discrimination by all public authorities (as defined) in the exercise of their functions. All forms of racial discrimination (direct discrimination, indirect discrimination and victimisation) are included, and the existing protections against discrimination in the 1976 Act are unaffected. In addition, Section 1 of the 2000 Act inserts new Sections 19C and 19F into the 1976 Act. These new sections provide that judicial and legislative acts and decisions not to prosecute or to discontinue criminal proceedings are exceptions to the new Section 19B.

The definition of what amounts to a 'public authority' under both the Human Rights Act and the Race Relations (Amendment) Act 2000 is deliberately wide and includes anyone whose work involves functions of a public nature, including private sector organisations. The new Section 19B simply applies to 'any function' of the public authority. The CRE general guidance document *Strengthening the Race Relations Act* (Commission for Racial Equality, 2000) and the Home Office Consultation Paper *New Laws for a Successful Multi-Racial Britain* (Home Office, 2001: para 2.13) give examples of the sort of public functions which must be exercised without discrimination. Of note, these specifically include mental health authorities when making determinations such as those for compulsory detention under the Mental Health Act 1983.

The Race Relations (Amendment) Act 2000 recognises that racial discrimination can be either direct or indirect (although the Act does not use these terms itself). In simple terms, discrimination is said to be direct when it is overt, explicitly on grounds of race. Discrimination is indirect when it is hidden behind a more or less plausible façade; where the discrimination is ostensibly on other grounds but has the effect of discriminating on grounds of race. It is useful at this point to recall the definitions in the 1976 Race Relations Act. Section 1(1) (a) of that Act states that discrimination comprises two elements: (a) treatment which was less favourable than the treatment which was (or would have been) accorded to another person and, if so, (b) that the less favourable treatment was on racial grounds. Examples of the sorts of direct discrimination which would be unlawful by virtue of the new Section 19B of the Race Relations (Amendment) Act 2000 include:

- Treating racist assaults, racist harassment of local authority tenants or racist bullying in schools less seriously if the victim is black rather than white.
- Assuming that all black prisoners are aggressive and therefore subjecting them to harsher discipline than white prisoners (a parallel can be drawn here with the issue of race being used as an index of dangerousness within the mental health system with all its implications for treatment).
- Making poorer quality social services or special education needs provision for those from certain ethnic groups.

Indirect discrimination is not immediately apparent but results from the operation of apparently neutral actions or events, requirements or conditions, policies or procedures. It is caused by treatment which may be described as equal in a formal sense as between different racial groups but which is discriminatory in its effect on one particular racial group. There is ample evidence that the apparently neutral action of detaining people under the Mental Health Act 1983 has resulted in the gross over-representation of young black men, in particular, in the coercive end of the mental health system.

Race Relations (Amendment) Act 2000 and Human Rights Act 1998

In this part I shall deal with the interface between Section 19B of the Race Relations (Amendment) Act and the Human Rights Act. Article 14 of the European Convention on Human Rights provides that: 'the enjoyment of the rights and freedoms set forth in this convention shall be enjoyed without discrimination on any grounds such as sex, race, colour, language, religion, political or other opinion, national or social origin, association with a minority, property, birth or other status'. This Article is incorporated into UK domestic law as one of the convention rights in Schedule 1 to the Human Rights Act 1998 (which came into force on 2 October 2000). Prior to the enforcement of the Human Rights Act, domestic law was limited to protection from discrimination on grounds of sex, marital status, race and disability.

Article 14 obviously includes the Race Relations Act concept of racial grounds as a prohibited ground of discrimination, but has a broader application, for example, to groups only defined by their religion. As with the Race Relations Act, there must be a clear correlation between differential treatment and the characteristic identified. It should be noted that Article 14 does not prohibit all kinds of discrimination. European Convention case law recognises that differential action may be appropriate, but any distinction needs to be soundly and objectively based (Belgian Linguistics case [1968] 1 EHRR 252, para. 10). The aim and effects of any measure and the proportionality between the means employed and the aims sought to be realised will determine whether or not the differential treatment is justified. The burden of proof will be on the applicant (i.e. the person bringing a case before the court) to show the difference in treatment. The burden of proof then shifts to the state authority in question when it comes to justifying the differential treatment.

Article 14 does not provide a 'free-standing right' to protection from discrimination. When exercising the other convention rights the individual has the right not to be discriminated against on any of the grounds listed in the Article 14 text. In other words, the scope of the protection from discrimination in Article 14 is limited to the right embodied in the convention and its protocols. As such, it can only be involved in conjunction with one of the other convention rights. However, a breach of Article 14 can be found even where there is no violation of a substantive right (Belgian Linguistics case, as above). The question to be asked is does the action in question fall 'within the ambit' or 'subject matter' of another convention right? This is illustrated in the case of Abdulaziz, Cabales and Balkandali v UK (1985) 7 EHRR 471. The applicants were women who were lawfully settled in the UK but complaining that, unlike men who were so settled, their spouses were refused permission to join them in the UK. The court found that although there was no violation of Article 8 taken alone (the right to respect for his/her private and family life) there was a breach of Article 14 in conjunction with Article 8. The court took no issue with the restriction on the admission of non-national spouses to the UK in principle but agreed that it was unlawfully discriminatory to permit entry to the spouses of males but not of females.

This opens up the possibility of a complaint, taking Article 14 together with Article 5 (the right to liberty), that mental health detention in circumstances where evidence shows that someone of a different racial group would not have been so detained might be unlawful under both the new Section 19B Race Relations (Amendment) Act 2000 and the Human Rights Act.

Mental health legislation

In July 1998, Frank Dobson, the then Secretary of State for Health, announced that there would be a 'root and branch review' of the Mental Health Act 1983 (Department of Health, 1998). An expert committee was appointed with the task of recommending a legislative framework to reflect government policy but at the same time reviewing and identifying 'a legal basis to ensure individuals get supervised care if they fail to comply with their medication' (1998: 2). The Committee, chaired by Professor Genevré Richardson, received over 600 submissions from individuals and organisations and delivered its report in November 1999 (Department of Health, 1999c). It recommended (among other items) that a new Mental Health Act should be underpinned by a set of guiding principles, such as non-discrimination and patient autonomy, and a broad diagnostic criterion with 'express exclusions, coupled with rigorous entry criteria' for those who are liable to come under a compulsory framework (1999a: 2). But in that very same month, a Green Paper (Department of Health, 1999b), presented to parliament by the Secretary of State, focused on risk as the key factor on which compulsion should turn and in effect rejected nearly all the recommendations put forward by the Richardson Committee. This government document was not well received by practitioners; Professor Nigel Eastman, Consultant Forensic Psychiatrist and Professor of Law and Ethics in Psychiatry at St George's Hospital Medical School is quoted by Peay (2000) as stating that it 'took part of the skeleton of the Richardson Committee but abandoned its ethical heart' (2000: 8). An alliance of mental health organisations – the 'Mental Health Alliance' – came into being to voice opposition to the government stance.

In 2002, a consultation Bill was published as Draft Mental Health Bill 2002 (Department of Health, 2002a). The Department of Health (DH) received over 2,000 responses and, although none was published, it is widely thought that the vast majority were critical of the provisions in the draft consultation Bill. However, in 2004, a (new) Draft Mental Health Bill 2004 was published (Department of Health, 2004b). This was an appreciably thicker document than the consultation Bill of 2002 but with very few substantial changes to meet the critical responses to the draft consultation Bill. A cross-party pre-legislative scrutiny (PLS) committee set up to receive evidence on the Bill had over 450 written responses from individuals and organisations and fifteen live evidence sessions, mostly critical of its contents (Department of Health, 2004b). In making 107 recommendations for changes to the Bill, the PLS committee report in March 2005 (House of Lords, 2005) commented that the draft Bill was too focused on addressing public misconceptions about violence and mental illness and did not do enough to protect patients' rights. In particular, the PLS report asked for fundamental principles to be set on the face of the Bill, including the least restrictive alternative principle and that compulsory treatment should not be instituted unless capacity is impaired.

While rejecting or remaining silent on nearly all the PLS recommendations, the government response (Department of Health, 2005c) stated that they that were 'redrafting the bill to take account of changes to be made following consideration of the scrutiny Committee's report' (2005c: 6). In fact, the DH abandoned the idea of a new Mental Health Act and instead introduced a Mental Health Bill amending parts of the Mental Health Act 1983, namely:

1   Supervised treatment in the community.
2   Skill base of professionals.
3   Patient safeguards with regard to the Mental Health Review Tribunal.
4   A simplified definition of mental disorder.
5   Exclusion for drug and alcohol dependency and preserving the effects of the Act in relation to people with learning disabilities.
6   Availability of appropriate treatment.
7   Remedying ECHR incompatibility in relation to the Nearest Relative and bringing the Act in line with the Civil Partnership Act 2004.

(Department of Health, 2006a)

Two of the proposals at the centre of the change to the 1983 Mental Health Act were the replacement of 'treatability' and 'care' tests with an appropriate treatment test and the setting up of Community Treatment Orders (CTOs).

Treatability

The concept of treatability contained in Section 3(2) (b) of the 1983 Mental Health Act provides that persons suffering from psychopathic disorder or mental impairment may only be detained if the treatment proposed alleviates or prevents deterioration of their condition. This has become known as the 'treatability test'. Those who supported the government's position state that the treatability test has made it too hard to detain psychopaths in particular. But what is the actual situation? Medical treatment as defined under Section 145 of the current Act includes nursing, care, habilitation and rehabilitation under medical supervision. The DH proposes amendments to the definition of medical treatment in the Mental Health Bill 2006. Medical treatment will now include 'nursing, psychological intervention, and specialist mental health habilitation, rehabilitation and care'. A barely noticeable amendment! In any event, in R v Canons Park MHRT, ex parte [1994] it was stated that a patient could be detained if hospital treatment would prevent deterioration in his condition or make him less uncooperative or more insightful, or if detention was likely to impact on his symptoms even if it wouldn't touch the substantive illness. In Reid v Secretary of State for Scotland [1999] the House of Lords stated clearly that the definition of treatment was now so wide that its purpose may extend from 'cure to containment'. In R (Wheldon) v Rampton Hospital Authority [2001] the High Court stated clearly that the concept of treatability was a very wide one. It does not take much analysis to conclude that almost every patient will have symptoms of a condition that can be 'treated' by some form of clinical intervention even if it is just containment.

Community treatment orders

In the case of R v Hallstrom and another, ex parte W [1986] it was deemed to be unlawful to re-admit a patient into hospital from Section 17 leave and renew their detention before discharging them back into the community purely for the purposes of re-establishing the patient on medication. This was criticised by the court as being a 'long leash' approach which should be discouraged. How things have changed!

In R v Barking, Havering & Brentwood Community Healthcare NHS Trust ex parte B [1999], at the time when the consultant completed the form to renew detention under Section 20 the patient had been granted leave under Section 17 to be at home (as in the Hallstrom case) between Thursday and Monday inclusive, and leave to be away from the hospital during the other days. Four weeks after her detention was renewed she was granted leave seven days a week. The renewal was challenged on the basis that there was insufficient inpatient treatment to justify the test of Section 20(4) of the 1983 Act, i.e. that medical treatment in hospital cannot be provided unless the patient continues to be detained. The court determined that 'continues to be detained' should be construed to mean 'continues to be liable to be detained' and treatment as a whole – including returning from leave and being monitored for drug use – was sufficient to meet the test.

In R (DR) v Mersey Care NHS Trust [2002], DR was detained under Section 3 of the Mental Health Act 1983 having relapsed into a psychotic illness. She responded to treatment and was granted increasing amounts of leave. When application was made to renew her detention under Section 20 of the 1983 Act she was on permanent Section 17 leave of absence save for attending occupational therapy at the hospital during the day on Fridays and attending the ward round on Mondays for monitoring and review. She was given her medication at home. The court decided that the section could be lawfully renewed having heard evidence from the clinical team that DR would not take her medication except under section and would then deteriorate rapidly. The court further noted that the treatment could include leave of absence under Section 17.

In R (CS) v MHRT [2004], CS had a history of non-compliance with medication when discharged, leading to deterioration of her condition and re-admission into hospital. She was detained under Section 3 of the 1983 Act. At the time of her Tribunal hearing she was on leave at home and required to attend a ward round once every four weeks. She received her medication by injection in hospital because she did not wish to receive it at home. There was also a weekly session with the ward psychologist. The plan was to transfer her care to the assertive outreach team in the community. The Tribunal upheld the section on the basis that the history of non-compliance with medication and disengagement with services meant it was likely she would refuse medication and deteriorate rapidly if taken off section. Five weeks later her care was transferred to a community psychiatrist and then six weeks after that the section was lifted. At the point at which the patient was discharged from section she had spent approximately sixteen weeks entirely in the community under Section 17 leave with no plan for her to spend any time in hospital. The court decided that the element of 'treatment at hospital', though 'gossamer thin', was lawfully designed to break the historical cycle of relapse and re-admission.

It should be borne in mind that patients may have their Section 17 leave revoked and be recalled into hospital at any time by their responsible medical officer (RMO). There is no provision for there to be a reason for the revocation or recall; the RMO simply has to give notice in writing. The provision under the 1983 Mental Health Act (before the Bill to amend it) is remarkably similar to the proposed provision in the Mental Health Bill 2006.

Opposition to the Mental Health Bill 2006 (to amend the 1983 Act)

During consultations on how the 1983 Act should be amended, a network of BME organisations and individuals produced their own suggestions in official letters to the DH from the National BME Mental Health Network (BMENW). Corresponding to the seven parts designated by the government these were:

1   An amendment that makes it legally binding for the detaining authority to consult with such persons, community organisations and human rights bodies as have knowledge of the patient's social and cultural background.
2   Wherever the 'Approved Mental Health Professional' (AMHP) is mentioned in the course of amendments to the Act, there should be a clause stating that the person should have 'those skills that are appropriate for working in a multicultural society'.
3   An amendment to Schedule 2 of the 1983 Act should ensure that (a) the legal persons appointed by the Lord Chancellor should have experience in the race relations field; and (b) the non-legal, non-medical persons appointed by the Lord Chancellor should have experience in anti-discriminatory practice.

An amendment to Section 78 (Procedure of Tribunals) should state that the Tribunal, in arriving at their decision, takes account of cultural diversity and institutional racism.

An amendment to Section 72 (Power of Tribunal) should enable a Tribunal to direct the detaining authority to seek additional information on the cultural background of the patient.

4   An amendment to the Act should bring in a clause that states that the judgment of the presence of 'mental disorder' must take account of the patient's social and cultural background.

5   An amendment should ensure that (for the purpose of sectioning) mental disorder should not be construed by 'reason only of culturally appropriate beliefs and/or behaviours'.

6   An amendment should make it legally binding that any treatment that is imposed on a patient should take account of the patient's culture, gender, sexuality and social background.

7   An introduction to the Act should set out principles that define human rights and anti-discriminatory practice. The principles should be modelled on those within the Scottish Mental Health Act 2003, including adherence to equality and non-discrimination.

(National BME Mental Health Network, 2006)

It was pointed out to the DH by members of the BMENW that the so-called 'treatability' test had already, to all intents and purposes, been removed and CTOs were, to all intents and purposes, already *de facto* in existence even before the changes were proposed (see above). The view was expressed very forcibly to the DH (and later to members of parliament) that widening the definition of mental disorder and shifting the emphasis for determining its presence onto *judgements* of a person's risk of being a danger to others would result in people from BME communities being at an even greater risk of being detained unjustly than they are already. And the BMENW attempted to ensure that a proper Race Equality Impact Assessment (REIA) was carried out on the Bill before it was presented to parliament (see below).

Race Equality Impact Assessment (REIA)

The DH, being under a legal obligation to assess the race equality impact of the proposed legislation in accordance with the Race

Relations (Amendment) Act 2000, did so in a desultory and negligent fashion in the case of the Mental Health Bill 2006. The CRE guidelines on how this should be done – followed by the Home Office when drafting the Identity Cards Bill 2004, Charities Bill 2004 and the Immigration, Asylum and Nationality Bill 2005 – were not adhered to by the DH, much to the consternation of the BME mental health community. The first REIA in relation to the 2004 Mental Health Bill (which was withdrawn by the government – see above) was criticised by the Department's own Advisory Group and questions about its process were asked in parliament. The REIA on the Bill amending the Mental Health Act 1983, presented as the Mental Health Bill 2006 (Department of Health, 2004b), drew criticism from some members of the reincarnated REIA Advisory Group (with a new chair) as not representing honestly the advice they gave (personal communication, April 2007). The CRE had previously pledged to look at this REIA with a 'critical eye' once it had been completed. And in June 2007 while the Bill was being debated in parliament a letter from the CRE to the (then) Minister for Health Rosie Winterton stated that the DH had failed in its duty to assess the Mental Health Bill's impact on BME communities (Samuel, 2007). Yet, the DH did not deviate from its stance in supporting the main thrust of the Mental Health Bill, virtually ignoring the views of the CRE on its failure to carry out a legal duty with respect to the Bill. The BMENW called on the CRE to seek a judicial review of the Act passed on the basis of the Bill, namely the Mental Health Act 2007 (Chapter 12), but without any effect.

All the proposals (outlined above) from the BMENW were supported by the Alliance and were the basis of intensive lobbying by the BMENW, whose members met ministers and had extensive discussions with civil servants from the DH. However the government rejected all of these suggestions and the 'Mental Health Bill 2006' (Department of Health, 2006b) was introduced in parliament on 16 November 2006 in a form that was likely to exacerbate rather than reduce inequalities suffered by BME communities. The Bill presented by government also proposed amending the Mental Capacity Act 2005 in response to the 2004 European Court of Justice judgement, HL v UK (the 'Bournewood Judgment'). In spite of opposition in the House of Lords, and lobbying of members of parliament by many groups including the Alliance and the BMENW, the government Bill with relatively minor changes was passed in the Commons and received Royal Assent on 19 July 2007 as the Mental Health Act 2007 (Chapter 12). One of the main changes was a right to advocacy for all patients liable to be detained, including under guardianship or a CTO. Even this limited right to advocacy applies only *after* someone has been compulsorily detained ('sectioned') under the Mental Health Act and so is unlikely to make a great difference to the plight of black people facing 'sectioning'.

Implications for the black and minority ethnic (BME) communities

The 'Count Me In' census (Healthcare Commission, 2005) of inpatients carried out on 31 March 2005 revealed that Black African and Caribbean people are 44 per cent more likely to be detained under the Mental Health Act 1983. Once in hospital they are 50 per cent more likely to be secluded and more likely to receive higher dosages of medication. These 'racial inequalities' have been recognised for many years (see Chapter 1). The concern from a BME community perspective is that this rare opportunity to redress some of these inequalities has not been grasped by government. Fundamental principles on the face of the Bill as originally suggested by the government's own special committee could make a big difference, as they would undoubtedly include principles of anti-discrimination, equality and respect for diversity, as well as promotion of social inclusion, whenever discharging duties under the Mental Health Act. This would fit in well with the concept of joined-up legislation bearing in mind the provision of the Race Relations (Amendment) Act 2000 and the Human Rights Act 1998.

Conclusions

The legal framework for providing mental health care, in particular the provision of safeguards against deprivation of liberty in a context of 'mental health', is an important issue for all communities – but more so for BME communities because of the disadvantages they suffer in the mental health system. Further, in a multi-ethnic society, justice for all sections of society is an important part of establishing good race relations. This chapter reviews the main legislation that affects mental health care in relation to race relations and human rights. The government announced its intention to reform mental health legislation in September 1998. Since then, there has been a Green Paper, a White Paper, a draft Bill (with-drawn before being presented to parliament) and finally a Bill to amend the Mental Health Act 1983. This Bill went through parliament with minor amendments to receive Royal Assent in July 2007 as the Mental Health Act 2007 (Chapter 12). This Act does nothing at all to help redress racial inequalities. The government appears to have lost an opportunity to re-draft legislation in such a way as to reduce those inequalities and limit the impact of case law. It is a major concern of BME communities that the inequalities in mental health care provision that have resulted from the 1983 Mental Health Act and developed case law are very likely to continue.

Chapter 3

Inequalities and the politics of 'race' in mental health

Suman Fernando

While all health services have a political dimension, service provision for 'mental health' is more political than any other field of health care. It is very much about rights and justice, about alienation and inclusion, about power and privilege *vis-à-vis* professionals and service users, black and white, male and female, etc. When it comes to 'race', it is about white supremacy and black powerlessness in terms of what is seen as right and wrong, primitive and advanced, acceptable and 'alien' and so on. Although within an ostensibly 'medical' framework, mental health systems are more political than medical (see Barker and Stevenson, 2000; Castel, 1988; Ingleby, 2004; Miller and Rose, 1986). Further, the politics of mental health is inevitably located in the general politics of the wider world. The struggle for equity for black and minority ethnic (BME) communities in mental health service provision is a struggle for their human rights, the right to expect public systems to be equal in spite of (cultural) difference, and the right to freedom from racism. Therefore, race-based inequalities and culture-based discrepancies in mental health must be seen in context, both of the historical background of social systems, psychiatry and western psychology and of concomitant problems in other systems in society, such as criminal justice and education. This is the remit of this chapter.

The history of racism in psychiatry (see Fernando, 1988, 2003; Thomas and Sillen, 1972) and the nature of inequalities suffered by BME communities in mental health care today have been considered in detail elsewhere (see Bhui, 2002; Department of Health and Home Office, 1994; Fernando, 2002, 2003; National Institute for Mental Health in England, 2003). So this chapter will start by presenting these two topics very briefly before going on to give an overview of issues in British criminal justice and educational systems that seem to resonate with what is happening in the mental health system – at least in terms of statistics – and then to discuss recent attempts to bring about change at a national level and activities of the BME voluntary sector.

History of psychiatry and racism

The serious study of human behaviour which led to modern-day psychiatry emerged, together with (western) psychology, in the late sixteenth century in Western Europe; and almost at the same time, crude notions of white racial superiority were becoming embedded in the culture of that region, resulting in a variety of myths, stereotypes and superstitions about black people and about cultures seen as 'non-European', 'Oriental', or 'African' (see Bernal, 1987; Eze, 1997; Fernando, 1988; Said, 1978). The close association of the emergence of psychiatry and racism is illustrated in Figure 3.1.

Although the medical interest in matters to do with the 'mind' and medical control of people designated as 'mad' goes back in European history to the early seventeenth century, it was not until the nineteenth century that some sort of medical order in terms of (medical) causes for insanity and later specific diagnoses of mental illness emerged (Porter, 1990). Two main concepts prevalent in nineteenth-century Europe influenced thinking about (mental) illness – both imbued with ideas about racial difference: first, the concept of 'degeneration' proposed by Morel (1852) as a basis for understanding poverty, lunacy and racial inferiority – a concept in which 'race' was deeply implicated (Pick, 1989) and incidentally fed into the construction of schizophrenia as a primarily inherited condition signifying racial degeneration (see Fernando *et al.*, 1998); second, the idea of the 'born criminal' derived from criminology, bound up with concepts of backwardness and the 'primitive' (as seen through white European eyes) (Lombroso, 1871, 1911). But there was a wider socio-political context that also influenced thinking within the two disciplines. Although Charles Darwin (1871) in *The Descent of Man* argued against human 'races' being distinct species, the application of his theory of evolution to theories of social change led to eugenics (with its overt racism) and Social Darwinism (based on the idea of 'survival of the fittest' – a phrase coined by Herbert Spencer) (see Howitt and Owusu-Bempah, 1994). The idea (emanating from Social Darwinism) that different races

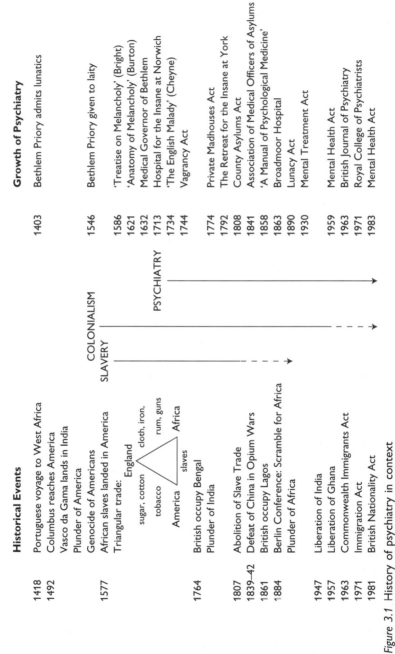

Historical Events

1418	Portuguese voyage to West Africa
1492	Columbus reaches America
	Vasco da Gama lands in India
	Plunder of America
	Genocide of Americans
1577	African slaves landed in America
	Triangular trade:
	England
	cloth, iron,
	sugar, cotton rum, guns
	tobacco Africa
	America slaves
1764	British occupy Bengal
	Plunder of India
1807	Abolition of Slave Trade
1839–42	Defeat of China in Opium Wars
1861	British occupy Lagos
1884	Berlin Conference: Scramble for Africa
	Plunder of Africa
1947	Liberation of India
1957	Liberation of Ghana
1963	Commonwealth Immigrants Act
1971	Immigration Act
1981	British Nationality Act

SLAVERY

COLONIALISM

PSYCHIATRY

Growth of Psychiatry

1403	Bethlem Priory admits lunatics
1546	Bethlem Priory given to laity
1586	'Treatise on Melancholy' (Bright)
1621	'Anatomy of Melancholy' (Burton)
1632	Medical Governor of Bethlem
1713	Hospital for the Insane at Norwich
1734	'The English Malady' (Cheyne)
1744	Vagrancy Act
1774	Private Madhouses Act
1792	The Retreat for the Insane at York
1808	County Asylums Act
1841	Association of Medical Officers of Asylums
1858	'A Manual of Psychological Medicine'
1863	Broadmoor Hospital
1890	Lunacy Act
1930	Mental Treatment Act
1959	Mental Health Act
1963	British Journal of Psychiatry
1971	Royal College of Psychiatrists
1983	Mental Health Act

Figure 3.1 History of psychiatry in context
Source: S. Fernando (1989) *Race and Culture in Psychiatry*, London: Routledge, p. 35

were on a hierarchy of development – socially, culturally and in every other way – became embedded in the theories and practices of both western psychology and psychiatry – something that emerges in modern times (see references below for theories of emotional differentiation and intelligence). I shall illustrate the representation of race in the history of psychiatry by picking out a few examples.

In the nineteenth century, psychiatrists in the US argued for the retention of slavery, quoting statistics allegedly showing that mental illness was more often reported among freed slaves compared to those who were still in slavery (Thomas and Sillen, 1972). And around then, the now infamous mental illness drapetomania was constructed – an illness diagnosed among black slaves which (according to Cartwright, 1851) manifests itself by 'this troublesome practice that many negroes have of running away' (1851: 319). When John Langdon Down (1866) surveyed so-called 'idiots' and 'imbeciles' resident in institutions around London, he identified them as 'racial throwbacks' to Ethiopian, Malay and Mongolian racial types – mostly, he said, they were 'typical Mongols' (1866: 16).

Early in the twentieth century, a standard text on adolescence by Stanley Hall (1904), founder of the *American Journal of Psychology* and first president of the American Psychological Association (Thomas and Sillen, 1972: 7), described Asians, Chinese, Africans and Indigenous Americans as psychologically 'adolescent races' (1904: 648). Throughout most of the twentieth century, the apparent rarity of depression among Africans and African-Americans was attributed to their 'irresponsible' nature (Green, 1914: 703), 'absence of a sense of responsibility for one's past' (Carothers, 1953: 148) or a 'striking resemblance between African thinking and that of leucotomized Europeans' (Carothers, 1951: 12) – in other words their under-development.

The idea of black- and brown-skinned people as under-developed white people (going back to Social Darwinism, eugenics and the concept of degeneration described above) has become woven into thinking in psychiatry and psychology, affecting diagnoses and assessments. It surfaces for example in the theory of emotional differentiation proposed by Leff (1973, 1981), namely that people from developing countries and African-Americans apparently have a lower level of differentiation when compared to people from developed countries and white Americans; and in recurring versions of the claim that black people have low IQs (see D. Campbell, 2006; Howitt and Owusu-Bempah, 1994). After visiting the United

States, Carl Jung (1930) proposed that white Americans were different in the way they expressed their emotions because they suffered from 'racial infection' from living too close to black people: 'The inferior man exercises a tremendous pull upon civilized beings who are forced to live with him . . .' (1930: 196). And when Freud (1915, 1930) envisaged that the 'leadership of the human species' should be taken up by 'white nations' as opposed to 'primitives', the latter (to him) included Melanesian, Polynesian, and Malay people, the native people of Australia, North and South America and the 'negro races of Africa' (Hodge and Struckmann, 1975). So it is against this background that we come to the present.

Ethnic issues in mental health

Issues around race and culture in mental health services in the UK have been highlighted in the literature since the early 1980s, mainly based on ethnic differences in admission to psychiatric institutes and compulsory detention under the Mental Health Act. The main thrust of these issues, summarised in Box 3.1, has been confirmed recently by a one-day census of mental health institutes (Care Services Improvement Partnership, 2005). The over-representation of BME communities, especially people from Black African or Caribbean backgrounds, is evident among patients detained compulsorily under the Mental Health Act (for example, see McGovern and Cope, 1987; Moodley and Thornicroft, 1988) and most strikingly significant in secure forensic settings (for example, see Coid *et al.*, 2000).

The reasons for the inequalities affecting BME communities are debated – just as statistics for over-representation of black people in the prison population, among people subjected to 'stop and search' by police, etc. (see below) are debated; and the content of these discussions has been well covered elsewhere (see Fernando, 2003). But to many black people who experience mental health services at first hand, and to anyone who understands the nature of institutional racism and/or the effects of racial prejudice, there is very little doubt as to what the real problem is, although (as with the criminal justice system) proving it in a legal sense is not easy.

Ethnic issues reflect complex problems involving racism in society at large but also problems and complexities in the practice of psychiatry and psychology in a multi-ethnic society (see Chapter 1). Psychiatric diagnoses carry their own special images which may

Box 3.1 Ethnic issues: British findings

Black/ethnic minorities more often:
Diagnosed as schizophrenic
Compulsorily detained under Mental Health Act
Admitted as 'offender patients'
Held by police under Section 136 of Mental Health Act
Transferred to locked wards
Not referred for psychotherapy
Given high doses of medication
Sent to psychiatrists by courts

connect up with other images derived from (say) common sense or tradition. Thus, alienness seems to be linked to schizophrenia (as a diagnosis) and to biological (or genetic) inferiority (as a human type). It is not difficult to see how 'race' comes into both these concepts – alienness and biological inferiority. The result is a racial bias leading to an over-diagnosis of schizophrenia among black people who are seen (in common sense at least) as both 'alien' and 'inferior'. When psychiatry is called upon to 'diagnose' dangerousness, common-sense images of dangerous people seem to be the guide that is resorted to, often without much insight into the problems this raises. Indeed dangerousness and schizophrenia appear to be confused together both in lay minds and among many psychiatrists, general practitioners and social workers – as shown in a study on decision-making by professionals (Browne, 1997).

What happens at the coal face of everyday psychiatric practice is characterised by: (a) the failure by most professionals in the mental health field, whatever their ethnicity, to allow for racial bias in practice and institutional racism in the delivery of services; (b) institutional practices, such as mental health assessments and risk-assessments, that are inherently institutionally racist (see pp. 13–15) being carried out in a colour-blind fashion that does not allow for bias; (c) social pressures that apply differentially to people from BME communities not being picked up so that (for example) justified anger arising from racism in society is not taken into the equation when mental health assessments are made; (d) the sense of alienation felt by many people from BME communities being interpreted as a sign of illness   often seen as *their problem*, rather than a problem for society as a whole. The net result of all this is that a disease model (reflected in 'symptoms') or a criminal model (requiring control) – or both – is seen as the most appropriate response to many BME people presenting to the service, or brought into the service compulsorily. For further discussion of these matters readers should consult well-known texts on the interplay between mental health, race and culture (e.g. Bhui, 2002; Fernando, 2002, 2003; Littlewood and Lipsedge, 1989). What is striking is that the statistics reflecting racial inequalities in the mental health system, especially at its hard end of compulsory admission and forensic psychiatry, are very similar to statistics about the judicial (prison) system and education. This leads on to the next section.

Judicial and education systems

In mid-1995, 13 per cent of adult prisoners whose ethnic origin was known were found to be from minority ethnic groups although they formed a mere 6 per cent of the population of corresponding age groups (Home Office, 1996). Over the years, ethnic statistics kept by the (British) Home Office have improved in reliability and extent of coverage. An overview of recent statistics (Barclay *et al.*, 2005) shows that BME groups are disproportionately represented in the criminal justice system (CJS) in a variety of situations – 'over six times more likely to be stopped and searched [under legal powers given to police when they suspect that someone may be carrying illegal drugs or weapons of some sort], three times more likely to be arrested [on suspicion of breaking the law], and seven times more likely to be sent to prison [as a result of court proceedings] than white people' (2005: iv). This report quotes evidence to suggest that this ethnic imbalance is not the result of people from BME communities actually committing more crimes than their white compatriots. It is a result of discriminatory processes.

According to studies by Hood (1992), a series of negative effects impinge on black people during the court trial itself. Of alleged offenders brought to courts, black people (compared to whites) are: (a) more likely to plead not guilty (and it is established that people who plead not guilty initially are more likely to receive higher sentences and less likely to have social reports asked for by courts); (b) more likely to be remanded in custody rather than given bail (and it is known that people so remanded are less likely to be able to show mitigating circumstances, for example by obtaining references from employers or reports on character); (c) disproportionately charged for drug-related offences (and most people so charged are charged as a result of police activity rather than because of complaints from the public). In addition, discrimination is likely to occur at a series of encounters with the police even before alleged offenders reach the courts: (a) at first contact with the police when the latter use discretion as to who they ignore or just warn and who they arrest; (b) after questioning when a decision is made on whether a person who is arrested is charged or not, and, if charged, the nature (seriousness) of the charge; and finally (c) how the case is presented to the courts.

The previous paragraph shows how an overall racist outcome may arise from a series of discriminations, relatively minor in each case and so difficult to demonstrate, but adding up to form a process of institutional racism. It is likely that similar cumulative processes occur in the mental health system, often subtle, sometimes overt, dependent on assumptions about people, stereotypes in society, cultural misunderstandings and so on. But, since the mental health system is seen as a *medical* system, this type of institutional racism gets covered over.

Education

The failure of the educational system *vis-à-vis* black children in British schools was noted way back in the 1970s (Little, 1975), attributed then to a mixture of 'prejudice on the part of teachers, prejudice on the part of fellow pupils, and a variety of background factors' (Bagley and Coard, 1975: 322). Statistics in Birmingham for 1989/9 showed that baseline attainment for African-Caribbean children was 20 per cent above average at primary school but declined at each key stage after that to 21 per cent below average at the end of secondary education (Gillborn and Mirza, 2000). Recent ethnic statistics are more detailed. The 2004 statistics for attainment, measured by the achievement of five or more grades A*–C at GCSE (General Certificate of Secondary Education) level or GNVQs (General National Vocational Qualifications), show that Gypsy (Roma), Black Caribbean, Pakistani and Bangladeshi pupils fall below average while Chinese and Indian pupils do better than average (National Statistics, 2004). These ethnic differences are evident from the start of education (in primary school), but the gap widens in the case of Black Caribbean pupils and pupils from other black backgrounds while the gap narrows in the case of Bangladeshi pupils (Department for Education and Skills, 2005).

A report from the Runnymede Trust (Amin *et al.*, 1999) criticises the focus during the 1990s on discussing 'under-achievement' (by minority ethnic groups), thereby strengthening popular stereotypes, lowered expectations and self-fulfilling prophecies; it suggests that discussion should be about *disadvantages* of opportunity and *inequalities* in the educational system itself. Also, ethnic differences in educational achievement should be taken in context: a variety of other issues may impact on educational achievement. For example, children of recent immigrants and those whose parental language ('mother tongue') is not English are at a disadvantage in the examination system. It has been found that Pakistani children (compared to white children) are 2 to 5 times more likely to have been identified as having visual impairment or hearing impairment and hence requiring special attention; Black Caribbean and other black boys (compared to white British) are twice as likely to be categorised as having behavioural, emotional or social difficulty and hence as having special educational needs (Department for Education and Skills, 2005).

School exclusion

The disproportionate exclusion from school of minority ethnic pupils has been a concern for many years (Parsons, 2005), but ethnic monitoring of school exclusion was poorly carried out through the 1990s (Appiah and Chunilal, 1999). It was estimated that in the mid- and late 1990s,

> African-Caribbean pupils were four to six times more likely to be excluded from school than white pupils, although they were no more likely to truant than others, and many of those who were excluded tended to be higher or average ability, although schools saw them as under-achieving.
>
> (Social Exclusion Unit, 2000: 22)

The first reliable data on school exclusion to emerge using detailed ethnic codes relate to the year 2002/3: exclusion rates when compared to the national average were between 2 and 2.5 times for 'Black' children (including those categorised as 'Black Caribbean', 'White and Black mixed-race' and 'White and Black African'), 3 to 4 times in the case of Travellers of Irish Heritage and Gypsy/Roma, and well below average for Indian, Pakistani and Bangladeshi children (Department for Education and Skills, 2005). The reasons for these ethnic disparities have not been adequately researched. A briefing paper for the Runnymede Trust (Appiah and Chunilal, 1999) cites teacher–pupil conflict and the stereotyping of black boys as being aggressive as likely explanations for high levels of exclusion of African-Caribbean pupils. A report by Peter Wanless, Director of School Performance and Reform at the Department of Education and Skills (DES), has attributed the exclusion gap to 'largely unwitting, but systematic, racial discrimination in the application of disciplinary and exclusion policies' (Griggs, 2006: 8). In fact, the situation may be similar to that in the mental health system where young black men are compulsory detained, given the diagnosis of 'schizophrenia', etc. (as described earlier).

Redressing inequalities

Although race-based inequalities in mental health service provision have been evident for over twenty-five years (see above) it seemed for a long time that government was not interested in addressing these problems. Also, for a long time, psychiatry as an institution – represented by the Royal College of Psychiatrists – vigorously avoided any reference to racism or even allowing any discussion (within the profession) of whether psychiatric methodology needed to change to meet the needs of a multicultural society. But gradually total denial was replaced by admission of 'cultural' problems. Yet, whenever training was instituted to address (what were usually called) 'cultural' issues, the schemes were generally implemented half-heartedly and without much financial support – and racism was carefully avoided or side-stepped. In the late 1980s, the Mental Health Act Commission (MHAC), a government inspectorate, took up issues of race and culture at an official level through its reports (Mental Health Act Commission, 1987, 1989 1991). Some groundwork done within statutory organisations such as the Central Council for Education and Training of Social Workers (CCETSW) was significant at the time too. The Transcultural Psychiatry Society (TCPS) highlighted racial injustices within British psychiatry and psychology in conferences held around the country. Public consciousness was raised; government began to take notice; several health authorities appointed development workers in an effort to explore what needed to be done, and indeed some projects aimed at meeting needs of BME communities were developed within

National Health Service (NHS) facilities; and, most importantly, BME communities began to get together to develop services for their communities outside the statutory mental health sector, often with government support. Some examples of projects within the statutory and voluntary sectors are described elsewhere (Fernando, 2005), and of course this tendency for BME communities to take the initiative continues (see below) and is a major theme of this book.

In the early 1990s, the government introduced ethnic monitoring of admissions to psychiatric institutes, but its implementation was half-hearted. A government document, *Black Mental Health – A Dialogue for Change* (Mental Health Task Force, 1994), noted the need for action to redress injustices in the mental health system affecting people from black and Asian communities, but nothing much was done. There were increasing pressures at the time on services and professionals working within them, accompanied by strenuous criticism of mental health services by users of the services and, for very different reasons (for example, alleged risk of violence perpetrated by 'mental patients'), by the public at large. Meanwhile, the 'ethnic scene' in the workforce of the statutory health services had changed considerably from that in the early 1980s. Black people were a visible presence at many levels of the health professions and management – although still relatively poorly represented in its higher echelons. In this context, the interest in race issues lapsed in the mid-1990s, possibly because there was a general feeling (at governmental levels) that having a fair number of black professionals in positions of influence represented 'change'. So-called 'development workers', who had been appointed in the late 1980s, were eased out of their commitments, usually by ostensibly 'absorbing' their work into mainstream services –'mainstreaming' being used as a euphemism for abolishing. Projects for BME communities found it more difficult to get funding allocated within the NHS, and some projects that were active were dismantled, through mainstreaming. Significantly, by then there were many policies supposed to counteract inequalities and there were a fair number of black and brown faces at management level. But changes at the level of 'patient care', in the experience of BME service users, were not forthcoming. The fundamental issues of institutionalised racism within the disciplines that inform mental health services were not even being touched.

The way in which a report into deaths of black people at Broadmoor Hospital (Special Hospitals Service Authority, 1993) was handled exemplifies the problems of addressing racism in psychiatry in the 1990s. This report was commissioned by the Special Hospitals Service Authority (SHSA), a government body that supervised all special – or high security – hospitals at the time. But when the report highlighted racism as a major factor in the events leading to the deaths, recommending 'further research into the diagnosis of schizophrenia in Afro-Caribbeans . . . [and the monitoring of] patterns of diagnosis among minority ethnic groups in the special hospital system' (1993: 52), the hospital authorities rejected the report and the Royal College of Psychiatrists failed to take up the challenge thrown out to the profession.

The advent of a Labour government in Britain in June 1997 raised the hopes of many people for positive action in redressing various injustices – not least issues around racism. Following the Macpherson report (Home Department, 1999), referred to in Chapters 1 and 2, many public bodies, including the Department of Health, instituted audits of institutional racism. Many health authorities and social service departments began to promote training of their staff directed at counteracting racism and they seemed to focus specially on mental health services. The Royal College of Psychiatrists appointed an external consultancy to carry out an independent review of institutional racism within the College structures (see Cox, 2001); and two papers (Cox, 2001; Sashidharan, 2001) published in its official organ (the *Psychiatric Bulletin*) attempted to open a debate on institutional racism within British Psychiatry, making official something that had been debated outside the College for many years. The government commissioned a new report on what needed to be done about ethnic issues. After much delay (and it seems much argument about its content) *Inside Outside* (National Institute for Mental Health in England, 2003) was published, calling for radical changes in the statutory services (the 'inside') together with work with BME communities and the voluntary sector (the 'outside').

Although *Inside Outside* was far from being a comprehensive policy for changes in statutory services (i.e. the '*inside*'), the report was well received by BME communities. Its emphasis on the need for radical changes in the statutory services (the 'inside') was balanced by a call for policies directed at empowering BME communities – the '*outside*' – to feed into changes (in statutory services) that should come about through 'community development'. The underlying message of *Inside Outside* highlighted two issues that had never been directly pinpointed in an official report before: first, that current mental health services, being underpinned by models of illness, therapy and care, are rooted in narrow western thinking – in other words are ethnocentric; and second, that services had been designed with 'white people' alone in mind, reflecting attitudes towards 'others' that are essentially racist – or at least not designed to address racism. The next stage was clearly to work out an implementation plan for *Inside Outside* – a framework for bringing about changes that confronted both ethnocentricity and institutional racism.

So what happened? Even while the author of *Inside Outside* was preparing to get together a team to plan its implementation, the Department of Health had apparently approached someone else, someone from a different place and a different background, to devise a plan that did not come out of *Inside Outside* at all. The outcome was *Delivering Race Equality* (Department of Health, 2003), drawn up in a university department without any consultation with BME communities. This new report, 'DRE 2003', was couched in similar terminology to that used in *Inside Outside*, but very different in implication. The emphasis on changing statutory services in line with what BME communities want (being empowered to voice their views) was shifted to an emphasis on collecting information. And, even more importantly, instead of 'community development' there appeared 'community engagement' – the idea being that BME communities needed to engage with services more effectively.

For the first time, individuals from several BME organisations came together, calling themselves the National BME Mental Health Network (BMENW) (http://www.bmementalhealth.org.uk), to voice concern at the government's retreat from the position taken by *Inside Outside*. Meanwhile another inquiry – this time into a violent death in a mental hospital of a black patient (David Bennett) – reported that institutional racism was to blame for some of the events leading to his death (Norfolk, Suffolk and Cambridgeshire Strategic Health Authority, 2003). The government then announced that DRE 2003 was intended for 'consultation' (although it had been announced earlier as a definitive final plan) and brought on board several professionals from BME communities to help in reworking it. A revised version together with the government's response to the David Bennett Inquiry – largely rejecting most of the recommendations in it – was issued by the Department of Health (2005c).

Box 3.2 Expected outcomes by 2010

The vision for DRE is that by 2010 there will be a service characterised by:

- less fear of mental health services among BME communities and service users;
- increased satisfaction with services;
- a reduction in the rate of admission of people from BME communities to psychiatric inpatient units;
- a reduction in the disproportionate rates of compulsory detention of BME service users in inpatient units;
- fewer violent incidents that are secondary to inadequate treatment of mental illness;
- a reduction in the use of seclusion in BME groups;
- the prevention of deaths in mental health services following physical intervention;
- more BME service users reaching self-reported states of recovery;
- a reduction in the ethnic disparities found in prison populations;
- a more balanced range of effective therapies, such as peer support services and psychotherapeutic and counselling treatments, as well as pharmacological interventions that are culturally appropriate and effective;
- a more active role for BME communities and BME service users in the training of professionals in the development of mental health policy, and the planning and provision of services; and
- a workforce and organisation capable of delivering appropriate and responsive mental health services to BME communities.

Source: Department of Health (2005b).

The new version of DRE ('DRE 2005') repeated much of the earlier plan but added on a process for bringing about 'whole systems change' to be pursued on the basis of research funded by the National Institute for Mental Health in England; a scheme to try out (pilot) changes in the statutory sector in selected 'focused implementation sites'; and, most importantly, a list of expected outcomes by 2010 (Box 3.2), which meant that its success or failure could be judged on clear criteria. BME voluntary groups and individuals who had been very critical of DRE 2003 generally accepted DRE 2005, although by the time it came on line, the original DRE had already been acted upon with the appointment of Race Equality Leads. The government appeared to look to DRE as the remedy for (what it called) 'racial inequalities' in mental health service delivery, and made much of the fact that it was led by people from BME communities – i.e. black- and brown-skinned people –

although they were handpicked by government and did not necessarily carry the confidence of BME communities.

During 2006 it seemed evident that DRE was in trouble (Fernando, 2006) and in early December 2006 the main author of DRE resigned his position as DRE lead, confirming an impression gaining ground at the time of writing (September 2007) that little change is likely to ensue in the statutory sector as a result of DRE. It appears that resources directed to university research (for example to produce a plan for 'whole systems change') may be unproductive and those allocated for grass-roots workers may be diverted to avenues other than DRE; that focused implementation sites seem unlikely to develop any special systems that can be followed by other centres; and that 'community engagement projects' resourced under the DRE umbrella have been organised as research programmes unlikely to be sustainable as services (Fernando, 2007a).

Conclusions

In this chapter I have traced institutional themes running through from the early history of psychiatry into (current) racial inequalities in the mental health system that resonate strikingly with what appears to be going on the CJS and education. We seem to be seeing a pattern in British society whereby there are three inter-connected phenomena: (a) disproportionate numbers of black men being compulsorily detained and diagnosed as 'schizophrenic' by the mental health system; (b) disproportionate numbers of black youngsters being subject to stop and search, arrest and then being charged, leading to magistrates and judges disproportionately sending black men to prison; (c) disproportionate numbers of black children being excluded from school. All this may add up to failures of the three social systems (mental health, criminal justice and education) to connect with BME communities or (more likely) to all three systems reflecting institutional racism in society as a whole.

Unlike the mental health system, where research and study tend to hover around, if not get submerged in, medical-type studies, the CJS is seen as something for predominantly sociological, rather than medical-type, study. Discrimination tends to be incremental throughout the passage (as it were) of a person moving from the street to prison, via police and courts. In the education system, some BME children seem to get a raw deal – and they happen to be black-skinned (rather than brown-skinned) or come from Roma or Traveller ('Gypsy') backgrounds. The similarities between what is happening in the CJS and the education system and what I have discussed as 'ethnic issues' in the mental health system are eerie. Extrapolating from the CJS to the mental health field, I believe similar forces operate at various points on the journey of people using mental health services (more often than not) under compulsion – a journey that takes the person through arrest, 'sectioning' (i.e. detention under mental health legislation), stigmatisation, exclusion, (compulsory) medication and control. Extrapolating from education to mental health, children excluded cannot but get the message that they are not wanted by society, that they are 'aliens' – the equivalent in psychiatric jargon to being 'schizophrenic'.

Identifying inequalities is one thing; redressing them is another. Although race-based inequalities in mental health care have been evident for many years, little progress appears to have been made in redressing them. This chapter has summarised recent moves to get to grips with the problems through a government plan which at the time of writing (September 2007) seems doomed to failure.

Chapter 4

Black and minority ethnic women

Nutan Kotecha

Although there has been considerable research into the over-representation of people from some black and minority ethnic (BME) communities among patients in psychiatric institutes and the inequalities they suffer in mental health services (see Chapter 3), the special position of women from these communities *vis-à-vis* these issues has received very little attention. This chapter addresses the experiences of women from BME communities, focusing on women from African, African-Caribbean and Asian communities, covering policy context issues concerning abuse, women as parents, and women refugees and asylum seekers (some of these issues are also addressed in Chapter 9). It reviews research findings on issues for women in general and outlines available research findings relating to BME women; and it examines official documents issued in the UK on mental health in relation to care for women, namely *Women's Mental Health: Into the Mainstream* (Department of Health, 2002c), referred to as *Into the Mainstream*, and the *National Suicide Prevention Strategy for England* (Department of Health, 2002b) and documents that are of particular relevance for BME women such as *Delivering Race Equality in Mental Health Care: An Action Plan for Reform Inside and Outside Services* (Department of Health, 2005b). Finally, the chapter describes some projects in the voluntary sector in London which aim to cater specifically for BME women with mental health problems, although admittedly London may not be representative of the rest of the UK. The chapter concludes by drawing attention to the likelihood of a significant level of unmet need among BME women within mainstream mental health services, and makes some general statements about the reasons for this.

General research findings

Evidence shows that there are clear gender differences in the prevalence and incidence of common mental disorders between men and women (Mind, 2003a). Figures suggest that more women than men will experience some form of mental disorder – 20 per cent of women compared to 14 per cent of men (Bird, 1999). Furthermore, two-thirds of people using mental health services are women (Black and Shillitoe, 1997). Social deprivation is strongly linked to the prevalence of mental health problems (Bird, 1999). Women tend to be subject to many adverse socio-economic experiences, making up two-thirds of the number of adults living in the poorest accommodation (Office for National Statistics, 2004). Women are also more likely to be lone parents and are therefore more likely to experience social isolation and lack of mobility (Office for National Statistics, 2004). However, the over-representation of women in mental health statistics is not only due to these socio-economic vulnerability factors, but also stems from discriminatory attitudes within health and social care (which are embedded in the structures and processes of most mental health services), rather than the attitudes of individual staff, many of whom are acutely aware of the issues women face (Raine, 2000; Williams and Scott, 2002).

Another variable in the complexities related to mental health service provision for women arises from the way mental health problems are conceptualised and perceived. Williams and Scott (2002) suggest that services approach women's mental health from an individual pathology perspective, whereas service users consistently ask for a more holistic view of their lives. They sum up this difference in attitude as the difference between asking 'What is wrong with this woman?' and asking 'What has happened to this woman?' Williams and Scott (2002) suggest that to overcome this fragmented view of women's lives, service planning and delivery need to be rooted firmly in people's social experience. Services must be able to understand and work with the fact that individual expression of mental distress and requests for help will be affected by a range of aspects of women's identity, including their class status, age and gender, and their previous experiences, including any previous stigmatising experiences when seeking support. Two overarching issues are common experiences for many different groups of women who experience mental distress, namely issues of abuse and violence and issues concerning children where mothers are caring for another dependent person apart from the child.

Abuse and domestic violence

Research indicates that 50 per cent of women who see a psychiatrist report experience of sexual abuse (including non-contact abuse) as children (Perkins, 1996). Young women who have been sexually abused are at risk of further abusive experience, early and lone parenthood and, in some instances, becoming vulnerable to drug misuse (Abel *et al.*, 1996). Women with enduring mental health problems and women within secure services are more likely than men in similar situations to have experienced sexual abuse by their father or stepfather, to have been the victim of more than one abuser, to have been 'in care', and to have had numerous changes of placement (Williams and Scott, 2002). Sadly, these experiences are often compounded by women not being believed by services when they take the difficult step of revealing their experience of abuse, or by further sexual harassment during inpatient stays (Warner and Ford, 1998). Domestic violence against women accounts for 25 per cent of all reported violent crime (Department of Health, 2002c), and the actual figures are likely to be much higher. Agencies dealing with this issue, along with organisations such as Rape Crisis (http://www.rapecrisis.org.uk), are often left on the margins of mental health partnership working, rather than being perceived as having useful knowledge and expertise to offer (Chantler, 2002). Even though the association between domestic violence and mental health has been established, Abel *et al.* (1996) suggest we need a great deal more research to analyse this relationship.

In addition to the factors experienced by male and female refugees and asylum seekers alike – such as exile, war, famine, persecution and separation from family – women refugees and asylum seekers may also have been subjected to violence and rape, and they are largely responsible for children. As such, they are likely to have high mental health support needs in a context in which they may face questioning about their experiences, often before they are able and willing to talk about these.

Women with children and dependents

Services seem to fail to take account of the needs of women with mental health problems who are also parents and may also be caring for another dependent person (Montgommery *et al.*, 2006). For example, a significant number of children are looked after by women who also care for another dependent person (Office for National Statistics, 2004). It is also known that women do the bulk of caring, which has significant implications for their emotional well-being. A significant source of fear for women is that if they reveal their mental health problems, their children are more likely to be taken into care (Oates, 1997). Moreover, male partners in child custody disputes can use to their advantage the mental health status of women and their need to access mental health services. In terms of generational issues, being in care as a child is a risk factor for the development of mental health needs in later life.

There are particular issues relating to care of children when women are admitted to hospital, stemming from the fact that women provide the majority of (and often sole) care for children and other dependants. There is now some recognition that further action is required in this respect (National Institute for Mental Health, 2003). The consultation document *Into the Mainstream* (Department of Health, 2002c: 57) recommends separate family visiting areas and visiting environments appropriate for children of a range of ages, with access to refreshments, toilets and baby-changing facilities.

Research findings on BME experience

There is documentation of the difficulties experienced by women with mental health problems (Abel *et al.*, 1996), but studies often fail to differentiate between the issues for all women and those for women from BME groups (Owen and Milburn, 2001). It has also been suggested that the position of BME women is closely linked to that of their respective communities (Wilson, 2001). The next section will consider issues for BME women in relation to primary care, inpatient services, parenting, suicide and prisons (not necessarily presented in order of priority).

Primary care

Research into the prevalence of mental health problems in BME communities confirms differences in patterns of primary care consultation and indicates high levels of general practitioner (GP) consultation for certain groups, although they may not necessarily specify (or be found to suffer from) mental health problems. In a community study to establish the prevalence of health problems in minority ethnic communities, by Lloyd and Fuller (2002), the Bangladeshi group had high levels of physical problems reported to GPs; the authors concluded: 'This raises important questions about the understanding of stress, access to services and the perceived value of consulting for emotional problems across ethnic groups' (2002: 106). This situation may well apply to other groups of BME women too. The 1997 King's Fund Inquiry (Bhui, 1997) catalogued a range of findings indicating adverse experiences by BME communities in primary care. These included embarrassment, language difficulty, and lack of access to information and gender-matched GPs. Specifically, it appears that Asian and Black African and Caribbean women (compared to their white counterparts) are less likely to have mental health problems identified by their GPs and to be offered follow-up consultations. For example, a study exploring perinatal depression in Black Caribbean women (Edge *et al.*, 2004) found that they were reluctant to consult their GP about depressive symptoms, and that when these women did consult GPs, the latter were unable to validate the women's depressive symptoms. Thus there are issues around how well primary care practitioners are equipped to recognise and address mental health problems in women from BME communities.

The experience of refugee and asylum-seeking women from a range of communities in accessing primary care is fraught with difficulty. Many are not only fearful of engaging with statutory bodies but clearly have a need for social and mental health support, however that is defined (see Chapter 9). It is crucial that strategies exist to respond effectively in primary care settings, including: establishing relationships of trust, ensuring that communication can take place, and ensuring that practical difficulties are not overlooked (Perkins, 1996).

Inpatient services

There is evidence of higher rates of compulsory detention ('sectioning') in the mental health system of African-Caribbean women compared to other women, as well as higher rates of detention by police (Healthcare Commission, 2007; Wilson and Francis, 1997). Overall, there is evidence that people of African-Caribbean origin receive more coercive treatment within mental health services than do patients from other groups, and this applies equally to African-Caribbean women and men (Healthcare Commission, 2007). Women are also over-represented in secure provision within mental health services. Knowles (1991) found that the first admission rates for African-Caribbean women with a diagnosis of schizophrenia were 13 times higher than those for white women, and double the rates for African-Caribbean men, except for those admitted under the Mental Health Act. But other figures suggest that the rate of first admission for African-Caribbean women diagnosed with schizophrenia is 3.9 times higher than it is for white people, while for African-Caribbean men it is 4.3 times higher (Mind, 2003a).

Parenting

Although national data are lacking, evidence from a number of local studies makes it clear that there are high numbers of children from BME communities being supervised within the child protection system – particularly those from mixed heritage and African and Caribbean backgrounds (Biehal et al., 1995). A recent study examining young women's experiences in one local authority over a nine-year period (Lees, 2002) found that 79 per cent of the sample were from BME communities, with 54 per cent from African or African-Caribbean backgrounds. This study, and others in this area, point to a range of factors, including Eurocentric assessment tools, lack of cross-generational support resulting from migration, language barriers, differences in child-rearing practices, and strains generated by poverty, racism and abuse resulting in pressure on family relationships. An important area for further research and analysis is the number of children from BME communities who enter care as a result of their mother's mental health status. The study by Lees (2002) found that in one-quarter of the sample who were in care as a result of a court order, one of the key factors contributing to their entry into care was the lack of a carer due to bereavement or hospitalisation, often as a result of mental illness. This finding has been confirmed elsewhere (Chand, 2000).

Suicide

Although the lack of ethnic monitoring data in death certificates and coroners' verdicts means that accurate statistics are not available, there is some evidence that suicide rates are higher among BME women compared to other women. The evidence so far shows that (a) Irish-born people have high rates of suicide, particularly among those aged 20–29 (Muinteras, 1996); (b) young Black African and African-Caribbean people may be disproportionately vulnerable to suicide (National Institute for Mental Health in England, 2003); and (c) suicide rates for Asian women aged 15–24 years are more than double the national average (Bhugra and Desai, 2003).

A study of young Asian women in the London Borough of Newham (Newham Innercity Multifund and Newham Asian Women's Project, 1998) found that the suicide rate among women born in Kenya or Uganda was double the expected rate, while young British-born Asian women also had relatively high rates of attempted suicide and self-harm. Respondents in this study pointed to a far wider range of factors contributing to self-harm and distress than conventional and over-simplistic explanations of 'culture conflict' within the family. These factors included an absence of someone to talk to about their distress, the difficulties associated with transition to different life stages, and a range of experiences of abuse, including bullying at school and racism. This study found that respondents had little knowledge of voluntary or statutory support services. Most of these young women respondents did not consider their GP to be a pathway to care because they feared loss of confidentiality and the stigma attached to accessing support. A study mainly of Muslim women in Manchester (Chantler et al., 2002) had similar findings. The women communicated their answers about definitions of mental distress, attempted suicide and self-harm in terms of a powerful combination of social, political and economic pressures, both from inside and outside the community. Again, women feared loss of confidentiality, but they also felt they would be misunderstood and judged by mainstream services, and were reluctant to talk about intimate matters in front of interpreters.

Prison services

The proportion of females in the prison population has been rising rapidly in recent years, mainly due to tougher sentencing policies and legislative changes. While women form a small percentage of all offenders and generally commit offences for shorter periods of time than men, a higher number of women than men in the criminal justice system have mental health needs – 56 per cent of sentenced women are reported to have a psychiatric disorder, compared with 37 per cent of sentenced men (Butler and Kousoulou, 2006). BME women are represented in prison at an even more disproportionate level than BME men, making up 31 per cent of all female prisoners (Ash, 2003). However, detailed information to clarify this worrying over-representation is lacking. The context for these figures requires further investigation and an analysis of the mental health needs of BME women within the criminal justice system is needed. There are also no accurate data on the proportion of women who are foreign nationals.

Summary

There are many gaps in knowledge about issues of race and culture *vis-à-vis* mental health and mental health services as they apply to BME women. The statistics of BME women caught up in the mental health system and those of their children in the care system suggest that the pathologising of the behaviour of African-Caribbean people – for example as 'loud, aggressive, and difficult' – may play some part in what is found in research studies (for example, Wilson, 2001). It is critical that BME women should be able to access appropriate care and support at an early stage to prevent all the negative consequences that this entails, not least separation from their children. However, the field is a complex one in practical terms. Apart from problems to do with stereotyping and racist attitudes that may distort judgements made by professionals, situations are likely to be even more complicated. For example, Chantler *et al.* (2002) point out that there is sometimes a tendency to privilege race and culture over gender, in that workers may feel that certain types of abuse were cultural practices and therefore should not be questioned (see Perkins, 1996). Such a response can easily leave women with a sense of isolation and discourage them from accessing services until crisis point.

Gender and race within government policy documents

Four substantive comments on the issues relating to BME women appear in the document *Into the Mainstream* (Department of

Health, 2002c), although they are scattered throughout it. The document:

(a) States that BME women are vulnerable to mental ill health and subject to the impact of a range of social, economic and political pressures; and acknowledges the existence of important differences between groups of women. Two particular patterns of mental health problems are highlighted, namely suicide, self-harm and eating disorders among young South Asian women, and post-traumatic stress disorder and other mental illness in some groups of asylum seekers and refugees (2002c: Section 2.3.3).

(b) Draws attention to the vulnerability of BME women to experiencing mental ill health at or around childbirth; and states that this vulnerability may be due to a range of cultural and circumstantial factors including isolation, lack of access to family support due to migration or family pressures, racism and lack of suitable responses from statutory services (2002c: Section 12.5.3).

(c) Points out that assessment and care planning must take into account the ethnicity and culture of BME women and must recognise that racism commonly affects women from BME communities; and notes that services often fail to meet women's cultural and spiritual needs (2002c: Section 9.1.5).

(d) Concludes that there is need for further research on the interaction of gender, ethnicity and culture, and its impact on mental health and illness (2002c: Section 7.3).

Into the Mainstream generated a wealth of feedback, including comment on the absence of both a fuller discussion of, and detailed plans to address, the complexities and simultaneous discriminations faced by different communities of vulnerable women, including BME women (St John, 2002; Ibrahim, 2003). However, the document fails to specify particular experiences and needs of BME women. Further, it would have been helpful if *Into the Mainstream* had cross-referenced policy and consultation documents that refer to BME mental health services, such as *Inside Outside* (National Institute for Mental Health in England, 2003); and if the *National Suicide Prevention Strategy* (Department of Health, 2002b) had made the point that strategies need to be sensitive to social and cultural backgrounds of women.

BME women's involvement in planning mental health services and the particular problems they face in accessing mental health services have been acknowledged in *Delivering Race Equality in Mental Health Care: An Action Plan for Reform Inside and Outside Services* (Department of Health, 2005b).

The *National Suicide Prevention Strategy* aimed to support the target, put forward in an earlier document, *Saving Lives: Our Healthier Nation* (Department of Health, 1997), of reducing the death rate from suicide by 20 per cent, by 2010. With reference to BME groups, the strategy refers readers to a toolkit of health promotion for people from BME groups published by the National Institute for Mental Health in England (NIMHE) in late 2003 (Duffy *et al.*, 2003) and states that the NIMHE will request the Coroners' Review Group to consider routinely recording ethnicity, to allow monitoring of suicide patterns.

Developing services for BME women: examples from London

Given the unequal treatment that women from BME communities experience in mainstream mental health services, organisations in the black voluntary sector have emerged to address these inequalities. These developments are more prominent in London and will be reviewed here, but this is not to suggest that these examples can be extrapolated to other areas that do not share the features of this city. London is, however, the place where the majority of BME communities are currently located and there are useful insights that can be gained from the services that will be described below.

Of the range of services for BME women that exist across London, some provide ethnic-specific services, while others support a range of communities of black women around domestic violence. An example of the latter is the Southall Black Sisters in west London (http://www.southallblacksisters.org.uk). The former type of service includes the Ashiana Project in Waltham Forest (http://www. ashiana.org.uk), which was set up in the late 1980s to provide a service to young Asian women but has successfully extended its service to Turkish and Iranian women. Some services have been in existence for some time but struggle constantly to meet the level of demand, such as the Irish Women's Centre in north London (http:// www.womeninlondon.org.uk/liwc.htm). Others have been set up or developed more recently: these include the African Health for Empowerment and Development Project (http://www.hivsouthlondon. org.uk/partners/ahead.htm), which provides support services for black people generally, but is in the process of implementing a specific service for women with mental health problems, in addition to its existing HIV/AIDS support services. Drayton Park (Killaspy *et al.*, 2000), a statutory-funded women's residential crisis project in north London, was set up in 1996 but remains one of the few of its kind in London and so very much in demand.

Many mental health services for women in the voluntary sector are located within projects that have a broader focus than mental health, reflecting the social base of mental distress for BME women. What most of these projects have in common is that they all provide outreach, information and social space for women to meet together. It has to be acknowledged that this approach may work in some instances, but these services may not always be fully equipped to deal with severe mental health problems. There is a need for mainstream services to develop ways of addressing the needs of BME women in this category.

Three projects are highlighted in the following case studies. The first is organised around a faith identity; the second is unique in being the first survivor-run black women's mental health project; and the third is based within a domestic violence project.

Case study 1: Muslim women's helpline

This service is unusual in being based on a faith identity rather than an ethnic one. Founded in 1989, it runs without any state funding and uses volunteers. It provides a listening service, emotional support, practical help and information and, increasingly, face-to-face counselling for hundreds of Muslim women and girls. This work includes home visits and accompanying women to appointments with a psychiatrist or social worker.

The service developed in response to an awareness that Muslim women in crisis were not accessing statutory authorities or mainstream voluntary services because the women felt they were negatively stereotyped because of their religious and ethnic backgrounds. Staff working in the services had viewed Islam, in particular, as oppressive to women, and they equated liberation from oppression with women leaving behind their adherence to their religion – which was often not what the women wanted. The service has reported high levels of need, particularly at community-based and primary care levels.

Case study 2: The Black Women's Mental Health Project

The Black Women's Mental Health Project (BWMHP), based in north London, is a self-help project managed by black women service users and survivors. The project was set up in 1996 with few resources and is unique in being managed mainly by women with personal experience of mental distress. Its aim is to support 'all Black women and women who define themselves as Black in this society, to collectively demand for themselves good practice in mental health', as well as to enable 'Black women to speak for themselves regarding the care and services they need to regain their own means of coping' (Black Women's Mental Health Project, 1999: 3).

The project developed in response to what the women showed they needed, and at its peak in the late 1990s had a very hands-on approach, taking responsibility where services were failing to address needs, and making sure that a wide range of information was available to meet the obvious needs of women attending the project. In addition to providing a drop-in service, members made home and hospital visits, supported women attending meetings with social or housing services, and helped find out more about medication, as well as helping women retain care of their children. Leaflets were distributed at the local market, and news of the group was spread by word of mouth. Currently, the future of the project is uncertain because of funding difficulties.

Case study 3: The Newham Asian Women's Project

This organisation runs a domestic violence refuge, a second-stage hostel and a resource centre for South Asian women. It established a further project to provide a social space that is non-threatening and confidential, where young women can escape home, school and society pressures via support groups, residential and local school-based workshops and counselling. This project is well attended by young women who self-harm and have felt suicidal. The counselling service has accredited counsellors who speak a range of languages. The organisation also runs a mental health scheme for older women. This comprises a weekly mental health support group and employs a full-time psychologist who has an advocacy and liaison function with statutory and other agencies, while women can also access one-to-one counselling.

Discussion and conclusions

The mental health needs of women, including women with children, have received some attention in national policies, and there has been an acknowledgement that social and economic reasons lie at the root of the development of many women's mental health needs. However, BME women remain marginalised within current policy debates around culture and race as well as those around gender. BME women seem to be viewed largely in terms of stereotyped ethnic images – for instance, as 'loud and difficult to manage' in the case of African-Caribbean women, or as having problems that are rooted exclusively in 'cultural conflict or practice' within the family, in the case of Asian women. This results in their needs as women being ignored and overlooked.

Generally BME women access services only at crisis point, due to experiences of services as inappropriate, a lack of confidence and trust in the service, and an inadequate knowledge of what is available. Services fail to take account of the needs of women with mental health problems who have children or other dependants. This is significant given the high numbers of African-Caribbean and mixed-heritage young women in the care system.

In general, it appears that BME women are less likely than women from other groups to visit their GP and receive treatment at primary care level, and there are indications that their experiences and outcomes within primary care are poor. Communication difficulties in this and other settings are a significant problem. BME women are over-represented in the criminal justice system, yet there is little information available on the reasons for this, or about the mental health needs of these women. There are indications that suicide and self-harm rates are higher than average among certain groups of Asian women and among young African-Caribbean and Irish women. Some Asian women (and young Asian women, in particular) tend not to use GP services as a pathway to care, for fear of loss of confidentiality. There is a lack of specialist crisis and respite services for BME women in London and in the UK as a whole.

A potent mix of gender blindness and negative views of minority cultures is contributing to BME women's mental health needs being severely neglected across the spectrum of research, policy development, service provision and practice. There is a significant level of unmet need among BME women, both within and outside of mainstream mental health services. Action on these issues is long overdue. Mental health services need to strive for a gendered understanding of race and culture for BME women which is reflected in service provision. A range of accessible services is needed, including those that support women and their children. Many BME women have insufficient knowledge of services and how they may help, highlighting the need for mental health aware-ness and promotion strategies. The challenge that services face will be easier to overcome by involving BME women themselves in the planning and commissioning of these services. Information is a powerful tool in promoting access to services, and should be con-sidered part of an overall strategy targeted at individuals, groups and organisations. However, careful attention needs to be paid to involving women in how services aimed at them are funded and configured. Services need to learn from, and secure, the good practice that is already present in some services – especially in the voluntary sector – and to evaluate these models from user-centred perspectives. Extensive support networks – especially crisis ser-vices, advocacy and self-help groups – need to be established, and fuller research should be commissioned into the needs of BME women and their children.

In examining some voluntary sector services for BME women in London it seemed that they operate at the margins of main-stream service delivery. They are under-funded and lack capacity to fill the gaps in service provision in the statutory sector. In any case, it is the right of BME women to expect proper services on a par with those provided for other sections of the population, but appropriate and sensitive to their needs. The ideal of course is that mental health services should be fully equipped to meet the needs of all women, including those from BME communities, but in the absence of this, there remains a vital role for projects that specifically focus on the needs of BME women.

Chapter 5

Race equality training in the UK: a historical overview

Joanna Bennett, Jayasree Kalathil and Frank Keating

Approaches to race equality training (RET) in the UK have followed a historical pattern almost identical to that of the United States. Increasing immigration after the Second World War led to racial tensions and race riots in the UK. In the 1960s a policy of multiculturalism or cultural diversity replaced the policy of assimilation. From this perspective it was perceived that immigrants have different cultures and that these would persist in Britain. The change in policy required a new response from public services, which focused on the need for service providers to be adequately informed about 'immigrant cultures' and the special needs resulting from their cultural differences. RET in Britain developed as part of a wider response to address racism and discrimination. This chapter provides an overview of these developments, identifies some models of training and reflects on some challenges when RET is used as a strategy for achieving race equality.

A key factor that influenced the development of RET was the perception of immigrants and their presence in the UK. Their presence was problematised and issues of race inequality were viewed as arising out of cultural differences. The problem was not racial discrimination but the inability of black immigrants to become sufficiently integrated. The main strategy that was employed at the time was multicultural training or 'learning about them', which provided the dominant training assumption throughout the 1970s (Luthra and Oakley, 1991). The emphasis in multicultural training is primarily on the provision of information on minority ethnic cultures and cultural differences. The underlying assumption is that the problem to be tackled is mainly one of ignorance by the host community of minority cultures and that the provision of information will itself lead to changes in attitude and behaviour.

Training was therefore seen as necessary primarily for practitioners responsible for delivering services, and the main aim of training was to improve knowledge of the differing cultures of minority groups or to develop multicultural awareness (Peppard, 1981).

From the late 1970s, training that focused on providing cultural information began to be questioned and multiculturalism and pluralism were attacked as masking the reality of racism and discrimination and doing little to address the issues of social justice and equality (Luthra and Oakley, 1991). Multicultural training was widely criticised for the narrowness of the perspective and the potential to focus on minority groups as the problem (Peppard, 1981). The Race Relations Act 1976 established the unlawfulness of indirect racism. Section 71 of the Act placed a duty on local authorities to ensure the elimination of unlawful racial discrimination and promote equality of opportunities between different racial groups. For the first time, addressing race equality was seen as an organisational rather than an individual responsibility. However, there were no sanctions on authorities which did not comply.

RET was not a requirement under the legislation and no specific funding was provided by central government. However, the Commission for Racial Equality (CRE) published guidelines on training and provided advice on good practice. The emphasis within training was on equal opportunities in employment. It did not focus on equality in service delivery. This has been addressed in the Race Relations (Amendment) Act (RRA) 2000, which places a duty on all public bodies to combat racism, to publish a race equality scheme and to provide training for staff on the RRA 2000 (Commission for Racial Equality, 2006). There was subsequently an increased demand for training aimed at promoting equal opportunities and reducing discrimination. Training typically comprised information provision about race inequalities and the 'psychology of prejudice'. The development of 'race equality units' in many local authorities led to a growing emphasis on staff training as a means of implementing race equality policies in both employment and service delivery.

Before the amendments to the RRA (2000), a further impetus to RET was the recommendations of the report by Lord Scarman (Home Office, 1981) after the 1980 and 1981 riots in London. The report emphasised the need for RET for improving policing. As more organisations developed policy commitments to tackle racism, the demand for training and trainers increased. There was no central strategy to promote and staff RET. Thus a range of *ad hoc* responses by a cadre of entrepreneurial trainers emerged. These used a range of different approaches with different premises and different aims and emphases (Luthra and Oakley, 1991). Training developments within the Metropolitan Police and within other public sector organisations reflected a diminished emphasis on minority cultures and a greater focus on US-style racism awareness training (RAT). According to Brown and Lawton (1992), course titles picked up the terms 'race awareness', 'racism awareness' and 'racial awareness' with no consistency; in fact at the height of popularity these terms were attached to any kind of training in the field of race.

The 1990s saw the emergence of a broader training encompassing other social inequalities such as gender and disability as well as race inequality, under the banner of equal opportunities. Davis *et al.* (2003) argue that there was a shift by the CRE and the Equal Opportunities Commission away from demands for social justice and tougher legislation to collaboration with government and business to achieve change through employment policies. This was in keeping with the conservative government policy, which preferred a business-led response to disadvantage rather than a state-led one. Equalities training shifted from an emphasis on awareness towards the functioning of the organisation. Differences emerged in the extent to which race equality was stressed as opposed to other equality issues. The International Labour Organisation's study of anti-discrimination training in the UK [International Labour Organisation/United Nations (ILO/UN), 1999] found that the majority of training activities were classified as equalities but that there were three sub-groups: equalities with broader issues of positive action; gender and disability; equalities, anti-racism and diversity training. This study showed that whilst the majority of training was focused on equalities or equal opportunities, a significant proportion of training activities could be defined as diversity management training. The concept of 'managing diversity', developed in the business world in the United States, was adopted in the UK. This has increased rapidly, with one-third of the 200 top British companies actively involved in diversity management in 2000 (Collett and Cook, 2000) and 70 per cent of all organisations having diversity management policies in place by 2005 (Mizra, 2005).

A review of training in racism awareness and valuing cultural diversity across local authorities found that the trend in RET in the

UK was towards diversity (Tamkin *et al.*, 2002). Tamkin *et al.* argue that race issues have been subsumed into a broader agenda which has moved from an emphasis on reducing difference through equal opportunities to a diversity approach with an explicit recognition of difference and trying to meet particular needs of individuals. Training in race issues is increasingly being delivered under the banner of diversity or cultural awareness, which is considered more inclusive than race alone, a less emotive way to approach race and a more modern term than equalities. Whilst equalities and diversity management are currently the overarching frameworks for addressing race inequalities in the UK, there has been some interest in adopting the US-style cultural competence model to address inequalities in health care (National Institute for Mental Health in England, 2003; Papadopoulos, 2003; Webb and Sergison, 2003).

The concept of cultural capability has recently emerged. Bhui (2002) suggests that it is important to emphasise practitioner capabilities and not just their competence to perform certain roles. The concept is further developed in the publication *Inside Outside* (National Institute for Mental Health in England, 2003), where it is proposed that it is essential to improve the cultural competencies and capacity of the mental health workforce in order to reduce racial inequalities. Cultural capability is proposed to consist of two elements: the first is training in cultural competencies, and the second is ensuring a multicultural workforce. Cultural capability is therefore a framework for service delivery rather than a model or an approach to training. Cultural competence is the accepted approach within the government's action plan (Department of Health, 2005b) to address race inequality in mental health services.

Models of race equality training in the UK

The literature on models of RET has tended to define approaches to training according to the methodological aims and objectives, the output aims, the content and the participants of training (Tamkin *et al.*, 2002). Examples of this are seen in the work of Luthra and Oakley (1991), Wrench and Taylor (1993), DeRosa (2001) and Rogers (2001). Whilst acknowledging that models of training are not mutually exclusive, the problem with this approach is that what is being described is often varying approaches to training within a given model (for example, DeRosa describes varying approaches within the diversity model). A historical analysis of RET suggests that six major models of training have emerged in the UK since the 1960s: multicultural, racism awareness, anti-racism, equalities, diversity, and cultural competence or cultural capability. The development of these models has been influenced by a number of factors including definitions of race and racism, legislation and social policy on race inequality.

Multicultural training

Multicultural training focuses primarily on the provision of cultural knowledge. Trainees are introduced to different aspects of 'culture,' including dietary habits, religious practices and rituals. Courses sometimes include elements on race relations such as factual information about the extent of racial discrimination and psychological theories of prejudice and racism. The approach is primarily didactic with little attempt to apply learning to practical situations. Other approaches to training within this framework include cultural information, cultural awareness and cultural sensitivity training. The underlying assumption of this approach is that providing factual information will increase practitioners' ability to work more effectively with black and minority ethnic (BME) communities.

Racism awareness training

RAT is based on the principles and method of the 'White Awareness' programme, developed by Judy Katz in the US in 1978. The premise of this approach is that racism is a psychological disorder suffered by white people. This disorder, racism, is embedded from an early age at both a conscious and an unconscious level. The overall objective of the programme is to help white people change their racist attitudes and behaviours.

The training uses confrontational methods to enable the individual to acknowledge their own racism and to resolve this pathology. The course consists mainly of pair and group exercises staffed by one or two facilitators who are expected to have a deep understanding of racism (Brown and Lawton, 1992). The original intention was that training would be a six-stage process conducted over several days. Based on the goals of the training programme set out by Katz (1978), the content of training includes definitions of the concepts of bias, prejudice and racism; individual, institutional and cultural racism; personal feelings and fears around racism; identifying one's own racist attitudes and behaviours; and developing and implementing strategies to combat institutional and individual racism. This type of training, however, elicited feelings of guilt, anger and resentment which in our view could not have been beneficial for improving competence in race equality.

Anti-racism training

This model is a modification of RAT, which maintains a strong emphasis on addressing racism directly but also includes more organisationally oriented elements. Anti-racism/racist training thus addresses both personal and organisational goals. Racism is seen as endemic in society and in the cultures of institutions and cannot simply be reduced to individual attitudes. The overall aim is to challenge and eliminate racism. Training methods include didactic and confrontational techniques, within a collaborative rather than judgemental framework (Luthra and Oakley, 1991). Course content includes exercises to develop awareness and job performance. Whilst the focus is on changing behaviour, attitude change is seen as a prerequisite.

Equalities training

The legitimacy of equalities training is based on the fact that racial discrimination is illegal. Employers and service providers therefore have a legal obligation to prevent discrimination whether in intent or effect. The focus is on the recognition of racial inequality and action to identify and prevent it, and not necessarily on the causes or extent of racial discrimination. Equalities training may be part of a wider programme that addresses equal opportunities in relation to other forms of discrimination such as gender, disability and sexual orientation. Courses generally include explanations of rules, legal obligations and formal duties, and information to dispel prejudiced beliefs and assumptions, and encourage an understanding of the impact of racism and discrimination on job performance.

Training methods are aimed at, first, establishing ownership of the possibility of discrimination and the need to address it and, second, devising a strategy for dealing with it. Luthra and Oakley (1991) describe three stages in the delivery of training:

1   Selling the idea to managers and policy makers.
2   Didactic methods to provide technical information and facilitate planning exercises.
3   Technical instructions and skills development.

Equalities training seeks to produce change in behaviour and specifically avoids tackling racial attitudes.

Diversity training

Motivations behind diversity training include compliance with legislation, fear of litigation, social justice, desire to expand into diverse markets, and overall organisational transformation. However, there is a lack of consensus on the meaning of diversity training. To some, the focus is narrowly on those categories protected by law, primarily race, gender and disability (e.g. Day, 1995). Others argue for a broadly inclusive definition that encompasses age, educational level, family structure, job function, sexual orientation, ethnicity, and values, among others (Pegg, 1997). With this broader approach the focus is on understanding and valuing the differing perspectives and approaches to work that people of all types of backgrounds bring. There is a range of approaches to training within the diversity framework including the intercultural approach, and managing diversity (DeRosa, 2001).

Intercultural approach

The intercultural approach focuses on the development of cross-cultural understanding and communication between people of different cultural groups. It tries to help people develop sensitivity to the cultural roots of one's own behaviour, as well as an awareness of the richness and variety of values and assumptions of people of other cultures. In this approach, ignorance, cultural misunderstanding, and value clashes are seen as the problem, and increased cultural awareness, knowledge and tolerance are the solution. Cultural identity and ethnicity are the focus, while racial identity is not often examined. Gender and sexual orientation are explored within the context of culture and tradition, but not within the framework of power and oppression.

Managing diversity

The emphasis in this approach is on awareness and appreciation of the contributions of different cultures. The main aim is to promote diversity in the workforce, to improve productivity, efficiency and achieve best value. Managing diversity is an extension of the business case for equal opportunities. It includes all ways in which people differ, not just race, gender and disability. Training usually targets the managers of an organisation. While some experiential activities may be included, examination of personal attitudes and behaviour is likely to be limited to the business context. Workshops often focus on how stereotypes and prejudice affect hiring and promotional decisions, and undermine team effectiveness, productivity, and, ultimately, profitability.

Lasch-Quinn (2001) suggests that common themes in diversity training materials include:

• The view that negative stereotypes are the cause of tensions regarding racial or cultural differences, simplifying the issue drastically.
• The need to overcome stereotypes through intervention along therapeutic or behaviourist lines.
• The aim of replacing negative stereotypes with understanding of group attributes and replacing old behaviours with new ones based on more enlightened ways of thinking about difference.

The most common purpose of diversity training is to raise awareness and understanding of cultural differences and to change behaviour of individuals in order to eliminate discrimination. Other training aims include attitudinal change at the individual level and cultural change at the organisational level.

Training courses generally start with an inclusive definition of diversity, and clear objectives that are linked with organisational goals. Employees are often involved in their design and top-level support is usually evident. Training includes awareness (examining assumptions, biases, stereotypes) and skill development (listening, communication, conflict resolution). Diversity trainers tend to use readily available materials, such as films, handbooks and other materials that are appropriate for use in short workshops. Little emphasis is given to the fact that the literature in this area is extensive with a range of views and perspectives on racial inequality. Resistance is confronted by providing facts, appealing to deep values, and identifying human commonalities while recognising the great variation in their expression. Overall, the focus is on finding ways for people to work cooperatively despite differing perspectives.

Cultural competence training

Although a number of models of cultural competence have developed over the last two decades, the most commonly used framework is based on the work of Cross *et al.* (1989). Cultural competence is not regarded as a purely clinical model as it addresses cultural intervention at the individual, organisational and policy levels. At the clinical level, it is defined as the acquisition of competence in three main areas: beliefs and attitudes, knowledge, and skills. At the individual level, cultural competence is viewed as a lifelong process, which requires practitioners to examine their own attitudes and values and acquire knowledge and appreciation of cultural differences and similarities within, among and between groups. It is argued that cultural competence should be incorporated into all aspects of policy making, administration, practice, and service delivery and should be informed through the involvement of service users, key stakeholders and communities. The model devised by Cross *et al.* (1989) identifies a continuum of cultural competence from cultural destructiveness through cultural incapacity, cultural blindness, cultural pre-competence, cultural competence and cultural proficiency. Cultural competence is considered a behavioural approach, which does not focus on implicit levels of racism but operates on the principle that changes in attitudes can be implied through behavioural change.

Cultural competence training describes a vast array of educational activities which are aimed at enhancing the capacity of service delivery systems to meet the needs of different racial and ethnic populations. Training can include educational activities which aim to increase cultural awareness and sensitivity; provision of demographic information on local populations; skills building in bicultural and bilingual interviewing and assessment; and increasing cultural knowledge and understanding.

Race equality training (RET) in the UK: current situation

We have recently completed a mapping exercise on RET for the Sainsbury Centre for Mental Health. The study found that there are no common standards for RET and no register for RET trainers or body to oversee RET. It is clear from the findings of the study that the majority of RET in mental health services in England is being delivered within the framework of diversity, cultural competence and cultural awareness, with a significant emphasis on improving cultural knowledge and changing negative attitudes on race. Whilst it is important to recognise that culture may play a role in health-related behaviours, the cultural competency literature tends to present this framework as a panacea against racism and health-care inequality. Gregg (2004: 960) argues that 'race is not culture and racism is not simply a lack of cultural competence'. Questions about disrespect and lack of care based on how a person looks and sounds are questions of racial bias. Racism that needs to be tackled is not just individual racism but the racism that is woven into societal and institutional practices, through centuries of colonialism and slavery. Taking the cultural approach dilutes the importance of racism in perpetuating disparities and suggests that the problem of inequalities is the result of the person's cultural difference and not the racial bias of institutional processes and practices.

The indication is that approaches to race-related training have been significantly influenced by the changing politics of race relations. The concept of race and racism has been replaced by culturalism as an explanation for the social inequalities experienced by BME groups and is the central framework for race-related training. As the focus on 'race' became unpopular politically, the concept of diversity was introduced as an explanation for all forms of inequality. Diversity and differences in language, religion and cultural norms and expectations are now seen as the explanation for inequality. The solution is posited as the provision of information on different cultures (Culley, 1996). The simplistic use of culture in public policy, as the superficial manifestation of health beliefs, values, communal rituals and shared traditions, suggests that ethnic groups categorised as African, Caribbean, Asian or White are made up of people who are all the same. In effect, it posits a definition of culture as shared and static.

In practice the aims or content of diversity training vary according to the individual training provider's interpretation. Whilst many training programmes do not use confrontational techniques they continue to be influenced by the assumptions of the original sensitivity training approach. Cultural knowledge is provided with the main objective of changing individual attitude. This suggests that racial discrimination is seen as a matter of individual attitude and practice. This approach is not in keeping with the requirements of the RRA (2000), the David Bennett Inquiry (Norfolk, Suffolk and Cambridgeshire Strategic Health Authority, 2003) or the action plan for *Delivering Race Equality in Mental Health Care* (Department of Health, 2005b), all of which emphasise racial discrimination and institutional racism as the cause of inequalities.

Additionally a major problem facing RET in the future is the shift in government policy away from multiculturalism, which historically has influenced the framework for training. Multiculturalism is seen to have resulted in separatism. Emphasis is now being placed on the need for minority groups to develop core values of 'Britishness' (see Ethnos Research and Consultancy, 2005, 2006). The move to de-emphasise cultural differences and the significant criticism, for example, of the cost of using interpreters present a challenge for public services, which have focused on cultural and linguistic differences as a basis for addressing ethnic inequalities. Further diversity does not appear to benefit BME communities. This is demonstrated by an increase in racial harassment and discrimination lawsuits in the US (Hansen, 2003) and continued evidence in the UK of racial inequalities in mental health (Healthcare Commission, 2007).

Conclusion

We have attempted to give a brief overview of the historical developments in relation to RET. It is clear that there is a lack of consensus over terminology as well as a lack of agreement on the focus of RET. Some models adopt an assimilationist approach, some a multicultural approach, and the current approach is to focus on cultural competence or capability for practitioners. A common theme in these models seems to be the fact that the emphasis in RET is on assisting professionals to help BME communities to engage with services, rather than equipping services with the skills and competence to engage with these communities. Essentially, 'training for race equality' should focus specifically on the areas of inequality in mental health services such as diagnosis, compulsory detention, reducing fear, etc. rather than having a generic focus on culture and race. The emphasis must be on improvement of professional practice and not merely on acquisition of knowledge of the cultures of the 'other'. The mapping exercise on RET for the Sainsbury Centre for Mental Health found inconsistencies in the prominence that RET is given in mental health services and in the content of training programmes, and a lack of comprehensive evaluation of the effectiveness of RET. We believe that this is a major shortcoming and that we cannot assess the impact of RET on service delivery and outcomes if we do not have adequate strategies to evaluate the training. It also seems that RET is often adopted as the only strategy for race equality. We believe that training should be an important dimension of any race equality strategy, but should be anchored in an overall strategy to improve organisational performance in meeting the needs of BME communities.

Part 2

Confronting issues

What has happened over the past fifteen years is that there have been various moves to confront issues of inequity and injustice in mental health service provision. In fact, there has been a plethora of policies and plans but little seems to have changed fundamentally in terms of confronting inequities that affect BME communities. Most plans appear to look to a mixture of good management and proper training to bring about change, coupled with attempts to tap into the expertise of experience by involving people who use services both in the planning of services and in the training of professionals. However, running through all this is the agenda – often understated and avoided – that institutional racism within services has to be tackled in some way or other.

The mood among many people today in confronting issues of racism and cultural diversity in the mental health scene is one of frustration, especially when it comes to bringing about systemic change. This part of the book explores ways of changing systems, focusing on strategies in management, innovation in the voluntary sector, race equality and cultural capability training, psychological services for refugees and asylum seekers, service user involvement and innovation in bringing about attitude change.

Chapter 6

Management approaches to effecting change

Alpa Kapasi

Thirty years after the Race Relations Act 1976, a revised piece of legislation, namely the Race Relations (Amendment) Act 2000 (see Chapter 2), set out to tackle the problem of institutional racism. This came about because the Stephen Lawrence Inquiry (Home Department, 1999), which found institutional racism in the Metropolitan Police, argued that institutional racism probably infected the majority of Britain's institutions. The government responded by devising a tool to help these bodies identify this type of racism and root it out. Whilst the legislative agenda to tackle racism has been progressive (see Chapter 2), it might be argued that there is a backlash sometimes, particularly amongst the very public sector bodies that are charged with the responsibility to eradicate the institutional racism inherent within their organisations. If used properly, the Race Relations (Amendment) Act 2000 should lead to an almost conditioned response, so that any time any person or any authority thinks about policy or action, they also think 'what does it mean for race equality?' Further, they will automatically know that to find out they must 'Assess', 'Consult' and 'Monitor' and, when they know, they must 'Publish' and 'Inform' – these being key requirements contained within the Statutory Order 2001.

It is evident that many public bodies have not fully understood the potential power of the Act or what they have to do. Across the public sector, there are variations in understanding, although many organisations demonstrate an enthusiasm and willingness to get it right. Hence it is important, if the health and social care sector is serious in its intent to deliver on race equality and to cut institutional racism, that public bodies optimise this opportunity. This chapter will discuss the ways in which these bodies can challenge and eradicate discrimination by developing race equality frameworks that are systematically mainstreamed into the organisation. In so doing, mental health commissioners and service providers can ensure compliance with the Race Relations (Amendment) Act 2000 (see Chapter 2) and proactively work towards the development of culturally appropriate services and reduce the degree of racial inequality in the commissioning and provision of services. The chapter will go on to outline the limitations of a purely management approach but argue that without a clear race equality vision backed up by a robust framework and strong action to bring about systemic changes, real change is unlikely to be sustained. Although new ways of working can be initiated by individual projects, individual initiatives of professionals, or new systems of training, unless these are mainstreamed at every level of the organisation, resulting fundamentally in a 'culture change' within the service, lasting change is unlikely to endure.

Developing coherent race equality frameworks

To challenge racism and eradicate it from our public sector bodies and create sustainable change, there needs to be a corporate management approach which at the same time permeates the organisation and is capable of involving all in the delivery and understanding of requirements. My work with a diverse range of public sector organisations has led me to identify the following key success criteria underpinning the development of a robust race equality strategy:

- Sponsorship, role modelling and championing at senior management/board level (political and managerial).
- Ownership of equalities through the business planning process tied to individual objectives.
- Ensuring that robust measuring systems are in place and that progress is reported using realistic but challenging targets.

The 'Best Value' regime was designed by central government to improve local public services (see Local and Regional Government Research Unit, 2003). Whilst working at the Greater London Authority (GLA), I was involved in reviewing this regime across the GLA Group, namely the GLA, Metropolitan Police Authority, Metropolitan Police Service, London Development Agency,

Transport for London, and the London Fire and Emergency Planning Authority ('Equalities for All' Best Value Review Team, 2002). We prioritised the following areas as being vital in the development of a coherent race equality framework that engenders a fundamental culture change to ensure lasting change:

- Vision and leadership
- Employment
- Improving services
- Consultation
- Culture change
- Performance management

These priority areas are inextricably linked with each other but they also stand alone. I shall examine them in turn to consider the way in which public bodies need to develop their policy and practice to address these priority areas. A small number of organisations have comprehensively addressed these areas; however, most have adopted a selection of some of these priority areas.

Vision and leadership

In a review of race equality schemes, the 1990 Trust states:

> It is imperative that there is a corporate commitment and political will underpinning race equality work. This needs to be backed up by a robust framework to support race equality work in an organisation; the framework will also need to be resourced properly with dedicated people, time, money and space.
>
> (2005: 6)

To achieve this, public bodies must begin by developing and promoting a shared vision for race equality within their organisations. The development of this vision needs to be led by senior management and the aim should be to achieve collective ownership across the organisation. The vision should make a clear, unequivocal statement about the commitment of the organisation in respect of equalities. It should be linked to a range of key objectives (which are integrated into the business planning process) and it should establish standards of conduct.

An equalities vision statement should recognise the multiple forms of discrimination experienced by people from marginalised and excluded communities. The development of such a vision would provide the opportunity for the whole organisation to engage in the crucial debate about equality target groups and the categories to be monitored on an ongoing basis – consistency in the categories is essential for planning, comparison and monitoring purposes. The agreed vision should be supported by and linked to the managerial and policy framework, i.e. shared objectives, agreed definitions, adoption of best practice, etc. This is an important first step in developing a robust performance management framework.

Employment

Public sector organisations should lead by example, in respect of employment practice. Many health and social care bodies choose to adopt a minimalist approach which simply ensures compliance with key legislation; it is argued that resource constraints prevent them from being creative. However, it is important for public bodies to exceed existing minimum statutory obligations, and strive to be not just compliant, but exemplary employers. Success as an exemplary employer can be defined in the following terms:

- Low turnover of staff
- High levels of staff retention
- Positive feelings about wanting to work for the organisation
- Positive feedback from exit interviews

Employers need to address the full range of human resources development and training as well as such issues as combating bullying and harassment, the development of work–life balance policies, equal pay, and pension and benefits rights for unmarried partners, etc. Therefore, the responsibility goes further than the popular focus on recruitment, retention and promotion.

The majority of health and social care organisations are engaged in some monitoring of staff recruitment and retention; however, there are limited analyses of the monitoring data and it is not clear if the analysis has made any impact on the development of policy or practice. The Employment Duty within the Race Relations (Amendment) Act 2000 is perhaps the most clear and prescriptive part of the Act, and yet there are a considerable number of organisations that are still struggling with proper implementation of this Duty.

Improving services

Having developed a robust equality and diversity strategic framework, it is important for an organisation to assess the degree to which their policies have made an impact on actual service provision. Organisations need to consider how it is that they determine the needs, priorities and concerns of their local communities and key target groups. Once again we turn to the legislation. The Race Relations (Amendment) Act 2000 requires organisations to *assess, consult and monitor*. Under the Race Relations Act 1976 (General Statutory Duty) Order 2001, public bodies are required to state the arrangements they have in place to enable them to meet the requirements of this Order by drafting a Race Equality Scheme (see Commission for Racial Equality, 2002), which must include details of the arrangements in respect of:

- Assessment and consultation on the development of new functions and policies or those subject to revision
- Monitoring of existing functions and policies for adverse impact
- Publishing the outcomes of assessments, monitoring and consultation
- Ensuring access to information and services
- Training staff to carry out the duties

In practice, it is evident that there is very little consistency in the degree to which organisations systematically determine the needs or concerns of their local communities or target groups. Where information is collected, it is often difficult to see how the monitoring data feed into the policies that inform service development. In fact, information is often patchy and incomplete; in some cases, organisations are not even familiar with the demographic profiles of their local communities.

Race equality impact assessments (REIAs)

Chapter 2 refers to the REIA being applied to recent legislation. Essentially an REIA is carried out to detect any potential adverse impact of legislation or policy on one or more racial groups. In other words, the body carrying out an REIA must look actively for potential discriminatory effects of legislation or policies. So, public bodies must always hold reliable information on all the communities in their localities, including their socio-economic profiles. Although some health and social care organisations are fairly adept at extracting this information in accessible formats, others are not.

A key indicator of the degree to which discrimination is taking place is the complaints procedure. Evidence suggests that not all organisations within the health economy have formal complaints procedures in place and, where they do exist, there are different approaches for publicising them and monitoring information received from complaints. It is vital that the availability of complaints procedures is properly publicised and forms/guidance are made available in a range of formats, for example, community languages, Braille, large print, etc.

Community development work is also critical in supporting the improvement of services. Community development workers operating at a grass roots level are best placed to advocate for local communities – they can act as 'honest brokers' facilitating the sharing of information and the development of a dialogue between public bodies and their stakeholders. However, it is important that these roles are properly funded and supported to enable these workers to be effective. They should be mainstreamed and sufficiently resourced to enable them to work with communities in a creative and meaningful way – only then can they engage the communities that are the most excluded and marginalised.

Consultation

In the drive to modernise public sector organisations, there has been a keen emphasis on the need for public bodies to be demo-cratically accountable. A number of commentators and political activists have made reference to the pattern of '[c]onsultation overload or fatigue' (Cook, 2002: 517). Members of local communities are tired of being researched and constantly asked about their needs and concerns; to eradicate the negative impact of this pattern, it is important that consultation is carried out in a meaningful way and that people feel valued and listened to. Public bodies must monitor more regularly the range of consultation exercises undertaken, with whom, and the outcomes. This information should be regularly fed back to local stakeholders, along with some analysis of the way in which these exercises have informed the development of policy and practice. This is important so that people feel that their contribution is valued and it has made an impact on the services being developed.

Research has shown that communities feel that consultation exercises are often poorly organised (Cook, 2002). Time frames are often too short for people to engage properly, information is either too little or too much, information is jargonistic, and there is inadequate feedback provided. Sadly, this is a common complaint from communities across the spectrum of public sector services. In light of this, organisations would benefit from the development of consultation frameworks and good practice guidelines to support officers when conducting consultation exercises. There are some good practice models available from a number of organisations in the health sector.

Culture change

The writer Charles Handy (1993) provides a helpful definition of the 'culture' of an organisation which refers to its unique characteristics, traditions and ways of working. Public bodies should be prepared to undertake a fundamental culture change if they are serious about eradicating institutional discrimination. The development of a strategic approach to equalities, backed up by a robust performance management framework, must be accompanied by the creation of 'safe spaces' to enable staff and managers to engage in an open and dynamic dialogue about their experiences, perceptions and expectations of equality matters. Once an organisation undertakes a mainstreaming process, it will inevitably stimulate a debate and discussion about equalities issues. Therefore, managers need to allow for this by creating safe spaces where people are able to explore in a frank and open environment their views, perceptions and experiences.

Managers need to demonstrate visible leadership, both at political and managerial levels. Elected members and managers should be supported in undertaking this role. All staff, managers and political leaders have a role to play in promoting the equalities vision and framework – members need to learn from each other and support each other in developing their organisation.

Performance management

Underpinning this whole process must be the development of a robust performance management framework. As the definition of the term 'mainstreaming' developed by the Greater London Authority suggests: 'Each part of the organisation accepts its own responsibility for promoting equality of opportunity and challenging discrimination' (2003: 3–4).

There must be a degree of accountability to ensure that all staff members, managers and political leaders are fulfilling their responsibilities in the mainstreaming programme. Equality objectives and tasks need to cascade through the organisation from high-level strategic objectives in the business plan through to the work plans of individual officers. This can only be achieved if the organisation has invested considerable time and energy in developing a robust performance management framework which allows for rigorous monitoring and forensic analysis of the work undertaken in respect of equalities. There is a range of equality standards and toolkits available in the public sector to enable organisations to carry out a self-assessment of their performance and the progress made thus far; this level of analysis can then determine the equalities performance indicators that need to be developed.

In 2004, a performance framework to support the health sector in auditing its performance in respect of race equality was devised by the National Health Service (NHS) and Commission for Racial Equality (2004). This document has performed the vital role of supporting organisations in the implementation of race equality. A recent study by the 1990 Trust (2005) found that the organisations with the most sophisticated Race Equality Schemes were those that had managed to address the requirements of the legislation, namely those of the performance framework referred to earlier, as well as other health programmes, such as that in the public health White Paper *Choosing Health: Making Healthy Choices Easier* (Department of Health, 2004a), all within the one document.

A critical factor to consider here is the process for commissioning services. An increasing number of health and social care services are now being outsourced – i.e. not run by the NHS or social services departments. It is therefore important to consider whether race equality matters have been fully integrated into the commissioning process. Public bodies need to adopt a twin-track approach here; there should be a careful examination of the way in which the procurement process can be 'opened up' to attract and include small businesses run by people from black and minority ethnic (BME) communities and, at the same time, capacity building work needs to be undertaken to support those small businesses in competing within mainstream commissioning programmes.

In my experience, a number of organisations struggle with the development of such a robust mainstreaming programme as their performance management frameworks are still in their embryonic stages. Many health care bodies are still struggling with the establishment of basic policies and procedures which will govern their overall performance management frameworks, and implementation of the Race Relations (Amendment) Act 2000 is still patchy.

Conclusions

We live and work in a dynamic and constantly evolving environment within the health care sector where it is important to develop frameworks that will secure sustainability for those in our communities who are in greatest need. BME communities have been badly served in the mental health field for many years and it is now imperative that serious attention is given to the needs of these communities. Management has a major role in making this happen. The laws are there, the procedures that need to be followed are not too difficult, and there are a number of organisations offering help and support. In this chapter I have outlined the fundamental approaches in developing a coherent framework for implementing change.

Chapter 7

Innovation in the voluntary sector

Tanzeem Ahmed, Yasmin Jennings and Jagroop Kaur Dhillon

As with most sectors, the voluntary sector covering non-governmental agencies is not uniform. However what makes it even more ambiguous is the disparity of organisations covered by this sector and how they might define themselves. The nature of this particular sector is even more difficult to describe because it is extremely fragmented and continuously and rapidly changing. What is more, there is little if any agreement on the role of this sector, which is also continually changing. Although, there is no set definition for what exactly the sector is, grouping the diversity of organisations into a sector acts as a useful reference point from which to analyse the numerous organisations and projects that exist.

The voluntary sector is a large and fertile ground for any ideas, concepts, projects, programmes or organisations that are 'not-for-profit concern'. However, even this is no longer set in stone as voluntary organisations are facing the challenge to diversify their income streams. Some organisations are looking at earned income as a potential way forward by trading goods and services through a social enterprise model. The public sector, local and national government often instigate changes in the voluntary sector. As Hanvey and Philpot point out: 'the winds of change that have, in the last decade, transformed commercial life so fundamentally have also blown fiercely across the face of charities' (1996: 1).

There has been change in this sector on many different levels: how these organisations are organised; the kind of work that they do; how they approach the work; the size; the incomes; the procedures; the legislation – the list is long and continues to grow. Over the last decade there have been immense moves to 'professionalise' the sector, as demonstrated through agendas such as

Change Up (Frazer, 2005). On the one hand this puts a great pressure on the sector and departs from the informal, locally mobilised roots of many groups. On the other hand, however, this response has been necessary in light of the recognition that voluntary and community organisations are instrumental not just to public and civic participation but also to service delivery, especially for 'hard-to-reach' communities (Griffith *et al.*, 2006).

In this chapter we shall present a personal view of the current context within which the voluntary sector operates. We shall then present three examples of programmes within the voluntary sector that impinge on mental health and social care.

Current context

In order to provide some background context, it is important to define at least some of the demographics of the sector. This will enable a conceptualisation of not only the size of the sector but also the nature and importance of the sector. According to a research report conducted by the London Development Agency in 2003, employment in the voluntary sector increased by 29 per cent in the five years between 1994 and 1999 (R. Jones *et al.*, 2003). The sector created 85,000 jobs, and in London alone around 46,900 full-time workers are employed in the sector in over 30,000 charities and voluntary groups (R. Jones *et al.*, 2003). This gives an indication of the scale and the growth of the sector in recent years.

Increasingly, voluntary sector organisations are instrumental in meeting the needs of communities. They are seen as the organisations closest to the communities, which not only fill in the gaps in statutory provision, lobby against injustices, and hold public authorities to account, but also deliver support and services directly to communities. Within this plethora of organisations there is a subsection that is particularly dealing with the needs and issues of diasporic or minority communities: Black, Asian and minority ethnic voluntary sector (BAMEVS) organisations. Generally these organisations are created on the principles of self-help, whereby communities that understand the issues that are specific to them are able to develop and deliver provisions and services that are also specific to them.

In recent years there has been increasing tension between the BAMEVS and the mainstream voluntary sector. In the past, black and minority ethnic (BME) organisations were on the whole smaller and more informal, and as such they were not competing for resources with the mainstream sector. Many BAMEVS organisations emerged from small groups of like-minded people who came together to tackle a particular issue or to meet a certain social need. As the number of service users increased and other resources were required there was an increased pressure on these organisations to formalise themselves and their practices. Issues around legal compliance and quality and professional standards have emerged, as services have grown and become better recognised. In such a climate there is a need for greater resources to support the smaller BME organisations so that they have the capacity to engage with the funding system or contracting arrangements and are able to fulfil the requirements set by them. Although there is increased recognition of the innovation and the need for such services (Treasury, 2002), the resources available and access to these resources have remained a specific problem for these organisations and projects.

Acknowledging the role of the voluntary sector

In acknowledging the role of the voluntary and community sector in reaching government targets around issues such as mental health and social care, the Treasury (2002) carried out a *Cross Cutting Review* exploring how central and local government could work more effectively with the sector to deliver high quality services. This review was underpinned by a recognition that the voluntary sector had made a substantial contribution to the delivery of high quality services.

However, it was recognised that, in order for the voluntary sector to be more effective in service delivery, there is a need for more skills, knowledge, structures and resources within the sector. In response to this, the government-led Change Up agenda (Frazer, 2005) intends to develop the capacity, skills and professionalism of the voluntary sector to enable organisations to better access resources and bid for governmental contracts.

Mental health and social care

The not-for-profit sector is significant in the implementation of *Delivering Race Equality in Mental Health Care* (DRE) (Department of Health, 2005b). The sector has been a partner in pilots delivering more appropriate and responsive services, in hosting community development workers through whom more effective community engagement has been achieved, and in being a vehicle through which information has been delivered.

When considering issues of mental health and social care, especially in relation to BME communities, the voluntary and community sector has taken the lead. Most of the organisations operating in this sector emerged with principles of self-help at their core and they developed from the communities whose issues they were trying to address. Mainstream services that had developed over many years and catered for the majority were unable to cater for or provide a specialised service for minority communities. These communities face a whole plethora of other issues that prevent access to mainstream services and compound the difficulties faced by these communities. Amongst these issues are factors such as a lack of information; a lack of awareness of what services are available; a lack of awareness about how to access services; and a lack of understanding of the issues faced by these communities amongst mainstream providers. These issues are further compounded by cultural insensitivity, discrimination and institutional racism.

However, the increasingly competitive environment, the complex tendering processes and the stringent reporting requirements of funding and commissioning bodies all act as particular barriers for BAMEVS organisations in utilising the opportunities that the new environment presents (Ellis and Latif, 2006). There is a danger that unless organisations can demonstrate strong organisational capacity, they will miss out on the tendering opportunities presented by local and national health and social care agencies. Their weak asset base makes them high risk for contract holders.

Social enterprise as one way forward

Increasingly, the government is placing emphasis on social enterprise and how the voluntary sector can be involved in delivering health and social care services. The then Prime Minister Tony Blair, in his foreword to the strategy report produced by the Social Enterprise Unit (2002), said that his government's vision for the social enterprise sector was 'bold'. Social enterprises, he said,

> offer radical new ways of operating for public benefit. By combining strong public service ethos with business acumen,

we can open up the possibility of entrepreneurial organisations – highly responsive to customers and with the freedom of the private sector – but which are driven by commitment to public benefit rather than purely maximising profits for shareholders. Many social enterprises are already showing how this can be done. There is the recognition that they are currently only a small part of our economy. We want to build on this foundation and create an environment in which more people feel they are able to start and grow such businesses.

(2002: 5)

The White Paper *Our Health, Our Care, Our Say: A New Direction for Community Services* (Department of Health, 2006c), published on 30 January 2006, sets out a role for local organisations as partners with local authorities and reformed Primary Care Trusts (PCTs). The health and social care sector is to have an innovative and wide range of providers. Decisions about communities are to be taken more closely with or within those communities, with social care and primary care embedded in the communities served. The White Paper contained a commitment to social enterprise, and a new Social Enterprise Unit was created within the Department of Health in October 2006. The Secretary of State for Health launched a pathfinder scheme to support social enterprises to provide innovative health and social care services.

Increasingly in the UK, social enterprise is being used to develop work opportunities for some of the most disadvantaged unemployed people. Across London at present, BME social enterprises – most of which are at the start-up stage – are making a real difference. They play an important part in the fabric of London's communities through offering services that statutory bodies are unable to provide. BME social enterprises, as is the case for some mainstream social enterprises, are often situated within, or benefit, disadvantaged areas. They often target niche needs within their own community, including tailored care, translation services, cultural and leisure activities, employment, and educational activities. They are able to look at the needs of BME communities in ways that others cannot. BME social enterprises are influencing the education agenda by working with schools and colleges to raise standards for under-achievers and to develop the existing workforce. They are also encouraging and promoting cultural diversity across London amidst discrimination and ethnic stereotyping.

Examples of voluntary sector programmes

Social enterprise

It has been said that mental health is 'the aftertaste of society's other activities, the residue of all its policies' (Karpf, 1988: 21). Thus services that impinge on mental health can come from a variety of approaches related more or less to what is good for society. The voluntary sector is well placed to innovate across boundaries and indeed does so very successfully in some instances. Scotch Bonnet is an example of an organisation that innovated within an overall social enterprise model. Although not setting out as a mental health project as such, Scotch Bonnet has succeeded in promoting mental health in the African Caribbean community.

Scotch Bonnet was established as a project to promote social inclusion by addressing the lack of supported opportunities for training and employment in the local area and responding to service users' demand for variety in opportunities. In building a service from within the organisation, Scotch Bonnet Catering provides Caribbean catering services within the health and community care sectors and training and employment opportunities for adults with mental health needs and learning difficulties. It was created by Southside Partnership, a charity which supports people with mental health needs and learning difficulties to lead independent lives. The remodelling and modernisation of the Fanon Day Centre in Brixton began in 2001, prompting the opportunity to develop its café into an external catering service, building on its popularity and reputation. The buffet catering service has been running since 2002, creating opportunities for trainees to gain waiting experience for which they are paid. More recently Scotch Bonnet extended its activities to provide a frozen meal service.

The rapid expansion of the business and the receipt of a grant from the Guys and St Thomas charity are facilitating the development of new full training programmes, which are offered in all areas of the business. In addition to catering, training is offered in customer service, marketing, business planning, finance, web-design and delivery. Scotch Bonnet will soon offer accredited NVQs in catering as well as running shorter courses focusing on building confidence and general work and life skills, in addition to specific business-related training.

The key components of the supported training service include an individual assessment for all participants to determine their specific needs and requirements, and what they intend to gain from their training. An individual training programme is then created to respond to those requirements. As the programmes expand, Scotch Bonnet will develop its ability to support trainees into further employment by working closely with local businesses and contacts within the community. Scotch Bonnet is aiming for fifty beneficiaries to complete the training programmes in their first year of operation, rising to sixty per year thereafter.

The supported training service is designed to positively impact upon the mental health of service users. The training offers trainees opportunities to develop self-esteem and confidence in their abilities, allowing them to learn and re-learn skills, and develop goals and ambitions, offering accredited training. This experience will allow them to access other services from which they are commonly disengaged, such as college courses and employment opportunities. It will also equip them with the confidence to engage with other essential services from which they have been disengaged in the past such as housing and health.

It is the focus on African Caribbean communities, together with the provision of a variety of training opportunities offered within different areas of the business, that makes Scotch Bonnet a unique social enterprise within the London area. Scotch Bonnet has delivered its business back into the mental health services and in doing so has created opportunities for adults with mental health needs and learning difficulties. The skills gained through the programmes are transferable into many fields.

As a training provider Scotch Bonnet is innovative in the purpose of its training, which is to focus on the personal development of each participant – supporting them to increase their involvement in their community, increase their confidence and self-esteem, and take steps towards further training and employment. Scotch Bonnet's training programmes are well supported by the statutory sector through the sale of their produce to organisations within the sector, although it receives no formal funding. As a project within Southside Partnership Group, it is still rooted in the voluntary sector. With an annual turnover in 2006/7 of approximately £50,000, Scotch Bonnet relies on the financial support of the charity, and is seeking to raise funds from charitable trusts. In the longer term, Scotch Bonnet seeks to become financially independent, relying solely on trading income and removing the need for short-term funding. Future development for the social enterprise will involve mutually expanding and growing both its frozen food and buffet services and its training programmes.

As a voluntary sector organisation, the major achievements of Scotch Bonnet have been to meet the challenge of effective business planning, and to acquire the necessary expertise to provide its training services.

Housing

Housing associations are new arrivals in the BME mental health sector. Their financial strength allows them to bid for and manage contracts from the health and social sector. Smaller BME voluntary sector organisations are often disadvantaged by their lack of track record of delivering large-scale financial contracts. BME housing associations have therefore provided a good balance of providing appropriate services whilst maintaining a business focus. Ujima Housing Group was set up in 1977 in response to the lack of access to housing services for black men who were young, single and homeless. The group first acquired short-life unwanted properties from the local council, and ran community activities such as cafés and shops to fund its services and acquire more properties, before developing into a housing association of Registered Social Landlord status.

Ujima is one of the few BME housing providers which offer mental health care services. Amongst other affordable housing services and tenant support provided primarily to vulnerable adults and families from the local BME community, Ujima provides mental health care services for adults of African and Caribbean origin in its care homes and supported living schemes. Service users are referred by Community Mental Health Teams in the statutory sector, often prior to discharge from hospital. They receive a package of care elements which is intended to assist them in their path to recovery and independence. This includes assistance with daily living and the re-learning of skills, help with managing and understanding their mental health, developing or repairing relationships with friends and family, support with access to training, employment and education opportunities and support with drug-related problems.

The positive impact of Ujima's services on the mental health of their clients is evident in the reduction in re-admissions to hospital and improvement in the level of compliance with treatment and medicine. The service acts as a bridge between clinical services and the community, where service users (customers) feel that their needs and difficulties are well understood and supported. Seventy-six service users benefit from the service at any one time.

As its services are commissioned by the local PCT, Ujima is well supported by the statutory sector. It maintains strong links with other voluntary sector services through the cultural support elements of its services, delivered in collaboration with localised religious and faith groups. With an annual turnover of £28 million, the services of the Ujima group are maintained by both its own income and its contracts with the statutory health care sector.

Ujima's key achievements have been to overcome opposition to specialist services for minority ethnic groups, to develop an awareness of both the changing and continuous needs of its client group and the requirements and objectives of those who commission its services, and to devise a service that is most appropriate to both. Ujima also seeks to develop relationships with other ethnic-specific mental health providers, in order to share experience across the boundaries created by the commissioning system between different BME communities and geographical areas.

Training

Innovators in the health and social care field have come from organisations that have taken the challenge of delivering a service to the community by engaging the community in developing skills and expertise so that they themselves can be the providers. It is through the skilling up of people that confidence has been developed and self-esteem. This has had a positive impact on mental health and has led to more appropriate service delivery.

Gharana Community Care (GCC) was founded in 1995 to respond to the lack of provision of high quality culturally appropriate care services. It delivers social support and domiciliary care to vulnerable people from BME (mainly South Asian) communities and creates employment opportunities for those communities in Northamptonshire, building capacity for delivering services to 'hard-to-reach' communities. Each service user is offered a package of services that they require to both maintain their independence and remain socially interactive. This can include practical support, personal care, social and community support, advocacy and assistance with access to other services. Support packages are tailored to each individual in accordance with a care plan which is based on assessment of particular vulnerabilities and needs. Whilst the elderly are the main target group of this service, with 90 per cent of GCC's care services delivered to this client group, services are also provided to disabled adults. The service benefits eighty people at any one time.

GCC provides a service that allows its users to feel confident that their requirements are understood and that they are protected from abuse. As service users remain visible to social and mental health services, those services remain accessible to them. A trusting relationship is developed between the service user and the carers, who are from the same community, helping them to overcome fear of isolation. There is also an opportunity to interact with other service users.

The organisation's approach to capacity building is to focus on providing culturally relevant care for people who belong to communities that are considered 'hard to reach'. By involving people from these communities in the delivery of highly personalised care to those communities, GCC addresses the widespread refusal of treatment and support which occurs out of fear that cultural differences are not taken into account and that values will therefore be compromised by engaging with services.

GCC is recognised as an innovator in its field for the measures it creates to break barriers to the involvement of people from BME communities in the social care profession. By 2008 all social carers will legally require a qualification, yet many culturally specific carers are excluded from training by language barriers. GCC supports its employees in obtaining the NVQ in care work by creating access to documents in community languages and allowing for alternative methods of assessment for those who have trouble with reading and writing. GCC has been given a National Award for this programme and is recognised by the local authority as an example of good practice. As social care is not highly valued as a profession in many of GCC's target communities, it is hoped that the availability of the qualification may address this problem.

GCC is seeking funding to replicate the model in other organisations who work with hard-to-reach communities, particularly communities that are relatively new within the UK. These communities will soon begin to require training to care appropriately for their elders.

GCC works in partnership with the statutory sector. The majority of its services are commissioned by the local authorities, although some services are obtained directly by service users. GCC continually refers service users to statutory mental health and social services. This can involve working with other counties, such as Leicestershire, in order to ensure that the most appropriate services and treatments are made available. Local authorities are also participating in promotion of the social care qualification across communities.

With an annual turnover of £330,000, all income is obtained through contract with statutory services and some private services that are provided. A key point of learning for GCC has been the need for understanding of the variety of health care needs amongst communities. This education is essential for GCC to achieve its aim of re-integrating individuals back into their community. Another difficulty has been gaining recognition in the commissioning system of the capability of smaller organisations to provide a higher standard of care.

Current policy developments and local targets may go some way to address this in increasing demand for the services GCC offers. Northamptonshire has identified the need for a range of culturally appropriate services to empower people to remain independent. This has created an opportunity for GCC to work more closely with local government and possibly expand its services by becoming a preferred partner. It plans to expand into other local authority areas where a gap in provision is recognised, to possibly include Milton Keynes, Leicester, Bedfordshire and Luton.

Conclusion

The voluntary sector is growing and dynamic, continually proving to be an innovator in delivery of appropriate mental health and care services. The government is increasingly recognising the potential role of the sector both in its legislation as well as in the programmes of support it has set up to improve infrastructure and grow capacity.

The weak asset base of many BME voluntary sector organisations has often excluded them from benefiting from this new recognition. Nevertheless there are examples of organisations that have developed their asset base, such as social housing providers, and are able to compete as critical players in delivery of appropriate services. There is also increasing pressure for the sector to diversify its income base through social enterprise routes. Again the government sees the value in this, with a dedicated unit in the Department of Health for social enterprise and a pathfinder scheme soon to be set up. BME voluntary organisations are engaging in the realm of social enterprise. Organisations such as Scotch Bonnet are showing their capacity to compete in the commercial sector, yet their focus is to provide training and employment opportunities for people with mental health problems. The positive impact of employment and training programmes on mental health is demonstrated by reduction in re-admissions. The models that work rely on both the organisations' links into and support from the statutory sector, as well as their links in the community.

Chapter 8

The challenges of race equality and cultural capability (RECC) training

Peter Ferns

Having conducted race equality training in mental health over many years, the kinds of comments discussed later (pp. 115–118) are all too familiar. What is it about RECC training that elicits such responses? Why is RECC training so notoriously difficult for services to deliver? What are the main challenges for practitioners, organisations and trainers in undertaking RECC training?

In 2005, a panel of people were brought together by the Sainsbury Centre for Mental Health to consider an appropriate term for training in 'race' and 'culture' for professionals in the mental health field. The term agreed as the best that could be devised at the time, although not without controversy, was 'race equality and cultural capability' (RECC).

'Race' is used here as a social concept without any biological significance and refers to the social and political impacts of skin colour and physical appearance. 'Culture' is recognised as a complex and dynamic term that operates in social groups on many different levels. (These terms are discussed further in Chapter 1.) Capability denotes a combination of knowledge, skills, values, personal qualities, experience, wisdom (or learning from experience), and 'conation' or the ability to apply capability in practice. It is not just about current capability in job role but encompasses future capability or potential competence to perform in an untried role. 'Cultural capability' has to address all of the factors associated with capability, but within a diverse cultural context, thus helping to define and inform transcultural practice in mental health. 'Race equality' implies that mental health services, including clinical practice of professionals, are delivered 'equally', i.e. in a manner that is fair, just and appropriate for all 'racial groups'. The idea that such 'racial groups' are politically recognisable within

British society is something implicit in (British) race relations legislation (see Chapter 2).

Several points should be noted with regard to the context in which RECC training has to be delivered in Britain. First, there is a long historical legacy of racism in psychiatry and mental health generally (Bhui, 2002; Fernando, 2002, 2003). Therefore, it is essential that the complex nature of institutional racism as it applies to Britain is taken into account in any training initiative that is designed to help in developing a workforce that is culturally capable of combating racism as it impacts on services at many different levels. However, at present there is a crisis of leadership and a lack of expertise in dealing with racism in mental health services in the UK. Further, many so-called 'experts', often chosen by government, although without much credibility in black and minority ethnic (BME) communities, tend to lack understanding of service user, carer or family experience of services.

Second, there is the structure of service provision. Statutory mental health services are centrally funded under the aegis of the National Health Service (NHS) and free at the point of delivery. However, locally managed 'Trusts', co-ordinated by Strategic Health Authorities, are responsible for delivery of services and hence for ensuring that their staff are properly trained. But (and a big 'but'), the *basic* training of these staff is supervised by professional bodies, such as (in the case of psychiatrists) the Royal College of Psychiatrists. It is not always clear to what extent Trusts within the NHS carry responsibility for providing training themselves, though they are responsible for the quality of professional practice. To complicate matters even further, Primary Care Trusts are increasingly influential in decision-making on what services are commissioned for any particular area and hence carry some responsibility for ensuring that staff on their patch are properly trained.

Third, government has increasingly looked to mental health services for reducing the risks to the public rather than improving the quality of life of service users. The result is that coercive methods of control based on 'risk assessments' are now central to mental health practice – something that disadvantages BME communities disproportionately because of popular stereotypes of 'dangerousness' (Fernando *et al.*, 1998).

Fourth, although funding for social workers is derived from local authorities and not central government, they often work closely with professionals employed by the NHS in mental health, so that training is sometimes delivered jointly for both sets of staff. Recent restructuring of services has brought mental health social workers under effective control of health services, thereby strengthening use of medical approaches to mental health in general over 'social approaches'. Finally, although Britain has an active 'voluntary sector' providing mental health care for BME communities, this sector is under-resourced and poorly supported (Fernando, 2003).

It is important to note that RECC training should not be seen in isolation from the rest of what goes on within mental health service provision. Such training without a clear and effective strategy to address individual and institutional racism, based on a thorough analysis of power dynamics and structural inequalities, has limited impact on discrimination in services and on improving 'cultural capability' of staff. RECC approaches are integral to good practice – they are not 'special' or 'different' approaches to practice; RECC training is about improving mental health services for everyone and must be seen as a part of developing good practice all round.

I have been responsible for leading a team of people developing RECC training packages for the Care Services Improvement Partnership (CSIP) (http://www.csip.org.uk) and the National Institute for Mental Health in England (NIMHE) (http://www.nimhe.csip. org.uk). The main lesson I have learned over many years of conducting race equality training in mental health is that it is not easy. Box 8.1 gives some typical responses of people who have participated in such training. In this chapter I shall describe some aspects of the process of developing RECC packages by outlining the *challenges* that may arise in developing and implementing this type of training, beset as it is by political controversies and pressures, having to tackle institutional racism, professional resistances to changing long-established methods of clinical practice and the conservatism of many institutions. At the end of the chapter I shall outline briefly the new RECC training materials currently being developed as part of the government's national strategy *Delivering Race Equality* (Department of Health, 2005b) and due to be rolled out to all mental health practitioners during 2007–8.

Challenges in developing training materials

Institutional racism operates in organisations at individual, team and organisational levels. At an individual level racism can influence the beliefs and values of practitioners through personal prejudices and stereotypes shaping their behaviours and decisions. At the team level discriminatory cultures can be created by team members through their group dynamics and the 'unwritten rules' in teams. At an organisational level a racist culture may go unchallenged by the leadership and become further embedded in the organisational culture through the development of discriminatory systems, structures and policies. If these three levels of a service organisation are aligned, the whole 'system' then becomes one that is likely to be self-perpetuating and so become stronger over time. RECC training has to address three key drivers of organisational culture change if it is to be effective in improving practice and services generally (Figure 8.1).

Figure 8.1 Context of training

- Leadership capability
- Design of systems and structures
- Practitioner capability

The nature of the challenge from institutional racism in relation to these three key drivers in mental health services is not straight-forward and is currently changing rapidly.

Strategic approach to RECC training

RECC training must be seen within a larger strategy to bring about change towards race equality and cultural capability. Figure 8.1 summarises the prerequisites for such a strategy. Most importantly, there must be genuine and unequivocal support from leaders in service organisations for training to be successful. It is essential that leaders communicate a vision of RECC in the everyday work of people in the organisation. The vision needs to be easily under-stood, memorable and not over-technical in its presentation if there is to be wider ownership of the vision across the whole organ-isation. The aims of the organisation should reflect this vision and help to set a common purpose for all employees to achieve fair service provision for service users on the basis of race and culture. This purpose has to be reflected in policy statements and strategies to improve and develop services for BME people. Implementation of policies should include action plans and tasks so that employees are clear about their roles in promoting race equality.

A major factor in creating the right environment for RECC in an organisation is to design systems and structures that support the common purpose of fair service provision for BME people. Sys-tems such as referrals, assessments and care plans must be designed to encapsulate RECC in practice so that anti-discriminatory prac-tice is supported. Structures such as the way that teams are organ-ised, their geographic locations and their authority hierarchies must enable practitioners to use their judgement in decision-making where flexible and creative approaches are required. Moni-toring and review systems should highlight any areas of possible discrimination and unfair treatment of BME service users and other groups vulnerable to oppression. Early warning systems such as this can avoid the worst excesses of institutional discrimination rather than waiting for racist incidents that require public or internal inquiries.

Finally, practitioners need to be clear about their individual accountability to deliver appropriate and effective services to BME people, both individually and as a member of a team; this determines the team culture which shapes the culture of the workplace. For a team to function effectively, cultural differences must be valued in teamwork and practitioners must be prepared to engage in reflective practice and view values-based practice as an inherent part of 'professional work' in mental health.

Principles

I have outlined below some principles that should underpin any strategic approach to implementation of RECC training.

Promoting a 'social perspective' of mental health

The service user/survivor movement has long championed the social model approach to mental health and now new organisations are being developed to form alliances to promote a social model approach across traditional professional, service user and community divides (see Social Perspectives Network: http://www.spn. org.uk). A social perspective enables the richness of a person's cultural context to be properly examined and seen as an integral part of mental distress and its consequences for a person's life. Within this perspective, 'mental health assessments' take on a holistic character incorporating mind, body and spirit. This is in stark contrast to a narrow medical approach where the 'real' work is seen as 'diagnosis of mental illness'. Issues around power dynamics in services, institutional discrimination, and oppression are all encompassed by social perspectives of mental health.

Ensuring involvement of service users, families and communities

The most effective way forward for developing culturally appropriate and anti-discriminatory responses to the mental distress of BME people is to ensure service user, family and community participation in service planning, design and delivery. Genuine participation would result in radically altering the balance of power amongst the stakeholders in mental health services and lead to a transformation of services for a range of social groups who are vulnerable to oppression and discrimination. Services can then focus on real needs and not assumed needs based on stereotypical thinking and beliefs. Constructing a genuine dialogue, establishing common ground and common purpose, focusing on shared priorities and linking creative ideas to practical implementation offer a positive way forward.

'Whole systems' approach to service development and improvement

A systemic analysis is essential when tackling racism as it impacts at different levels within services and communities and has a wide range of interconnected factors that demand a deeper level of analysis. A superficial level of analysis of institutional discrimination leads to a reactive approach and short-term solutions, which result in long-term problems. Responding to an analysis merely based on incidents of racism or reacting to short-term political agendas condemns any RECC training initiative to an ineffective and tokenistic outcome. A 'whole systems' strategy would need to address not only skills development of practitioners but also that of the leaders in mental health services. There would need to be a new culture of RECC generated in mental health organisations; systems and structures would have to be designed to support and drive good practice. Interventions to improve and change services would have to be co-ordinated and undertaken at several different levels throughout service organisations to counteract the negative, multi-layered impacts of institutional racism.

Responsibility of professionals to service users and communities

Systems consist of people as well as policies, procedures and structures. It is imperative that practitioners engage in reflective practice that challenges their prejudices and stereotypes; critically evaluate their decisions; understand their work roles clearly; acknowledge the use of power and authority in their work; and operate in a holistic way. Greater BME service user participation in service delivery will help in this process, especially in assessment and individual planning. Increased independent advocacy for BME people subjected to compulsory detention must be established as a legal right, particularly for people whose first language is not English. Finally,

BME service user-led audit of services can be extremely effective in helping services to focus on relevant improvements as well as giving practitioners constructive feedback about their practice.

Preventative approach to service delivery

In order to build credibility and engage BME people who are in mental distress, services have to put as much time and resources into preventative work with BME communities as they do into crisis interventions. Mental health promotion, outreach work, accessible information, anti-stigma campaigns and promoting social inclusion in BME communities are all essential activities in a preventative approach. The use of increasingly coercive methods by services with BME people in mental distress is bound to lead to increased fears of social control and injustice amongst BME communities and ultimately an avoidance of services altogether (see Keating *et al.*, 2002). There is a growing problem of stigma attached to mental distress within BME communities which has not been addressed by mental health services despite pockets of good practice – for example, Mental Health Media and North Birmingham Mental Health NHS Trust have developed a video, '*Mann ki baat*', about mental health problems in Asian communities presented by 'Bollywood star' Dharmendra Deol in 2000. Lower level community support initiatives that are not labelled as 'mental health' are urgently required, especially with 'hard-to-reach' groups such as young people, black men, refugees and asylum seekers and people from non-English-speaking backgrounds.

Challenges in presentation to participants

The typical comments from course participants reproduced in Box 8.1 hint at much deeper structural problems associated with race and culture in mental health services. These problems have proved to be quite intractable over a number of years despite a great deal of research evidence and several strategies to tackle the problem of racism in mental health services. I shall highlight just a few key issues that are currently emerging as major challenges to making progress on RECC in mental health services. Some of these responses may be related to the quality of delivery by trainers but I shall discuss this later.

Box 8.1 Typical comments of participants in race equality training

> 'It's all very well telling me about this stuff but it's my manager you want to talk to!'
> 'Our managers don't listen to us.'
> 'We did this kind of training years ago and nothing has really changed.'
> 'We just don't have the time to do it like that – they expect us to take on more and more work.'
> 'There aren't the resources for us to develop anything new at present.'
> 'We do all this anyway.'
> 'I'm part of a Health dominated team now so we can't do things in this way as we operate with a very medicalised approach.'
> 'It feels like you are attacking me for all of this – there is nothing I can do about it.'

Hostility

Sometimes the response from people is hostile due to anger at being accused of 'being racist', as it is perceived by them. More often, it is a response that suggests a failure to recognise institutional racism as a problem at all. People try to claim that they are just as likely to be discriminated against and treated unfavourably as BME people. Trainers who try to highlight institutional racism are presumed to have a hidden political agenda and white trainers who do this are somehow 'betraying their own people'.

Denial

This response may recognise that institutional racism exists elsewhere but 'not here'. People will claim that there are no problems with their services in relation to BME people even when presented with evidence to the contrary. People often make false or exaggerated claims about their services – claims that are not supported by BME service users in that area. If people in 'denial' are pressed harder they may enter into a 'hostile' response instead.

Apathy

This response essentially does not view institutional racism as being 'all that bad', and discrimination is seen as 'to be expected', ordinary and unavoidable. Individuals who experience racism are expected to accept it and 'make the best' of their situation. Service change is seen as being 'too hard' or 'unrealistic'. Apathy is arguably the most effective 'driver' of institutional racism as people with power and influence in services need only be apathetic and not question discriminatory systems, policies, procedures and organisational cultures for institutional racism to thrive. In other words, practitioners do not have to be actively racist to racially discriminate, they just have to be apathetic and the 'system' discriminates.

Pretence

In this response people recognise there is a problem with racism but deal with criticism by claiming that problems have been addressed when they have not. People may exaggerate small steps towards progress or take credit for a few excellent agencies in their area whilst not tackling serious problems within the majority of local services. Challenging this response in training courses is quite difficult as trainers must have evidence of local service delivery to BME people to be able to effectively get participants to critically reflect on their practice. The net effect of this response is to increase the covert nature of institutional racism, leading to tokenism and the creation of further barriers to progress.

Avoidance

People engaging in this response recognise that institutional racism is a problem in services but they will deflect criticism about racism by claiming that other forms of discrimination are worse, such as sexism or discrimination against disabled people. A 'hierarchy of oppression' is thus constructed in people's minds which is both divisive within the training group and does not lead to a coherent value-base for equality as a whole. The effect of this response is to deflect energy and time away from real change towards wrangling about 'who is worst off' and therefore most deserving of attention and resources, rather than actually addressing discrimination.

Puzzlement

Another response following recognition of the problem of racism could be one of puzzlement at to what to do about it. People may express feelings of being 'deskilled' and unconfident about dealing with BME people. There may well be a desire to improve practice but a lack of clarity about how to do this. Trainers should acknowledge the desire to improve practice and work constructively with participants to use the RECC materials to give people confidence and help them appreciate that they are engaging in good practice and not doing anything 'special' or different.

Challenges for trainers

Some of the challenges have been referred to above. The general approach of trainers to the responses highlighted in the previous section is important. Trainers need to weigh up the strength of any challenge and be prepared to justify it, as people will be making a judgement about whether they perceive the 'challenge' as an 'attack'. Many of these responses of participants may not arise from logical reasoning and so mere presentation of evidence, to counteract the views expressed, may not in itself be sufficient to shift people's thinking. Trainers have to look beyond immediate problematic responses and have a positive expectation of longer-term impacts of learning, as it is quite possible that some learning may take place months after the training is completed: what was taken in during training may only become effective when it links up with a new experience of the participant or realisation of its relevance in practice. The challenge of linking learning with practice improvement is one for any type of training, especially training aimed at tackling systemic problems as in RECC training.

Since the topics covered in RECC training and its aims are now fairly well known, participants in training may be quite sophisticated in their responses to it. For example, politically correct statements may be expressed with little substance behind them. It is important for trainers to keep in mind that the aim of the training is to bring about improvement in quality of mental health practice – something that is particularly important in situations where there is an established, discriminatory service culture and poor practice has become embedded into the habitual behaviour of practitioners.

Commitment

Trainers need first and foremost to be aware of and understand their own motivation for taking on such training. It is this motivation that trainers will fall back on when the going gets tough in delivering such challenging and complex training. If trainers do not do this for themselves, the issues raised by participants certainly will. The motivation of RECC trainers must relate to the overall purpose and learning outcomes of the RECC materials if trainers are going to be able to deliver the materials over an extended period of time.

Getting to grips with materials

Before trainers even embark upon RECC training they have to be prepared to deal with resistance to the issues and to the material itself. The demands on trainers to be able to handle difficult questions and have a good grasp of the underlying principles and theories will be great. The lack of established good practice in dealing with BME people in mental distress will require trainers to be able to readily apply the models in the materials to realistic local mental health issues.

Taking on local issues

The materials will have to be adapted by trainers to ensure that they are relevant to local issues that practitioners raise in training sessions. Time for discussion of local concerns about services for BME people must be allowed and constructive discussion facilitated. The nature of BME service user experience will vary from area to area according to factors such as rural versus urban, size of BME populations and the history of migration into different areas.

Involving service users and families

One of the most important features of the RECC training materials is that they are designed to incorporate inputs from BME service user/survivor trainers. However, despite the undoubted benefits of such involvement, there are dangers involved for co-trainers. They have to model a positive partnership with BME service user trainers and facilitate the effective use of service user expertise in the training sessions. If this can be achieved, the benefits for the quality of training are considerable and a much more effective and constructive challenge of professional practice is possible.

Dealing with culturally strong teams

Although training whole teams can potentially lead to greater changes in practice and service development, there is also an increased risk that teams with strong cultures may not be so open to change. Dealing with such teams may be very difficult for trainers as long-standing alliances and 'cliques' will tend to emerge if team members are challenged about discriminatory practice. Traditional ways of doing things may 'feel right' even though they are discriminatory; if they have remained unchallenged they will become part of the 'unwritten rules' teams operate by.

Multi-agency working

Multi-agency working is still not fully developed in many areas despite several years of multi-disciplinary working in mental health services. The power dynamics between different professional groups can be complex and take on greater significance than the needs of BME service users. Sometimes certain professional groups will see themselves as being more anti-discriminatory than others, or one group will tend to be 'scapegoated' as being the only problem in a simplistic analysis.

Training materials

The aim of these materials was to produce something suitable for all mental health practitioners regardless of qualification level or work experience. They were also intended to incorporate other forms of equality as much as possible. The materials were arranged into twelve learning sessions of approximately one and a half hour's duration, delivered as a series of regular short sessions for practitioners or combined to form a variety of workshops or programmes.

As part of a 'whole systems' approach to training, several of the exercises are designed to generate data and evidence of practice for managers. The purpose of feeding through such data to leaders is to enable them to make better judgements about policy and procedures and ultimately design better systems and structures to support and deliver anti-discriminatory practice. In this way leaders will get an invaluable insight into the culture of the organisation and the views of service users and staff about the quality of services. One of the central design principles is to present BME service user perspectives and interests throughout the programme. Finally, following each session there are suggestions for small workplace projects designed to link learning in that session to practice.

One of the most innovatory aspects of the RECC training is that it has been designed to be delivered in partnership with BME service user/survivor trainers. Co-training between BME service user/survivor trainers and other mental health trainers adds more complexity to the implementation of RECC training but it is essential in achieving its fundamental goals. We have found that issues of power, institutional discrimination, service user experience and cultural appropriateness have been discussed and dealt with much more effectively when BME service user/survivor trainers have been involved than when they have not. It is our aim to include 'training for trainers' as part of the implementation process for RECC, along with the establishment of a pool of BME service user/survivor trainers who may be called upon.

Future

Although the RECC materials are pitched at around 'foundation level' training, a second level of RECC training is being developed to focus on RECC skills development in specific areas of practice, such as assessment and person-centred planning, working with interpreters in interviews, and in service areas such as Children and Adolescent Mental Health Services, forensic services, drug and alcohol services and services for elders. A third level of training is being developed for team leaders on managing diverse teams and taking on a leadership role in promoting RECC. Finally, a fourth level is being planned for senior managers and service planners, which will focus on systemic approaches to RECC, changing organisational cultures, designing systems to promote RECC, and creating sustainable service improvements for BME communities. Detailed information about the RECC materials and the additional levels of RECC training is available on the website: http://www. fernsassociates.co.uk.

Chapter 9

Developing psychological services for refugee survivors of torture

Nimisha Patel

Refugee people, including those who have survived torture, are amongst the most vulnerable, disconnected, isolated and excluded people within British society. Compared to many people from well settled Black and ethnic minority (BME) communities in the UK, most refugees and asylum seekers are relatively recent arrivals, many with very complex and multiple health concerns. For survivors of torture, the relationship between human rights and well-being takes on an added significance when not only have they had their basic human rights violated, but their right to health eroded and their well-being further affected as a result of treatment by the very authorities from whom they have sought sanctuary, the 'host' society. It is argued in this chapter that mental health and psychological services as they are structured in the UK reinforce inequalities and contribute to the marginalisation and exclusion of already marginalised and vulnerable refugee survivors of torture. This chapter outlines the experiences and issues faced by many refugee survivors of torture fleeing to Britain, highlighting key human rights principles in developing mental and psychological health services which facilitate the protection of people's most basic human rights to dignity and health. Finally the chapter outlines some ways in which services may address the problems faced by refugees in ways that respect their human rights.

Refugees and torture

In order to be recognised as a refugee, an asylum seeker must fulfil the terms of the UN 1951 Convention Relating to the Status of Refugees ('Geneva Convention 1951') (United Nations High Commissioner for Refugees [UNHCR], 1996) and demonstrate that:

owing to a well founded fear of being persecuted for reasons of race, religion, nationality, membership of a particular social group or political opinion [he] is outside the country of his nationality and is unable, or owing to such fear, is unwilling to avail himself of the protection of that country . . .

(1996: 16)

A significant proportion of refugees (including asylum seekers) are survivors of torture, war or organised violence. Torture includes physical violation of the body with emotional consequences, such as beatings, suspension, use of electricity, and rape, as well as psychological methods, including solitary confinement, sleep deprivation, forced nudity and being forced to witness others being tortured, etc. Torture is deliberate and systematic, aiming to dehumanise, disempower and terrorise individuals and whole communities. It is the use of absolute power as a tool of oppression.

Currently, over 104 countries in the world practise torture (Amnesty International, 2006) although it is prohibited by international human rights and humanitarian law, from which no derogation is ever possible, even in times of war or emergency. Many refugee people have experienced torture, yet they and their health needs are often forgotten in health services.

In search of safety

During their flight searching for safety, many refugees endure further hardship and suffering. They may face long, arduous and dangerous journeys, physical dangers, and financial and/or sexual exploitation. They may experience malnutrition, lack of health care, hunger and assault. Although refugees form a heterogeneous group in terms of languages spoken, culture, and political and religious affiliations, they all share the experience of exile. Forced exile challenges the foundations of people's previous lives and of their communities, often radically interrupting the trajectories of their lives, confronting their identity and sense of dignity. Refugee people can experience profound and multiple losses of relatives, friends, community, health, status, role, etc. A predominant theme is the loss of hope: the hope of justice, of recognition and of safety. As one client said: 'I just want to be safe, is that asking too much?'

Inequalities that refugees experience in the 'host country', sometimes through institutional racism in Britain, further marginalise and disempower them. This is further compounded by hostility and suspicion from the authorities, their plight being manipulated by the media, and other abuses and hostility they experience as 'foreigners' looked on with suspicion. Following the September 11 attacks in the US and the London bombings in July 2005, by introducing anti-terrorism laws that erode human rights, Britain has fostered a political environment adversely affecting people seen as 'the other', the potential 'enemy within', namely ethnic minorities (particularly, though not exclusively, people of Arabic origin and Muslims) and migrants (International Council on Human Rights Policy [ICHRP], 2000, 2002). Many refugee clients report being too afraid to go outside for fear of racist verbal and physical abuse they have previously experienced and which they say they are too afraid to report to the authorities: 'they kicked me, spat on me and called me names; they said I was a terrorist and should be shot'.

Asylum, immigration policy and the legal system

Asylum seekers with active claims are dispersed to areas outside of London and the southeast; they are entitled to financial support (only 70 per cent of Income Support) and accommodation in the areas they are sent to. They are not allowed to work, unless granted asylum, after which they are also entitled to make an application for welfare support and alternative accommodation, and they have a right to family reunion. However, leave to remain is also temporary for the majority of people: Indefinite Leave to Remain (ILR) is only granted after five years' leave to remain, subject to review; or Humanitarian Protection (HP) is granted for five years before review and Discretionary Leave (DL) is granted for three years, only to a small proportion of applicants.

In the last eight years there have been four new Immigration Acts affecting refugee people, with an increasingly complex, and rapidly changing, asylum system. Successive governments have introduced policies aimed at controlling asylum applications and removing failed asylum seekers, exacerbating refugee people's sense of uncertainty, helplessness and feeling at the mercy of the government. As one client put it:

> nobody cares why we are here, we are a political football, no one asks, why did you leave your country to come here? Do

you think I would leave my country for a life of uncertainty, loneliness and this humiliation, no, I came because I had no choice, I came to be safe, but who cares, they just use us to fight their elections.

Detention and removal

Refugee people, including survivors of torture, can be detained in the UK in high security settings, reinforcing trauma from previous detentions, leaving them bewildered and terrified at the prospect of being held against their will until their case is positively or negatively resolved. In 2004 a study by the Medical Foundation reported a number of cases in which immigration detainees (all Black) suffered injuries as a result of excessive, and in many cases gratuitous, force being used during attempts to remove them from the UK (Granville-Chapman, 2004).

Health services

Whilst access to health care available to asylum seekers and those with a positive decision (refugee status, ILR, HP, DL and Exceptional Leave to Remain) has been left intact, entitlement to secondary health care has been significantly restricted by the Department of Health (DH) for failed asylum seekers with potentially lethal conditions (Burnett and Rhys Jones, 2006; P. Hall, 2006), and access to general practitioner (GP) practices has become, in effect, discretionary. These restrictions pose serious concerns: the provision of free secondary mental health services, except in 'life threatening cases', is at the discretion of the Mental Health Trust (the body providing services), which may charge failed asylum seekers for any such treatment received. Those particularly at risk include people with enduring mental health problems and those who are at high risk of suicide. Accessing appropriate psychological health services can also be difficult for refugee people: they may be unable to access primary care services when they are unable to find a GP who will register them; some psychological services may place them on a waiting list; they may lack familiarity with psychological approaches, or clinicians may lack experience in working with interpreters, or with torture survivors; and finally, there may be strict criteria for inclusion, for research (or other) reasons.

The total experience in the UK of a harsh (legal) asylum system, racism, detention, poverty, homelessness or very poor housing, difficulties in access to health services, isolation and continued uncertainty in exile is often subjectively described by refugee people thus: 'this is worse than the torture I suffered before' or 'this is torture in an open prison, there are no four walls, but we are imprisoned and treated like criminals, not even like humans'. It is in this context that mental health care for refugee people must be examined. Added to that is the often unquestioned application of western psychological approaches, resulting in a 'therapeutic' situation described by Patel and Fatimilehin (1999) as secondary colonisation, oppressing the already marginalised and disempowered, perhaps inadvertently, in the guise of professional 'help'.

Providing mental and psychological health services

Delivering an appropriate health service to a culturally and linguistically diverse population who have suffered gross human rights violations and armed conflict, and who continue to face many social, legal and economic difficulties in the UK, can seem an overwhelming challenge. In my view, such a challenge requires a deep and long-term commitment to upholding the fundamental rights of refugee people's access to health care which does not further marginalise, pathologise and disempower them. The following seven key principles offer such a human rights approach to developing health services.

1 Early identification of vulnerable refugee survivors of torture

The first principle is to enable the earliest possible identification of survivors of torture in health assessments, people who have a fundamental legal right to treatment under the United Nations Convention against Torture and Other Cruel, Inhuman or Degrading Treatment and Punishment (UNCAT) which came into force in 1987. Such identification can enable appropriate health care to be offered, as well as aiding legal protection. This principle requires a number of initiatives: early assessment by health professionals trained in exploring and assessing the health needs of refugee survivors of torture; mechanisms and resources to ensure that appropriate and culturally sensitive care can be offered; systems in place to ensure that appropriate interpreters are available when required; resources available to provide adequate and appropriate support and supervision for health professionals working with refugees; and mechanisms to provide legal representation for clients with quick access to relevant documentation (e.g. medico-legal reports) which may support the client's allegation of torture or organised violence.

2 Non-pathologising services and practices

Psychological treatment requires trust and safety, which for refugee survivors of torture can take time, particularly given that torture targets trust in others, control and agency. There needs to be an acknowledgement that torture is a deliberate political act, not an accidental trauma or a disease or illness, and its effects require not just psychological and physical care, but help in supporting people to re-establish a connection with society, with other human beings, and a belief in a just society. Professionals working with refugees must at all times seek to promote affirmation of their clients' humanity, dignity and basic human rights, developing services and therapeutic practices which acknowledge and respond to these fundamental issues.

3 Non-oppressive and non-discriminatory services and practices

Mental health and psychological health services risk reinforcing experiences of oppression and discrimination in many ways. An example is the restricted entitlements to free health care based on one's legal status, rather than clinical need. Professionals working with refugee people have a duty to try to ensure free access to health care, which is particularly significant for those who are most vulnerable (for example, those with mental health problems, survivors of torture).

Services need to respond to the linguistic needs of refugee people. Comments like 'we can't see people who don't speak English because we don't have the resources for interpreters' or 'there is no evidence that psychological therapy works when working with interpreters' or 'their needs are too complex and their lack of English does not meet with our inclusion criteria for research at this clinic/service' are not only ill considered but can amount to discriminatory policies and practices which exclude non-English-speaking refugees, thus breaching race relations regulations.

Other ways in which discrimination is practised, sometimes unwittingly, are illustrated by the following incidents known to me personally:

> *When referring on a woman seen in the National Health Service (NHS), someone who had experienced rape as torture in her own country and rape in the UK whilst homeless*: 'She is not suitable for our service, we deal with sexual assault not sexual torture, and she has had multiple rapes, which makes it a complex case.'

> *When referring on a family seen in the NHS, who did not speak English and who had experienced organised violence and the loss of one of their adult children in detention by torture*: 'We do not have the resources to see families like these, and they don't speak English, perhaps they would be better with someone from a community group.'

> *When refusing to accept a referral of a refugee survivor of torture*: 'There is no evidence that working with interpreters in psychological therapy is effective so perhaps it is better if you [a voluntary sector agency] can find someone who speaks their language or refer them to a community organisation?'

> *When negotiating with a colleague in the NHS to take a referral of a refugee survivor of torture*: 'Oh I've already got an Iraqi and they can be so demanding and difficult, and we've got quite a long waiting list . . .'

To ensure that services are non-discriminatory, it is necessary to question the way decisions are made on acceptance (or rejection) of referrals, how and why some people are prioritised, why particular interventions/therapeutic approaches are recommended or denied, etc. It is essential that there is adequate training and guidance to increase awareness of discrimination and racism in services, but in ways that enable staff to develop more confidence, skills and commitment to serving the needs of all equally, rather than

creating resistance and facilitating the development of more sophisticated ways of evading charges of racism. Developing non-
discriminatory services and practices also entails mechanisms to
ensure that refugee people are aware of their health care options,
that information about services and how to access them is
translated into relevant languages and distributed appropriately,
for example in refugee community organisations, GP services,
advice centres, etc. The provision of professional interpreters and
bilingual workers is essential and longer-term funding must be
prioritised and secured.

4 Culturally capable services and practice

Cultural capability requires that services are based on culturally
aware practices, which move beyond having posters of Black
people and 'ethnic' décor in the waiting rooms, and address skills
and knowledge and awareness of cultural issues in assessing refugee
clients' difficulties and experiences. Therapeutic skills that move
beyond the unquestioning application of traditional Eurocentric
psychological models are crucial in enabling clinicians to colla-
boratively develop more culturally meaningful and creative ways of
working towards rehabilitation and social integration.

However, for many refugee people, talking to a mental health
professional is seen as indicating enduring and serious mental
health problems, something which induces further shame and fear
of exclusion from their communities. For many, experiences of
torture have also directly involved health professionals, or been
compounded by professionals' silence and complicity in not con-
demning torture, or not documenting evidence of its effects when
reported.

Cultural and other contextual influences can shape the way in
which refugees present themselves and their difficulties to a health
professional, as well as influencing the culturally available options
for responding to and managing the effects of war, torture and
persecution. Working with refugees necessitates that we explore
actively our own model of working, explaining our approach,
concepts commonly utilised in therapy, the aims of therapy and so
on (Mahtani, 2003). Concepts and language used in therapeutic
work are not necessarily familiar to clients, including the concept
of therapy or counselling. Explaining confidentiality in ways that

can be understood within a cultural and political context is essential, particularly for refugee people, many of whom have suffered grave consequences as a result of information about them being misused. Fears of confidentiality breaches extend to concerns that members of their family or community may find out that they have experienced torture, or psychological health difficulties – which can add to their feelings of shame and lead to experiences of further marginalisation and even exclusion from their families and communities.

For professionals, cultural capability requires a commitment to self-reflection and exploration of one's own racism, biases and assumptions about refugee people, one's own ethnic/political history as well as one's motives for wanting to work or to avoid working with them, which in turn necessitates honesty, depth and sophistication in self-reflection skills. Needless to say, adequate and culturally competent professional support and supervision are vital to ethical practice with refugee people. Additionally, the employment of bilingual clinicians can help ensure continual skills sharing and learning between staff with differing expertise within service provision, thus avoiding ghettoising services for refugee clients, and leaving the responsibility for often the most complex and demanding cases with a handful of staff.

5 Contextually competent services and practice

As social beings, people do not exist in a vacuum; we and our worlds are context-bound and inevitably and inextricably connected to each other in complex ways. For refugee people, 'trauma' is not a single event, located in the past, but an ongoing and accumulated experience of exclusion, devaluation, hostility, indifference, poverty and discrimination: the harsh social context of their existence in exile. Individualisation of distress decontextualises and de-politicises distress, focusing on *effects*, not *causes*. It ignores relationships between structural inequality, injustice, oppression, power, privilege and violence, past and current.

Mental health professionals need to take an active stance against human rights violations in their work, dispensing their professional cloak, showing an interest not just in what problems a client presents, but in how they came to have these difficulties, what happened to them, why, by whom and what it means to them. Thus, the refugee person and the impact of their experiences are not assumed to be captured and represented in their psyches and in their symptoms, but are understood within their socio-political context. Symptoms tell a story, a story about injustice which needs to be heard, witnessed and acknowledged. Physical symptoms must also not be ignored as 'somatisation', but explored and where necessary investigated, for they can be related to experiences of torture.

Therapeutic approaches need to address the multiplicity of refugee experiences, countering the fragmentation of health and psychological well-being often experienced by survivors of torture, promoting their capacity to connect with other human beings. Therapy should not aim narrowly to 'fix' symptoms, but serve a significant function in bearing witness to atrocity, in offering humanity, compassion and honest communication. Therapists should attend to the layers of context, simultaneously and separately at different stages, locating pathology not in the individual with a mental health focus but in the structures, political and social processes and conditions which enable social injustices and torture to continue, with impunity – in other words, they should offer 'holistic' care that addresses the totality of health and well-being while exploring and wherever possible attending to the social and political conditions which impact on health. Therapeutic work should address injustices clients have experienced in the past and currently. Experiences of powerlessness, hopelessness and worthlessness need to be acknowledged and explored. In referring to his experiences in the UK, one client said, 'I came here to be safe, but I suffer so much, I can do nothing, the smell of fear, decay and death in prison were nothing compared to the smell of indifference and hostility here – is this what you call a Western democracy?'

Privileging constructions of self in individual terms within western psychological theories, research and practice has ensured that the significance of context and issues of power is minimised, or ignored (see Chapter 1). At the heart of almost all western psychological approaches is the idea that *talking is healing*, an issue highly pertinent to refugee clients. As White and Marsella suggest, 'the use of "talk therapy" aimed at altering individual behaviour through the individual's "insight" into his or her own personality is firmly rooted in a conception of the person as a distinct and independent individual, capable of self-transformation in relative isolation from particular social contexts' (1982: 28). In privileging his political and collective identity, a Kurdish man once remarked in therapy:

'talking makes things worse, talking costs lives and while I am here talking my comrades are being slaughtered by the dragon [the government], how can talking help them?' For him, talking about his feelings was inaction, self-indulgence and a betrayal of his people to whom he felt he owed his freedom. Talking, and the values central to psychological practice, contrasted with the values in his political culture of stoicism, secrecy and solidarity.

Psychologists and other mental health practitioners often position themselves as impartial, objective and politically neutral. Prilleltensky points out that, 'by portraying itself as a strictly "objective" endeavour, many of psychology's prescriptive biases are erroneously interpreted as merely descriptive assertions about human behaviour' (1989: 797), although prescriptions or 'solutions' often conform with dominant ideologies. Neutrality itself supports a denial of the significance of one's values, privileges and power, whilst alleged objectivity can result in not questioning socio-political origins of distress and not considering the part played by the professional themselves in supporting oppressive practices – even in the guise of 'professional help'. The professional cloak of impartiality, objectivity and neutrality may merely defend and legitimate human rights abuses, thus contradicting the humanitarian values of psychological and mental health practice with those who have suffered human rights violations.

Nevertheless, therapeutic interventions alone are insufficient. Clinicians need to engage in advocacy, for example for suitable housing, access to legal representation, access to education for children, and access to other health services. It is vital that health professionals challenge health regulations that victimise the most vulnerable refugee people who have become failed asylum seekers, destitute and facing the threat of return. The following example is illustrative:

> A young woman who had been raped and subsequently affected by a civil conflict became separated from her four younger siblings and mother who remained in her country of origin. She was helped to escape to the UK by an agent. He raped her during their journey to Britain, and she became pregnant by the rape. During the course of psychological work with her, she became a failed asylum seeker and, with her child, became destitute and suffered ill health as a result of a difficult birth which necessitated a Caesarean section. Terrified to

sleep rough for fear of further attacks on her, or her baby, she slept on the floors of people she had previously met at church, too afraid to seek further help, including that of her previous general practitioner, in case she was returned to her country of origin.

Therapeutic work in this case was about ensuring that she was able to access necessary medical investigation and treatment, that she and her baby were safe, that she had access to food for herself and her baby, and exploring options for urgent housing and for further legal representation. It also involved active exploration of where she could access support and be connected to social networks, such as in a relevant community organisation or church. Having explored with her the possibility of tracing her family to have some knowledge of their whereabouts in her country of origin, the Red Cross family tracing service was contacted for help, emphasising the need for collaboration with other agencies.

6 Collaboration

Collaboration with refugee community organisations (RCOs), who may be the first port of call for many refugee people, is essential given their invaluable and unique expertise, skills and knowledge about other available services – something often lacking in statutory services. Further, many RCOs have knowledge about the cultural, social and political context of people in their community and about the difficulties experienced by them in terms of accessing appropriate health care. However, it is important to be alert to differences and political, ethnic or religious divisions between RCOs, exploring the client's views prior to referring directly to an RCO.

Collaboration between statutory organisations and RCOs can also be at the level of service planning, delivery and evaluation. This may take the form of joint training or developing joint projects, for example those which do not have a 'health' focus, but instead (for example) provide information, raise awareness or increase access to help with housing and welfare. But genuine collaboration requires sustained funding (for RCOs), and energy and commitment from both sides. A guiding principle may be that RCOs should not be exploited in any way directly or indirectly. RCOs must benefit from partnership as much as, or more than, the statutory sector may benefit.

7 Addressing power: maximising choice and control

Human rights violations, particularly in the context of historical devaluation, persecution and economic hardship, can strip people of their dignity, autonomy and opportunities in life. Torture aims to render people helpless and terrified, such that they come to believe that they are helpless victims to tyranny, abuse and violence. The concept of informed consent (Mahtani, 2003), choice and control then becomes crucial in any related psychological practice – the antithesis to coercion, secrecy and oppression.

Addressing power can mean maximising opportunities to create options and opportunities for refugee people and enabling them to make choices and to have a voice about their own health care. User rights are natural partners to human rights. The offering of choice is a recognition that they have a view, that they have the right to express that view without adverse consequences and that every effort will be made to address their choices, in discussion with them. As one client said, 'Look at me, look what they [torturers] did to me, I am half a man, do I not deserve half a chance to have my health, to feel like a whole man?'

Many refugee people have been politically very aware and active prior to becoming exiled, many have held prominent leadership positions, many have fought for their basic rights, and been subsequently persecuted and tortured as a result. The meaning of voice and choice is not academic. For many refugees it has profound meaning and significance – as does being denied those rights. Informing clients about user groups and/or networks, and facilitating them in being connected to those groups, can be very helpful in terms of support, information about available services and enabling people to be aware of and to exercise their rights within services. However, not everyone will choose or feel able to engage in user groups, for a variety of reasons, including timing – for example when clients are in a crisis situation in terms of not having their immediate needs met for safety, housing and food, which can be a predominant concern. Fears of services being withdrawn, or of reprimand (given their past experiences of political violence as a result of speaking out), or fears that their asylum claim will be jeopardised, or that others will know about their difficulties, compounded by shame and distrust, can all deter a person from engaging in user networks. Nonetheless, clients can be encouraged and supported in connecting to user groups where they may find solidarity, support and a greater opportunity to have their collective voice heard in influencing health service delivery.

Conclusions

The provision of mental health services to address the experiences, difficulties and concerns of refugee survivors of torture requires an approach which is not narrow in focus, rigid in design and practice and fragmented in delivery. This chapter has outlined seven key principles to guide service design, delivery and practice within a human rights approach. To return to the man who asked, 'what are my human rights when I am not even human?' – perhaps we could all do well to remember that our democracy, our health services and our commitment to human rights can be judged by our treatment of and humanity towards some of the most vulnerable and oppressed people in society: those who have suffered gross human rights violations.

Chapter 10

Black service 'user involvement' – rhetoric or reality?

Premila Trivedi

Service 'user involvement' can be defined as the active engagement of people who use mental health services in the development of mental health policy and practice, for example, in the planning, delivery and monitoring of mental health services, in the training and education of mental health staff and in mental health research. Such 'user involvement' is predicated on the idea that service users are experts on their own experiences and involving them will ensure that their needs and concerns become central to mental health clinical practice. The importance of this has been increasingly stressed over the last decade (Crawford, 2001; Department of Health, 1999a, 2000a) and 'user involvement' (including Black 'user involvement') is now repeated like a mantra in most national and local mental health policy documents (e.g. Department of Health, 2003; Keating *et al.*, 2002; National Institute for Mental Health in England, 2003). This has resulted in more and more service users becoming 'involved', but, significantly, those from certain groups, for example people from Black and minority ethnic (BME) groups, homeless people, and gay and lesbian service users, have not become involved to an appreciable extent (Health and Social Care Advisory Service, 2005; Wallcraft, 2003).

Although Black service users, especially those from African-Caribbean and African communities, are under-represented in 'user involvement' settings they are massively over-represented within clinical settings, often at the harshest end of services (Mental Health Act Commission, 2006). In recent years, several high profile reports (Department of Health, 2003; Keating *et al.*, 2002) have stressed the importance of 'involving' more Black users, with their crucial experiential expertise, creativity and ideas for improvements, in improving services for Black people, but have not examined in any depth why so few currently engage in 'user involvement'.

In an excellent and comprehensive review of BME service user participation in social care, Begum (2006) attributes a dearth of 'involved' BME users in these settings to the fact that services too often sideline them and instead look to other groups, such as BME professionals, community leaders or voluntary sector workers, to represent their interests. Although this may be the main reason in mental health settings, other equally (or more) important reasons need to be explored, particularly in the context of role and power relations between Black service users and mental health professionals (Bertram, 2002; Dalal, 2004; Linnett, 1999). In this Chapter I attempt to do this, drawing on my own personal experience of being 'involved' in various capacities over the last ten years. I conclude this chapter by identifying some of the key issues in mental health services that need addressing if Black users are to engage in 'user involvement' and begin to bridge the massive gap which currently exists between the rhetoric of Black 'user involvement' and reality. At a time when the mental health of Black people and the way they are treated within mental health services are causing such political and social concern (McKenzie, 2007), mental health services cannot afford to go on losing all that Black users could bring to mental health service development.

Personal experience

My personal journey though 'user involvement' has consisted of four distinct stages when I have become 'involved':

- As part of a generic user group ('Communicate'), where I participated (for example) on committees (Trivedi, 2001), in the training of mental health staff, as a user researcher (Kavanagh et al., 2003; Philpot et al., 2004; Trivedi, 2002), and in making presentations and writing articles (Anonymous, 1999; Trivedi, 1996, 1999).
- As a member of a specifically Black user group ('SIMBA' – see Chapter 18), involved on our own terms in raising awareness of Black issues in mental health and suggesting ideas for improving services through creative work (Trivedi, 2007a; Trivedi et al., 2002), liaising with other like-minded groups, such as 'Mellow' (see Chapter 11) and the 'Transcultural Psychiatry Society' (see Fernando, 1988), to campaign for change.

- As a volunteer and freelance worker, focusing in particular on training mental health professionals regarding race, racism and mental health (Ferns, 2005), and writing to raise awareness of Black issues (Maule *et al.*, 2007; Trivedi, 2002, 2004).
- As an education and training adviser (service 'user involvement') employed part-time within a large Mental Health Trust to ensure service user perspectives are at the heart of training within the Trust and to build capacity amongst a range of service users so that they can be actively 'involved' in training mental health professionals (Tew *et al.*, 2004).

This seemingly simple progression has not always been smooth, and each stage of my journey has had its own benefits and challenges. Overall, though 'user involvement' on a personal level has given me important opportunities to grow and develop, it is not clear to me whether my 'involvement' has actually had any influence on clinical practice since I have rarely received any specific feedback on this and little seems to have improved for Black patients at a grass roots level (Mental Health Act Commission, 2006).

The latter was shockingly brought home to me last year when I was forcibly admitted to an acute ward and personally faced with the harsh reality that, in spite of service 'user involvement' and many ostensibly positive changes in mental health services (e.g. home treatment, better ward environments, protected time for staff and patients to communicate, more Black staff, etc.), little seemed to have actually changed at a grass roots level at the point which is most crucial to service users, namely the interface between themselves and mental health staff. With one or two notable exceptions, I experienced uninterested and disempowering staff attitudes, negligible levels of communication, a purely medical focus and a lack of cultural competence both during the admission process and during subsequent 'incarceration'. Even more shocking to me was how, on my admission, I suddenly seemed to switch from my role as self-determining, actively 'involved' and respected service user (whose voice was actively sought) to one of coerced, 'un-involved' and disrespected psychiatric patient (whose voice was actively ignored or dismissed as being part of my symptoms). This deeply disturbing contradiction brought home to me how rigidly roles are allocated to service users (and staff) in clinical settings and how such rigidity may preclude 'user involvement' (Linnett, 1999), especially Black 'user involvement'. I know that many Black users have had such negative experiences in their 'role' as Black patient. The traditional and rigid ways in which mental health services perceive Black users may be a significant reason why so few become 'involved'. As one Black service user said to me when I was badgering him to become 'involved': 'No way. Why would I want to go back to where I was treated so badly? That would prove I *really* was mad' (Falconer, 2005, private communication).

Roles and power in mental health services

In a perceptive critique of user involvement, Linnett (1999) has discussed the rigid roles service users (and staff) are traditionally allocated in mental health services and stresses the need for more flexibility if 'user involvement' is ever to succeed. Allocation of roles inevitably comes with allocation of power and the whole process serves the purpose of establishing a version of reality in which certain identities, differences and roles (e.g. patient, mental health professional) are made critical and accorded different status in society (Dalal, 2004). Once this is established, then ideology does the work of sustaining these roles and power relationships by convincing all that this is the natural order of the world – that the mentally ill must be contained, disempowered and 'treated' – and that this must be maintained if society is to remain stable and cohesive (Dalal, 2004).

For Black service users, this may be of particular importance since allocation of role and power within mental health settings will be determined not only by the identities and differences between service users and professionals but also by those between Black and White people. These may then compound synergistically to severely disadvantage Black service users (especially African-Caribbean users), keeping them at the most coercive end of services and labelling them as 'a problem' (see Fernando, 2003). Reflecting on my own experience of trying to involve Black users in 'user involvement', I suspect that role and power allocation within clinical settings goes a long way to explaining why so few Black users become engaged in 'user involvement'.

Issues in clinical inpatient settings

Although the issues described below apply in particular to Black people, they may indeed apply to all service users regardless of race or ethnicity (Keating, 2006; Trivedi, 2002).

- Many Black users are often left in too poor a physical and psychological state (for example as a result of high dose medication), with little energy or motivation, to become 'involved' in anything, let alone 'user involvement'.
- Many Black users are fearful of mental health services and want to keep as far away from them as possible (Keating *et al.*, 2002).
- Many Black users have not had their very basic physical and social needs met and have to spend their time and energy focusing on these before – according to Maslow's heirarchy of need (Mathes, 1981) – they can even think of things like 'user involvement'.
- Many Black users are very angry at the way they have been treated in mental health services – and just want to keep as far away as possible from services which they perceive to be damaging.
- Many Black users are deeply sceptical about the likelihood of mental health services improving at a grass roots level for Black users, considering that the issues that need addressing have been known for more than twenty years.
- Many Black users are highly cynical about the idea of them being able to bring about positive change, often saying, 'If they don't listen to us on the ward, how can we believe they will listen to us in other settings?'
- Many Black users may be trying (consciously or subconsciously) to gain some power by staying away from 'user involvement' and depriving services of their experiential expertise (Tew, 2005).

Black users may avoid 'user involvement' for one or a mixture of these reasons. Reflecting on my own personal knowledge and experiences, it does seem as if users only become 'involved' when they have sufficient physical and psychological resources, social stability, energy and self-confidence to do so. Many of the Black users I have tried to 'involve' over the years have tended, as a result of mental health interventions, not to be in this position and it is not surprising that they have shown little interest in engaging in 'user involvement'. One particular example of this was when, despite vigorous efforts by statutory services, the voluntary sector, carers, families and Black women service users, not one single male Black service user could be persuaded to become 'involved' in a

Black Participation Project I was 'involved' with. Initially, some did show an interest, but this was rapidly lost as soon as it became clear we were not in a position to help them with their housing, or benefits, or medication issues, i.e. that we could only *talk* about improving services but not actually *do* anything; it was hardly surprising then that they did not see any point in becoming 'involved' with us.

A lack of personal, social and other resources is not however the whole story, since many Black users who have been through the mental health system may actually make a conscious decision not to become 'involved' because they feel so angry with mental health services and/or cynical about their ability to change. This was illustrated in a Black user-focused monitoring project I was 'involved' with where we found Black users extremely angry and very sceptical about 'user involvement' (Sainsbury Centre for Mental Health, 2007). By enabling this to be honestly expressed and allowing Black users to determine their own role in the project we managed to engage them in the project with a very positive outcome, but it was an exhausting and time-intensive process. In other situations, it was much harder to engage cynical Black users in 'user involvement', particularly since we could find little hard evidence to show Black 'user involvement' having a positive effect on clinical services for Black users at a grass roots level.

Issues in 'user involvement' settings

As in clinical settings, many of the issues are the same for all users, regardless of ethnicity. They include:

- Mental health professionals being unaware of how to work with users in non-clinical settings – 'role confusion' (Linnett, 1999).
- Having to work to service-led, professional agendas within professional settings and with professional procedures which are user-unfriendly and allow little scope for users to introduce their creativity and ideas for how they could be 'involved' more positively.
- Lack of clarity as to the purpose of 'user involvement', and whether its aim is to benefit individual service users or improve services.

- Too much focus on consulting with users rather than enabling them to have any real control in terms of final decision making.
- Focus on content rather than the process of 'user involvement', with little monitoring or evaluation of how the process works for users and what influence their involvement has actually had on grass roots clinical services.
- 'User involvement' being seen as a tick-box exercise and/or an end in itself, with little emphasis on change in service delivery or professional practice.
- A serious lack of infrastructure to support 'user involvement'.

But for Black (as opposed to White) users there will also be other important issues because of cultural differences and the personal and institutionalised racism they may encounter. For example, when Black users are involved in generic 'user involvement', they may:

- Find it hard to raise issues of race and racism because they are perceived as 'having a chip on your shoulder' (particularly if they are the only Black person present), with little awareness among others of how much racism impacts on our lives and mental health (Trivedi, 2002).
- Be in danger of being pathologised if professionals feel uncomfortable with (to them) unfamiliar ways of expressing feelings or making criticisms.

Reflecting on my long experience of 'user involvement', I can see that when I have been 'involved' in generic work and have specifically raised 'race' and racism as an issue (for example on a Government Working Group in connection with devising a National Service Framework, and during discussions in a local Research Ethics Committee), I have often been left feeling invalidated, intimidated and silenced, and became reluctant to engage further (Trivedi, 2001). On one committee I was even summoned by the Chair and warned that if I did not stop raising race as an issue (I was the only Black person on the committee and the only one who ever mentioned race), prestigious members of the committee were going to resign and they could not afford to let that happen! In contrast, when I have not raised race as an issue, for example when working in partnership in research (Philpot et al.,

2004; Trivedi and Wykes, 2002), my involvement has been much more positive, suggesting that there may be a fundamental difficulty for Black users raising issues of race in generic settings, perhaps because institutionalised racism operates to silence us.

Being engaged in specifically Black 'user involvement' activities may prove to be more successful, but even then there may be issues. For example, Black users may:

- Feel very pressurised (and in some cases emotionally blackmailed) by some Black professionals who do not pursue issues they know about unless service users become involved.
- Feel let down by some Black professionals who are more interested in furthering their career than improving the plight of Black users.
- Feel invalidated when some Black professionals overstate their similarities with Black users and in the process ignore very real differences, especially in terms of role and power.
- Feel marginalised when mental health services use Black professionals or community leaders to represent Black users rather than making the effort to involve Black users themselves.
- Feel unsupported by some professionals due to 'role confusion' when our life experiences and other factors impact on our mental health (Maule et al., 2007; Trivedi, 2007b) and send us into crisis.

In my experience, when Black 'user involvement' has been successful, it has tended to be where Black users worked as part of a cohesive and committed group campaigning specifically around BME issues. These groups had autonomy and control over what they became 'involved' with and were very clear about their terms of engagement (Trivedi et al., 2002), and this seemed to play a vital role in ensuring that involvement was as positive as possible for Black users and they were not pressurised into being 'involved'.

Conclusion

Thinking about Black 'user involvement' for this chapter has been a difficult and painful exercise, especially since the latest BME census report suggests that, in spite of years of 'user involvement', nothing has changed at a grass roots level for Black users (Mental Health Act Commission, 2006). This is not to say that Black 'user involvement'

Box 10.1 Experiential expertise and personal qualities that BME service users bring to 'user involvement'

Diversity – which allows alternative values and viewpoints to be considered

Experiential expertise – from living across cultures, with institutionalised racism an everyday part of our lives, and being on the receiving (often harshest) end of mental health services

Resilience and endurance – which enables survival and growth despite racism and disadvantage

Understanding of mental health problems – within the contexts of their own lives

Knowledge of how personal and institutionalised racism can seriously impact on mental health – both within and outwith mental health services

Awareness, knowledge and insights – gained from contact with other BME mental health service users

Creativity, skills and talents – which enable generation of innovative and more user-friendly options

should be abandoned. Meaningful Black 'user involvement' has tremendous potential, as summarised in Box 10.1, but in most cases does not even really get off the ground because so few Black users become 'involved'. This can only be improved if mental health services begin to address some of the issues discussed in this chapter, and recognise the need to:

- Value Black users, enable them to have a voice and respond positively to them not only in 'user involvement' settings but also in inpatient clinical settings.
- Recognise how roles and power are allocated to Black users (and staff) in clinical settings and how this may result in coercive and disempowering care which then impacts negatively on the likelihood of Black users engaging in 'user involvement'.
- Improve clinical services because 'user involvement' can only work if Black service users emerge from clinical services with the physical, psychological and social resources and motivation to become 'involved'. In the current situation, it seems that Black users are not becoming 'involved' because of the way they are treated clinically within services, and services are

saying they can't improve until there is more Black 'user involvement'. This chicken-and-egg impasse must be broken; drastic improvements in clinical practice must be made before Black service users can get 'involved' to a significant extent.

- Recognise the impact of personal and institutionalised racism in both clinical and 'user involvement' settings and work actively to counter this.

- Evaluate role and power relations between users and mental health professionals in 'user involvement' settings, so that professionals use their power positively not just by consulting with service users but by enabling them to have a real and meaningful say in final decisions (Bertram, 2002; P. Campbell, 2001; Peck et al., 2002). If services find themselves reluctant to do this then they seriously need to consider what the true purpose of Black 'user involvement' is in their organisation.

- Be very honest about how much influence Black users can actually have in terms of changing clinical practice. The rhetoric suggesting that Black user involvement leads to clinical practice that is appropriate to the needs of Black users fails to take into account many other factors that impact on clinical practice, the complexity of organisational change and the constant tension between meeting needs of Black users and risk management. This should be made clear to users embarking on user involvement so that unrealistic expectations are not raised.

- Recognise the cause of Black users' anger and cynicism about 'user involvement' and actively work to prove commitment to improving relationships between mental health services and Black people at a grass roots level.

- Provide hard evidence of positive changes in grass roots clinical practice as a result of 'user involvement'. Surprisingly in these days of evidence-based practice, very little research has been published to show how (if at all) 'user involvement' has influenced clinical services – and this matter needs to be urgently addressed (Campbell, 2001; Crawford et al., 2002; Tait and Lester, 2005).

- Clarify the purpose of 'user involvement' and whether it is a tokenistic exercise to fulfil policy requirements, a sort of 'therapeutic intervention' that mainly benefits individual service users, or a means of really bringing about positive change in grass roots mental health services.

Peter Linnett (1999) has stated that 'doing' user involvement means becoming a revolutionary. Recent evidence (Mental Health Act Commission, 2006) suggests the need for some sort of revolution in the way mental health services work with Black people. The key question is: 'Are mental health services courageous enough to have such a revolution and, crucially, will the wider society enable them to do so?'

A programme for changing attitudes in the statutory sector: dialogue is critical

Sandra Griffiths

> Communication and dialogue . . . enable face-to-face contact which relies on the power of human relations to transcend historical and political divides that thrive on racist constrictions.
>
> (Bhavnani *et al.*, 2005: 160)

Mellow was launched in 2000 with the aim of contributing to the reduction of the over-representation of young African and Caribbean men in mental health services in east London (see Chapter 3 for a discussion of over-representation). As well as developing alternative and sustainable responses to mental distress, Mellow works in partnership with statutory, voluntary and art-based agencies nationwide, both as a facilitator and as a consultancy resource, to reduce the racial disparities in mental health. Mellow formally became part of the East London and City Mental Health NHS Trust in 2004, and plays a central role in the Trust's cultural diversity and race equality programme.

This chapter will explore some of the barriers to engaging staff in a mental health trust with the race equality agenda set by the plan *Delivering Race Equality* (DRE) (Department of Health, 2005b); provide a study of a programme of intervention that Mellow developed to address staff's disconnection with this agenda; and share some lessons learnt. A key lesson, which we hope to illustrate in this chapter, is the recognition that *creating a dialogue* with staff is a key process in addressing race equality within the National Health Service (NHS).

Context

It is Mellow's experience that mental health trusts struggle to mobilise their workforce to engage with the race equality agenda set by DRE, but yet, despite the existence of internal working groups, race equality champions and action plans, there still appear to be a significant number of staff who remain unfamiliar with the tenets of the agenda on race equality. The report by the Audit Commission on developing a race equality framework for public services sums this up in the following statement:

> . . . the implementation of the Race Equality (scheme) often means no more than having a working group in place with an action plan that has been endorsed by a senior manager.
>
> (Audit Commission, 2003: 18)

Central to Mellow's work is how to assist the mental health workforce to connect, or in some instances reconnect, with the race equality agenda generally and the agenda on race equality set by DRE in particular. Mellow's strategy has involved the use of drama informed by the experience of service users and staff to initiate dialogue with the staff about race equality issues. These discussions have enabled staff to explore the dilemmas and challenges of delivering mental health services to Black and minority ethnic (BME) communities. Since the launch of *Delivering Race Equality: A Framework for Action* (Department of Health, 2003), Mellow has carried out a range of activities to both promote the agenda set by this framework and support its implementation within East London and other London mental health trusts. In this chapter we describe a programme which involved a co-operative venture between staff of the mental health trust and people from Mellow.

Interventions in achieving race equality have often tended to consist purely of telling people the facts, relying on a rational imparting of information to counter existing attitudes. Such interventions assume that imparting knowledge will have the desired effect and that participants will reflect on and change their behaviour. There is very little evidence to show that this type of approach actually changes behaviour (see for example Chapter 8). We assert at Mellow that services do not pay sufficient attention to those barriers that prevent staff from talking about race equality. We believe that, unless there is a culture of talking confidently about issues of race, discrimination and its impact, it is difficult to engage staff in discussions about strategies to address race equality. Keating *et al.* (2002) have illustrated how the fear of talking about issues of race in mental health services impacts negatively on the ability of professionals to provide an appropriate service to BME communities. Mellow's discussions with staff indicate that there is a significant recognition of the importance of the agenda on race equality but it is an agenda with a difficult past and powerful negative assumptions that can and do undermine its implementation.

Why the disconnection from race equality?

Barriers to mobilising staff derive from unexplored and unspoken assumptions and anxieties about race equality. The Audit Commission's list of barriers to addressing race equality (Audit Commission, 2003) resonates with Mellow's experience:

- There are rules about what language to use – there is an inevitable risk of explicit racist remarks or exposing ignorance of another culture.
- Race equality is not a mainstream issue – it is perceived as a 'special and one off' agenda item and thus competes with mainstream agendas.
- Engaging BME communities will inevitably raise expectations and place extra pressure on scarce resources.
- Addressing race equality explicitly will inevitably result in a 'backlash' from the 'White community' as some groups are perceived to be receiving more favourable treatment than others.

Bhavnani *et al.* (2005) note the importance of talking about racism openly, without fear of 'political correctness' and with a genuine aim of articulating confusion and ambivalence. But race equality is often an emotive issue and there are strong feelings and beliefs attached to this issue which are deep-rooted, personal and hidden. And these, knowingly and unknowingly, tend to prevent dialogue and keep race equality a low priority.

Dialogue is an approach for tackling problems in a wide variety of social and political arenas and also a process for facilitating shared understanding of complex problems. Bojer *et al.* (2006) describe a variety of dialogue approaches and methods promoting dialogue, which may include open communication, honest speaking, genuine listening, responsibility for their own learning and

ideas, generating new ideas and solutions, creating a different level
of understanding, and promoting a more contextual and holistic
way of seeing. Bohm (1990) suggests three conditions for dialogue:
(a) participants must suspend their assumptions; (b) participants
must view each other as colleagues or peers; and (c) in the early
stages there needs to be a facilitator who 'holds the context' of
dialogue.

Drawing on these ideas and noting the landscape described
above, we developed a programme where dialogue was a crucial
element in promoting and facilitating engagement of staff with
both their local and the national race equality agenda. And we
decided to adopt drama techniques to initiate this dialogue with
staff. We believe that our approach has provided a level of safety,
thus allowing staff to share the concerns of their real dilemmas.
Moreover, it has offered opportunities to challenge, in a constructive and supportive manner, definitions and understandings of race
equality.

The Mellow 4 Sight programme

Following the launch of the DRE plan (Department of Health,
2005b) East London and the City Mental Health Trust and
Hackney Social Services commissioned Mellow to support the
development of a creative training initiative that involved drama-
based training. The aim of the training was to raise mental health
staff's awareness of the impact of racism and discrimination on the
experiences of BME people within the mental health system and to
begin to identify what action needed to be put in place to reduce its
impact. Mellow was commissioned to do this because we had a
long tradition of using creative expression and drama to address
the causes and impact of mental distress within the African and
Caribbean communities in east London.

We decided to plan a programme of work which involved: (a)
developing dramatic presentations which addressed issues that
should form the content of the dialogue with staff; and (b) putting
on an event – an intervention that promoted this dialogue. A small
planning group was established to oversee the development of this
initiative as a co-operative venture between colleagues within the
East London and City Mental Health Trust: Mellow's art and
mental health co-ordinator (AMHC), its service development
manager, the locality services sector manager of the London

Borough of Hackney, a clinical psychologist and a community development worker (CDW). Two independent consultants were recruited to respectively provide specialist advice on the intervention and evaluate the impact thereof. The evaluation was published by the Sainsbury Centre for Mental Health (Keating, 2005). Mellow commissioned a drama team of a professional actor and an actress, both experienced in issue-based theatre, to work alongside Mellow's AMHC to develop the drama element of the programme.

Developing dramatic presentations

To start with we held two focus groups in the London Borough of Hackney, one targeting service users and the other targeting staff. The aims of the focus groups were: (a) to gather their views on the impact of racism and discrimination on the experiences of BME clients; and (b) to identify actions that would improve that experience. The service user participants were recruited from members of African and Caribbean communities who had used mental health services, this group being selected because they continue to be over-represented in mental health services. Staff participants were recruited from both inpatient and community settings.

The focus groups were facilitated by the AMHC and the drama team, and supported by the CDW. Specific themes were derived from the focus groups. Then, using these themes, four short plays, each lasting fifteen minutes, were developed by the drama group and Mellow's AMHC in collaboration with the planning group. The four plays were collectively called '4 Sight', the title reflecting the act of looking forward (fore-sight). The plays were performed by a team of five professional actors and the AMHC. Below are summaries of the themes from the focus groups and the four drama pieces that were derived to address them.

Themes from service user focus groups

- *Impact of racism*: negative stereotyping of Black men within the mental health system.
- *Staff attitudes*: some staff do not exhibit a positive attitude towards Black clients which then leads to poor engagement. Staff attitude needs to inspire more hope of recovery.

- *Impact of medication*: insufficient information given about prescribing levels and medication side effects. The suggestion emerged that Black men get higher dosages than other people and are not offered alternative treatments, such as talking therapies.
- *Prevention and management of aggression and violence*: episodes of violence and conflict could be avoided if staff improved their communication with clients. Staff appear to view Black men as more violent and aggressive.

Themes from staff focus groups

- *Race equality terminology*: staff described the complex relationship between race, culture and discrimination and its impact on service delivery. They expressed confusion about the terminology used in addressing the experiences of BME communities. Should there be a focus on understanding different cultures and/or on tackling racism?
- *More focus on prevention*: there was a concern that NHS services are too focused upon crisis and less on prevention. As a result staff argued that this context prevented staff from actively engaging in recovery. In addition staff felt that 'delayed seeking help' behaviour meant that they only saw Black clients at the point of crisis.
- *Promotion of recovery role models*: staff felt that it was difficult to promote and inspire hope of recovery when they saw so few clients who had recovered successfully. Staff felt that it would be useful to recruit ex-clients who were in recovery to act as role models for those 'stuck in the mental health system'.

Play 1: Blame and shame

This piece involved two characters – an African psychiatrist and an African-Caribbean patient. Each character had a narrator on stage expressing their inner thoughts. Both have 'escaped' from the ward and slipped, unknown to each other, into a small room just off a hospital ward. The psychiatrist has escaped 'yet another seminar about the over-representation of Black men within the mental health system'. The patient has escaped the boredom of the ward.

The patient observes the psychiatrist's reaction to these seminars – the blame and shame staff experience and the psychiatrist's sense of powerlessness in addressing this issue. The psychiatrist, embarrassed by this exposure, orders the patient back to the ward. The patient refuses to go back and in the ensuing discussion the psychiatrist learns about the death of the patient's child which triggered his mental health distress.

Play 2: Daddy's last Christmas

This play tells the story of how everyday pressures and stresses lead to the mental ill health of a family man and its impact on his family. The play charts the difficulty a father experiences trying to get help from his general practitioner (GP), which culminates in a lengthy hospital admission. On release he finds everything has changed in his community, including where he used to live, and he becomes angry. He vows never to admit to feeling mentally ill ever again.

The play highlights the problems of early intervention for BME people with mental health difficulties, and the impact of lengthy hospitalisation on the service user and their family. The play illustrates the need for more family support and advocates for alternative care pathways.

Play 3: Bright minds

This scenario was based on the TV show *University Challenge*. Two teams – one comprising service users, the other university students – are tested on their knowledge of Black people and mental health. The scenario promotes the talents and potential of Black people who have experienced mental health problems. It also highlights the stereotypical views staff may hold about the Black community generally and Black service users in particular.

Play 4: The review

This play presents a view of the world where all the professionals are Black, and White people are over-represented in mental health services. The scene is a case review within a hospital setting. The staff team conducting the review are all Black, comprising a psychiatrist, a community psychiatric nurse, a social worker and the care co-ordinator. The patient is a White female who does not accept that she has a mental illness and accuses the professionals of racial discrimination. The team dismiss her claim of discrimination and ignore her requests to have her cultural needs met. Her care plan is developed without reference to her needs and concerns and is focused on her refusal to accept that she has a mental illness.

This play highlights the sense of powerlessness patients/service users experience in expressing their needs and aspirations at case reviews, particularly in relation to their cultural needs, and illustrates some of the challenges staff experience in understanding, valuing and meeting the cultural needs of BME clients.

The intervention

The intervention was a one-day event which consisted of the following elements:

- An introduction from one of the Trust Directors – outlining the Trust's commitment to equality and diversity and the DRE agenda.
- Presentation of the 4 Sight plays.
- Facilitated workshops which enabled staff to explore their reactions to the plays, their connection with the themes, and developing possible action to address the themes.
- Feedback from the workshops.
- A summary of the day and the key themes explored.

The intervention was repeated over three days to allow for maximum participation. A total of 142 staff attended the sessions, representing a wide range of professional groupings. Based on the returned evaluations ($N = 128$) the largest professional group was from a nursing background (43.7 per cent, $N = 56$). Fifty per cent of all participants were based in hospital settings, 43 per cent in community settings and the remainder (7 per cent) were based at the Trust's headquarters. There was some representation (7 per cent, $N = 10$) from staff at senior and management levels, a small representation of administrative staff (7 per cent, $N = 10$), and very little representation from psychiatrists (1.5 per cent, $N = 2$).

Reactions to the intervention

Reactions to the intervention were categorised into (a) emotive responses to the plays and (b) cognitive responses to the plays. At an emotive level participants used terms such as 'powerful', 'challenging', 'shocking', 'scary', 'uncomfortable', 'moving' and 'sad' to describe their initial reactions to the plays. The following comments summarise these reactions:

> 'I felt anger and frustration when the themes were acted out before me as it was a realistic picture of how the situations are.'

> 'It scares me to think that I am part of a service that is so dis-empowering.'

> 'It really gets to the emotional side of learning.'

At the cognitive level there was overwhelming agreement that the plays were thought-provoking and helped participants to gain insight through a reversal of roles (for example, when an all-Black team interviewed a White patient) and the misunderstandings that ensued. As some participants commented:

> 'It was mind blowing to see both sides in the reversal of roles.'

> '. . . an excellent way of producing insight into service users' experience.'

> 'This gave me a lot of food for thought.'

What's happened since

Since delivering this programme in Hackney, Mellow has delivered the same programme to all staff in an adjoining London borough, namely Newham, where approximately 340 staff from inpatient and community settings, drawn from all professional groups, attended. It is now being acknowledged by managers within the mental health trust that this programme is a 'starting point'. It has begun a process of dialogue between and across staff teams about the challenges and dilemmas of delivering mental health services to BME clients as well as working within ethnically diverse staff teams.

The original focus group that met in March 2005 has continued to meet as the 4 Sight Service Users group. This group, with an active membership of twenty men, has subsequently been consulted by the Trust on a range of service improvement reviews. For example, some members have been involved in working alongside an independent consultant to review Hackney's Care Programme Approach (CPA). CPA is the fundamental process used by specialist mental health services for documenting clinical and social care – see *Reviewing the Care Programme Approach (CPA)* on the website of the National Institute for Mental Health in England: http://www.nimhe.csip.org.uk. As a result, two members of the group have been contributing to CPA staff training. The group has also acted as a hub of information on personal development opportunities for Black men with mental health difficulties in Hackney. The involvement of this group in local service improvement programmes has led to further investment in its long-term future. In 2006, Mellow was able to secure funding from Hackney mental health services to: (a) employ a consultant to produce a sustainable business plan in response to members' identified needs and interests; and (b) employ an ex-member of the group to co-ordinate day-to-day group activities and the implementation of the business plan.

What have we learnt?

Through the dialogue process we have learnt the following about engaging mental health staff with the race equality agenda:

- *Spaces of understanding*
  Talking about issues related to race equality can cause discomfort, feelings of shame, anger and frustration. It can be difficult to hear another colleague's position if it is radically different from one's own. Some challenges can lead to conflict and prevent understanding. Facilitated dialogue enables staff to explore different points of view and fosters better understanding and awareness.
- *Spaces for not knowing*
  Some staff expressed relief at the opportunity to seek further information about the different cultures and local race inequalities and improve their understanding of how race equality strategies both nationally and locally could improve the mental health experiences of BME communities.
- *Definitions are important*
  Introducing this agenda means providing from the outset a clear definition. We have found it useful to make it explicit that

this means addressing poorer outcomes for BME communities and providing staff with some local data that can illustrate this.

• *Build upon existing staff competencies*
There are some very powerful stories within mental health services about how they fail to meet the needs of BME clients. There can appear to be very few stories of positive engagement. Interventions should take into consideration that there will be positive stories of engagement within the service as well as negative stories. Unless you create space for these positive stories to be heard it will be difficult to instil a sense of hope and a positive attitude to tackling race inequality.

• *Team approach*
Dialogue within teams that work together creates a greater level of safety and ensures that the issues raised are relevant to the team's practice.

• *Connection to the wider service improvement agenda*
There needs to be recognition that race equality dialogue should not be confined to short-term initiatives and one-off training days. Front-line staff and senior managers need to be encouraged to connect the emerging themes from the race equality dialogues to the wider organisational agenda for improving service delivery and workforce development.

Conclusions

Changing attitudes within the statutory sector are essential if a race equality agenda as envisaged in DRE is to be delivered. The dialogue approach has generated new opportunities and confidence within the Trust to initiate and promote strategies to bring about change that has a real impact in service delivery for BME communities. Mellow's emerging intervention using drama has involved creating a safe space for staff to discuss and explore the meaning they attach to race equality and their situational concerns and dilemmas. Creating these opportunities is an important gateway to enabling staff to actively engage with the development and implementation of the race equality agenda.

Part 3

Making it happen

This third part of the book looks at working models of services and movements that attempt to meet – often successfully we believe – some of the challenges described in the first two parts. What are presented are indeed working models, but not necessarily ideal services or approaches that are in any way comprehensive in terms of what they provide. The services and movements described here have stood the test of time and appear to satisfy some of the current needs of BME communities. The chapters are written by people working at grass roots level – it is often the first time they have been given the opportunity to tell the wider public what they are doing.

We believe that this part of the book indicates the approaches that the statutory service in general should be taking in developing mental health services that are suitable for a multi-ethnic society. It shows what can be done with commitment, realism and the will to action – and that making it happen need not be just a dream, confined to policies and plans.

Chapter 12

Working therapeutically with hidden dimensions of racism

Aileen Alleyne

The impact of racism on people seeking therapy or help for mental health problems can present as a complex picture which is often misunderstood and can lead to misinterpretations, misdiagnoses and inappropriate interventions. 'Race' enters psychotherapy in ways that parallel its workings in society at large. Overt racism is easily recognised as traumatic for the people at its receiving end – and is relatively easy to address as 'trauma'. It is the shift into 'subtle' and 'institutional' forms that is a major challenge for therapists (and sufferers) to address in the consulting room. The impact of racism, whether experienced as a one-off encounter, or an ongoing experience, can prove debilitating and even damaging to the well-being of an individual. But something that is all too often overlooked and under-appreciated is the importance of the capacity for resilience in the face of racism. So, in addition to holding on to the theme of resilience, therapists faced with the challenge of addressing racism need to be equipped with a full working knowledge of the following key themes:

- Racism as cultural trauma or 'the grinding down experience'.
- Racism as undermining identity, or 'black identity wounding'.
- Racism threatening relationships and leading to isolation or 'cultural shame'.
- Racism leading to an unhealthy attachment that allows trans-generational trauma to be kept alive, or 'the internal oppressor'.

In this chapter I shall discuss these themes separately although they are clearly inter-related. They help us to understand and interpret what may come up in the consulting room during psychotherapy;

they are not in any way 'pathologies' or symptoms of (what may be seen as) 'mental ill health'. In this chapter, the term 'black' is used to include people with known African heritage, and the expression 'minority' to mean anyone who can be discriminated against because of the colour of their skin, or because of their religion or their culture.

Resilience

The 'universal strengths model' (Grotberg, 1995) sees resilience as a universal human capacity that enables a person, group or community to deal with adversity by preventing, facing, minimising, overcoming and even being strengthened or transformed by adversity. The model also maintains that this capacity needs nurturing and support within a facilitative environment. Essentially, it is the ability to 'bounce back' and cope well in the face of profound problems. Bhui (2002) points out that the perception of threat and the level of control over racist experiences are important in the amount of stress we suffer if exposed to racism; and that control may be exerted by *action* (to get rid of the stressor) or by *adaptation*. Being resilient in these circumstances may be seen as an aspect of 'post-traumatic growth', an emerging field of interest (Tedeschi and Calhoun, 1995) in the study of life change after crises. However, resilience in the context of racism is often at a cost. From an analytic perspective, attacks on the cultural and racial skin raise serious issues for psychological 'containment' (Bion, 1967; Winnicott, 1965, 1967) – which, in effect, means enjoying a sense of (psychic) equilibrium and keeping oneself grounded. Containment is important for the preservation of identity and the process of 'moving on', but both *action* and *adaptation* may threaten this containment.

The grinding down experience

An understanding of the eroding impact of racism – the cultural trauma of racism, which can be experienced both externally and internally – was developed as part of a phenomenological study of black workers' experiences in three institutional settings, namely the National Health Service, Social Services and Education (Alleyne, 2004a). The model is presented in Figure 12.1. Difficulties experienced by workers were frequently set off by subtle, 'not so easy to pin down' incidents that frequently targeted a racial or

Pressures from:
Outside
External challenges
Societal
Political

**social inequities and power imbalances
difference equated with problems and negativity
micro/macro-aggressions
racial stereotyping
racial prejudice
racism**

**unresolved intra-psychic issues
attachment to the historical past
susceptibility to re-wounding of identity
post-traumatic stress syndrome from racism
constant presence of a post-colonial backdrop**

Pressures from:
Inside
Internal conflicts
Intra-psychic factors
The internal enemy and oppressor

Figure 12.1 The grinding down experience

cultural aspect of the black person's identity. Although initially precipitated by no more than minor annoyances – for example a mispronunciation of a black or foreign-sounding name or an assumption that a black person was angry when all they had done was to speak passionately about something or assert their point – such incidents tended to develop into complicated major events over time, causing much offence and hurt.

Workers experienced these subtle organisational forces as oppressive and infantilising, and equated them with what was happening within the dynamics of power, control and power-lessness. However, this was not all. The research concluded that the unconscious aim of these subtle acts of oppression was not just to control, but also to *transform*, to reduce 'the Other' to a state or form that rendered them helpless, easy to manipulate and manage. It was this dynamic that black and other minority ethnic individuals found themselves struggling against in the midst of such workplace conflict. These difficulties chipped away at the emotional and psychological fabric of the person's identity and, over time, left them depleted, soulless and helpless.

Sampson states that, within the context of power and race, 'dominant groups and individuals create serviceable others whose creation gives both the self and the other the very qualities that define human nature' (1993: 19). Then, 'the other cannot be permitted to have a voice, a position, a being of its own, but must remain mute or speak in ways permitted by the dominant discourse' (1993: 13). Sampson concludes: 'the other is an essential presence without whom the dominant protagonist could not be who they claim to be' (1993: 13). I believe these are key dynamics to understanding the nature of black/white oppression and that of other cultural oppressions. We should be aware that the grinding down experience is not confined to dynamics of the workplace setting. Erosion of self-esteem and dignity from the grinding down experience within society can be seen in the lives of many black men; unfortunately their experiences may be interpreted as mental problems or even 'illness' and then get inappropriately treated within a narrow traditional Eurocentric template.

Black identity wounding

Sarup (1996) suggests that identity is a 'mediating concept' between the external and internal, the individual and society, theory and practice. Identity then is a convenient 'tool' through which we try to understand many aspects of our lives – the personal, the political, the racial, the philosophical, gender, class, sexuality, and so on. Sarup refers to the '*it is*' and '*I am*' aspects of identity, which he suggests can become entangled when there is continuous discord between the two (1996: 28–43). The 'it is' aspect is a public identity that is usually created from a set of misinformation, misinformed perceptions and stereotypes about an individual or racial group. Over time, these can develop into negative social constructs from which people relate to 'the Other'. The 'I am' aspect of identity is the private part of the self that most accurately resembles and represents what we feel, think and know about ourselves. How one is perceived in public and how one sees one's private self can differ widely and contribute to an inner conflict and dis-ease. My view is that it is the presentation of this dis-ease, perhaps compounded by the vicissitudes of our past and other underlying latent difficulties, that mistakenly get interpreted as mental illness and disease. A person's discomfort in coping with the 'public' and 'private' identity-split can eventually lead to an inner disturbance; a form of depersonalisation caused by this brand of cultural trauma. A client of mine who worked as a psychologist summed up her feeling in therapy thus:

> Illusion plays a very important part in creating identity. It can be someone's truth. When that goes, one is left shattered, even depersonalised . . . this has been my experience from the devastation of subtle racism operating in my workplace.

Here we can construe that the puncturing of one's truth can destabilise a person's deep sense of being in the world. From this, we can anticipate that the challenge for therapists is to understand the consequential effects of Sarup's (1996) '*I am*'/'*it is*' concept and enable our client to find ways of maintaining equilibrium in the face of racial adversity.

Some writers (Akbar, 1996; Cobbs and Grier, 1968; hooks, 1996; Lorde, 1984) emphasise the task for black people to educate themselves for critical consciousness. By this they mean the ability to show independence of mind by reasoning for oneself and having emotional literacy to be more culturally and racially competent. In hooks's (1996) *Killing Rage: Ending Racism*, she reminds people of colour not to see blackness solely as a matter of powerlessness and victimisation; rather there is a need to have a deeper understanding of institutional racial oppression, in all its facets, which over-determines patterns of black/white social relations. She issues a strong challenge for us as black people to locate black identity from other multiple locations, not simply and only in relation to white supremacy (1996: 248), and she also challenges the notion of a stereotypical monolithic black culture, which is perpetuated in both the black and white sectors of our society.

It would appear that the individual whose sense of self is validated only or mainly from the point of view of their blackness will have a different sense of personal consciousness activated when in the presence of white people. The psychic structure may be more prone to being off-balanced by racial affronts (subtle or overt), and consequent emotional states of hyper-alertness and hyper-sensitivity will be more highly developed and brittle in these encounters. In keeping with Kohut's (1997) 'grounded sense of self', my research findings (Alleyne, 2004a, 2004b), suggest that such mental states are capable of causing interruptions to 'coherency' (feeling of being at one with oneself) and 'continuity' (moving on with one's life). What is being suggested here is that racism and other environmental stress factors can cause psychic collapse and clinical presentations resembling psychiatric illness, when they are imposed upon individuals who are functioning in this hyper-alert, hyper-sensitive psychological state. Therapists who will be challenged to work with this particular form of 'mental health' presentation should take into consideration all the afore-mentioned tenets of culture, race, distress and dis-ease, before settling comfortably into Eurocentric notions of disease and mental illness.

Cultural shame

The phenomenon of cultural shame may be best understood through the following statements of people I interviewed as part of my research (Alleyne, 2004b):

'As black people we don't seem to come together and sustain anything good for any length of time.'

'We are not patient and as determined in business . . . we expect to get rich quick . . . look at the Asian, they struggle for years in their little corner shop, and before you know it, they've owned the whole block with their food shops, drycleaners, black hair products stores (*!!!laughter*) and restaurants . . . all we seem to want is for it to happen today.'

'We too can be guilty of thinking we are all the same and miss out on those important differences that make us individuals in our own group. Sameness breeds too much familiarity and too much familiarity can sometimes be bad for us.'

'I had to catch myself the other day when I realised I too was doing the same as my white colleagues . . . thinking he [the black manager] was up to no good . . . and the sad thing about it was there was no reason or evidence for this.'

'I know I am driven . . . no matter how much I do and achieve, I always feel I should do more . . . always going that extra mile . . . giving just that little extra to be noticed . . . it's like a neurosis.'

'Sometimes in meetings, my voice can sound so out of place . . . I can't describe it . . . I know my voice is deep and it's different . . . it's black, but it kinda sets you apart, alienates you . . . you know what I mean? My family all think I sound like Maya Angelou [a respected black American writer and poet], but at work people seem to see me as this big, aggressive and scary black woman. It's not how I see myself . . . (*long pause*) . . . it's enough to give you a complex.'

These revealing verbatim statements show clearly an interlocking of views, opinions and beliefs that suggest a presence of shame – both at an individual level and within the group. They amount to a collective experience of loss, guilt on behalf of the collective, disappointment within the collective, and a resultant self-conscious identity that functions within a set of reactive, compensatory personal scripts. The experience of internalised shame is projected outwards onto other black people and even onto one's race as a whole. Underlying this cultural shame is a sense of narcissistic wounding, which, when presented in the consulting room, needs to be sensitively addressed from the clinical perspective of working with self-hate. The externalisation of shame and self-hate may also be further projected onto, for example, white people, the white establishment and onto new migrants and political refugee groups.

Shame stems from internalised conflict with an external authority (for example, society) and guards against the boundary of privacy and intimacy. Shame in this sense is necessary, and protects the innermost vulnerable aspects of the self and defends against anxiety which threatens to destroy an integral image of the self. Yet, shame threatens our individual relationships with each other and this is deeply felt in the black community in forms where we act out our feelings of indignation, anger, and frustrations at other black people who 'show us up' (Lipsky, 1987). This acting out often affects those closest to us, harming our relationships with each other and ultimately ourselves. The effects of shame show their result in our relationship with our children, who face fierce criticism from black mothers and fathers whose intention of 'disciplining' is interwoven with notions of obedience, submission and compliance. The need to control and the fear of being 'shown up' in front of others can lead to aspects of parenting which destroy any development of self-confidence in black children.

Shame can lead to cultural isolation, which is the withdrawing from other black people. Consequently, we act out our hurt, embarrassment, fear, dislike and mistrust by dividing ourselves amongst each other and creating hierarchies. Further divisions are created in the way we label each other. Characterisations such as 'house slave', 'coconut', 'too ghetto', are terms used within the black community to divide and rank the group within a cultural and social order. Shame has left us with complexes about our skin colour and its representations, summed up in this quaint Caribbean ditty:

> If you're white, you are right
> If you're brown, stick around
>   If you're black, get the hell back
>   (Old Caribbean rhyme used by children during play)

These revealing three lines of poetry not only categorise people according to skin colour, they also create hierarchies that indicate negative internalisations of black people by black people. These internalisations suggest a lack of acceptance of the self and also a lack of an actualised experience of full humanity. Within this belief system are psychological issues and challenges for the prospect of healthy identity development.

Shame as a human emotion overarches much of our work as therapists. Cultural shame, with its debilitating aspects, brings specific challenges and sensitivities to the work itself and for the therapist. The following case vignette is offered as an example of how we can work with the presenting theme of cultural shame.

Denzel is a 30-year-old African Caribbean man who is single, gay and works as a housing officer with a local council. He came into therapy to work on problems of identity, much of which he felt had stemmed from unresolved experiences of not knowing his father and being brought up by an emotionally absent mother. As the youngest of twelve children, all of whom are from different fathers, Denzel was looked after by an aunt whom he regarded as his mother. As a child, Denzel remembered being left to his own devices, feeling very much alone in the world and an observer in his very harsh surroundings. In later life, he fabricated stories about his father's absence, making out that he was a captain of an important government cargo ship that sunk in the Bermuda Triangle. He described him to others as a man of reputable character and highly regarded, all of which hid Denzel's deep shame about his father's real reputation for being a violent man, womaniser, drunk and deserter of his family.

On arrival in the UK at age 15, Denzel became uncomfortable and self-conscious and hateful of his Jamaican accent. He felt it regularly singled him out in negative and unfavourable ways. Shame about his accent led to a denial of his Caribbean heritage and a refusal to mix with other black people. He wished to change the way he spoke and embarked on expensive elocution lessons which kitted him out with a middle-class, albeit forced, English accent. He changed his name by deed poll and later chose only white men as partners. He existed in a make-believe, grandiose world that he hoped would remove him as far away as possible from any reminders of his past and true self. Driven by a deep shame to rid himself of any reminders of being black, and feeding his need to keep up a 'desirable' front in the eyes of white society, he finally found himself involved in dubious activities, which eventually brought him face to face with the law. He sought individual psychotherapy following a long custodial sentence which he had to serve as punishment for fraudulent activities which boosted and maintained a lavish lifestyle.

The following issues may be noted in this case vignette:

- Early emotional neglect with experiences of abandonment and loss
- Early acquisition of independence and self-reliance
- Keeper of the family shame and compensation for this through fabrication, aggrandisement and destructive acting out behaviour
- Manifestation of cultural shame and consequences of internalised oppression
- Struggles with identity (includes male identity crisis and crisis of the emotional and cultural self)

In therapy, Denzel explored issues of his early self-reliance, a persona which he realised he had developed from having to do a lot for himself in the absence of guidance and help from parents. He was able to make connections between the difficulties of his early upbringing and subsequent difficulties in trusting, receiving and giving unconditionally in his attachments. He began to understand his role of holding the family shame and the ways he compensated for this shame through fabrication, aggrandisement and reckless behaviour. The goals of therapy were slowly achieved by Denzel interacting more from a place of knowing and embracing his true and authentic self.

The internal oppressor

Much has been written about internalised oppression, for example by Lipsky (1987), Lorde (1984), hooks (1989, 1996) and Freire (1970). These authors suggest that it is the process of absorbing values and beliefs of the oppressor and coming to believe that the stereotypes and misinformation about one's group are true (or partly true). Such a process can lead to low self-esteem, self-hate, the disowning of one's group, and other very complex defensive behaviours in relation to this group. Yet, only a few writers (e.g. Lorde, 1984; Alleyne, 2004b, 2005) have dealt specifically with the concept of the oppressor within ourselves.

Many years of practice as a psychotherapist and clinical supervisor, together with evidence from my research data (Alleyne, 2004a, 2004b), have all provided abundant evidence to suggest that when it comes to dealing with issues such as race relations and racism, the real battleground is the personal – not the political. This statement in no way implies that: (a) racism does not exist; (b) it is not a problem; or that (c) it is only a black or other minority ethnic group issue. Rather, the suggestion is that whilst the very real and damaging effects of societal racism are to be truly acknowledged, the reality of confronting and dealing with racial oppression today is more concerned with the *personal* positions black people take up in dealing with its impact. Understanding the workings of the 'internal oppressor' can help us become more aware of the challenge for 'true' resilience in the face of racism. Such understanding will not only challenge the individual's ability to withstand external impingements of racism, but also be more attuned to what is aroused within 'the internal oppressor' and gets acted out in these encounters.

George Bach (1985) once suggested that the inner enemy is as much a formidable foe as the most manipulative (or oppressive) of associates. I discovered and observed the workings of this inner enemy within the language of my respondents' stories during the fieldwork for my research (Alleyne, 2004a, 2004b). From these narratives, a set of cultural scripts were identified that highlighted particular ways in which black people tended to organise and deal with certain archetypal experiences, in this case experiences relating to subtle racism operating in the workplace. Presented below is a selection of verbatim responses extracted from the respondents' stories.

Individual scripts that indicate the collective black archetypal experience

1   'People will always see your colour first and personality second'
2   'We have to work twice as hard to be noticed'
3   'No matter how much we succeed, people will always try to beat us down'
4   'Black people can't be racist – we haven't got the power'
5   'We can't afford to wash our dirty linen in public – that's like giving white people ammunition – we must stick together'
6   'As black people, we don't seem to come together and sustain anything that's good for any length of time'

Individual scripts that indicate a defensive (protective) mindset and value system

7 'What's the point in trying – you'll only get no for an answer'
8 'I am not interested in promotion – it only forces you to conform to the system – I don't want to lose who I am as a black person'
9 'I don't do deference where white people are concerned'
10 'I can never trust white people – I have a healthy disrespect where they are concerned'
11 'You can't afford to show vulnerability – people will walk all over you'
12 'When things get too much, I just walk away'
13 'You take me as you see me – what you see is what you get – like it or lump it'
14 'This is who I am – I say what's on my mind – ain't changing for no one'
15 'I am not putting myself out for no one'
16 'I don't trust anyone but myself'

The above sixteen scripts highlight an ever-present sense of disillusionment, caution, disappointment, defensiveness and protectiveness. A reflexive identity (both self and collective) will not be allowed the chance to thrive and develop within such a belief and value structure. In the context of racism and racial oppression, to be reflexive is to have a sense of one's history which is in continual development in terms of self-awareness and self-assurance, leading to a degree of liberation and movement forward within the self and the collective. The challenge of reflexivity is an important modern-day (psychotherapeutic) task for black people, which challenges us to throw off the shackles of the past and emerge from the entanglement of historical briars. A reflexive identity will only begin at the point where unconscious identifications and fixations with aspects of one's history cease.

The internal oppressor appears to have the function of holding on to these identifications and fixations in ways that colour black people's dealings with white people and influence these interpersonal and attachment dynamics. For the most part, the internal oppressor appears to lie dormant, but is re-awakened when it is in contact with an external oppressive situation that is either real or perceived, or a mixture of both. When re-awakened, the historical wounds are re-opened. The internal oppressor as a concept is not just concerned with historical baggage, though. Alongside are our prejudices, projections, inter-generational wounds and the vicissitudes (the ups and downs of our fortune) of our past. Further shaping its complexity are elements of our narcissistic injuries, personal unresolved difficulties where power and domination feature. The nature of the internal oppressor is therefore complex and embraces both the unresolved past (historical and personal), as well as our present-day difficulties.

The picture that is being created here is one in which the past and present, as well as intra-psychic and external factors, are inextricably linked and fused. This fusion or attachment pattern becomes an important determinant in black people's health and psychological security. Mental health concerns producing dis-ease and distress, and mental illness and disease, will be more prevalent when there is ontological insecurity kept alive by the themes discussed in this chapter.

Summary

The relationship between racism and mental health is complex. Resilience encompasses our capacity for coping, and the need to 'bounce back' and be strengthened even by adverse experiences. However, in the setting of psychotherapy there is much else. I have explored in this chapter the idea of racism as a grinding down experience. When people seek help in psychotherapy, the wounding of black identity is a significant way of thinking about the damage done by racism. But, in my view, the theme of cultural shame is perhaps the single most important variable overarching much of what is seen and understood to be happening in black people's struggle for actualisation. I have suggested the need for a reflexive identity to redress cultural shame and blame. The fieldwork in my research led me to derive the idea of an 'internal oppressor' as a powerful feature of the self that helps us to understand the crucial role played by 'the personal' as opposed to 'the political' in the struggle we have in finding our way through complex issues subsumed under the heading 'race relations' in western society.

Chapter 13

The Marlborough Cultural Therapy Centre

Rabia Malik, Raina Fateh and Rakhee Haque

Research and Department of Health policy frameworks have repeatedly attested to 'disparities and inequalities between black and minority ethnic (BME) groups and the majority white population in mental ill health, service experience and service outcome' (National Institute for Mental Health in England, 2003: 5). Whatever the reasons for this, we remain in a position where there is a gulf between mainstream service provision and minority ethnic communities. Government initiatives (see Chapter 3) may bear fruit and produce sustained change in service delivery but this depends on a variety of problems being addressed and requires overcoming anxiety and defences within organisational settings (Lowe, 2006).

In this chapter we will reflect on our experiences in the Marlborough Cultural Therapy Centre (MCTC) over the past ten years, discussing some of the challenges that we have faced and risks that have been taken in shaping and developing a specialist culturally appropriate service for the south Asian and Arab communities in northwest London. We will highlight the key areas that we think have been vital behind the scenes in order to enable us to create a context for culturally competent services.

Setting the scene

Background

The inception of MCTC eleven years ago started with the recognition within the Marlborough family service (MFS), a children and adolescent mental health service (CAMHS), that despite a significant local BME population, clients from these communities were visibly under-represented in their use of the service. Moreover, amongst a team of thirty professionals there were, then, only two black members of staff. This triggered the team to take a closer look and reflect upon themselves and their practices. In an attempt to understand this chasm, an outreach service for the Bangladeshi community was set up by two white members of staff. It soon became clear that there were a number of barriers operating to prevent effective collaboration between mainstream mental health services and the local BME communities. These ranged from language to wider conceptual differences. One strategy for overcoming these barriers was to try to recruit BME staff with cultural knowledge and language skills.

However, cultural knowledge is not something that has been routinely expounded or valued in professional training and at that time there were relatively few BME professionals working in mainstream therapeutic professions within the National Health Service (NHS), especially in the field of family therapy; reflecting deeper underlying discrimination and exclusion. Indeed even professionals who were themselves of BME backgrounds were often thoroughly 'colonised' into an ethnocentric approach, where cultural difference was hardly recognised as an issue to be addressed. A more radical approach was required.

Two members of staff at MFS, namely Ann Miller and Inga-Britt Krause, proposed an innovative two-year project (called the Asian Families Counselling Project), which was funded by the local health authority. Some of the background to the project design is reflected in the chapter 'Culture and family therapy' (Krause and Miller, 1995) in the first edition of this book. In brief, the project involved the recruitment of six personnel from BME communities that were under-utilising the service, namely Bangladeshi, Chinese and Pakistani, and one researcher. Two people from each ethnic group, with some experience of community and/or mental health work and appropriate language skills, were recruited. To privilege cultural knowledge and to keep it in the foreground, workers were offered an in-house tailored training programme, which contextualised ideas about health and illness within a cultural framework, alongside the diploma in systemic (family) therapy training. Early work focused on raising mental health awareness in the respective communities and building links with community organisations in order to facilitate referrals. Clients were offered systemic therapy in their preferred language – Bengali, Syleti, Urdu, Punjabi, Cantonese and Mandarin. The team worked towards developing therapeutic practices which brought culture into the conscious domain and articulated how cultural processes impacted and were interwoven in the family's dilemmas and the interventions that ensued. Such discussions were facilitated by a team approach, with one worker from each of the community teams working with the family in the therapy room and the other interpreting for colleagues behind the one-way screen.

The project was evaluated through participant observatory research, which addressed service delivery, training and organisational integration and clearly indicated a significant increase in the uptake of services by the targeted BME communities. Consequently a proposal for mainstream permanent funding was put forward and taken up by the local health authority. The success of the proposal was due to the perseverance of the management at MFS and the backing of the, then, Operations Director of the Trust – who was herself of a BME background. Malek and Joughin (1998) in their review of mental health services for minority ethnic groups observed that many innovations in services for BME groups suffer from 'short-termism' because they are project-based and often disappear as funding periods come to an end. They also stressed the vital role of commissioning agents and processes in the development of mental health services for minority ethnic children and adolescents.

Progress

The service is now (February 2007) in its eleventh year and over time we have seen a steady rise in referrals. On average we see 125 new referrals each year in addition to ongoing cases. A large percentage of referrals come from voluntary community organisations, and self-referrals, as well as established routes through GPs, schools and social services. The service is well placed between the community, voluntary and statutory sectors. The skills mix among the staff in the service – which covers knowledge of mental health issues and mainstream services, and knowledge of BME communities and differences in cultural and religious beliefs – has been invaluable in helping us to liaise between marginalised minority clients and the wider mental health system, and to co-construct culturally appropriate interventions. Our dominant model of work-ing has been the systemic model, which offers a broad contextual perspective and focuses on a relational framework which accords well with Asian and Arab cultures that emphasise family ties and a relational self. Although much of the work involves families, we also see a significant number of individuals – including adolescents and adults. A large proportion of the work is carried out in clients' homes or community settings. More recently the service has expanded to include a full-time Arab worker, to address the needs of Arabic-speaking communities which currently make up a large percentage of the population in the London Borough of West-minster, where MFS is located.

Behind the scenes

Whilst the MCTC has made much progress – in terms of increasing access to services for BME clients, raising awareness of the needs of BME clients in the mental health arena, raising awareness of mental health needs amongst BME communities and building capacity amongst BME staff – it has by no means been straight-forward or easy. A number of struggles have had to be resolved (as it were) behind the scenes in order to enable the sustained development of the service.

The MCTC exists within the wider organisational contexts of the MFS and the NHS, as well as a wider socio-political context. Although these structures offer some possibilities they also operate some constraints. To accommodate 'difference', change is inevit-ably required, which invariably brings with it conflict and resistance. We would like to highlight some of the challenges we have encountered and track the changes that have ensued along the way in our development. These include negotiating hierarchies, pay structures, disciplinary boundaries and the privileging of cultural knowledge. Through engaging in this process we have built an identity as a specialist service that enables us to position ourselves and build relationships across mainstream and community sectors.

The socio-political context

Organisations operate in a socio-political context and there is thus a strong tendency for them to replicate wider social relations and structures. Prior to the inception of the MCTC, the MFS had already begun a process of reflection and had engaged in anti-racism training, as a result of which the boundaries that were operating in the organisation had been acknowledged. It was the commitment of two white members of staff to anti-discriminatory practice, though, that brought about the possibility for change and breaking down some of the boundaries that were operating. Although they were supported in this endeavour by the then head of the service, Alan Cooklin, they also met with some organisational resistance. Space needed to be created for the new project and the staff group had to accommodate six new part-time members of staff who had not followed the traditional routes into the profession and who were allocated the task of representing 'difference'. Raising issues of 'difference', as Lowe (2006) argues, is a precarious task and often triggers feelings of persecutory anxiety in white staff, which can then be projected onto those who raise such challenges. Such dynamics at times translated into conflict and splits amongst the project managers and within our staff team. Whilst we, the project staff, were encouraged to hold onto and assert our difference, there was the paradoxical danger that 'difference' would be exoticised, reified and embodied in the BME staff and clients alone, leaving 'whiteness' everywhere and nowhere (Dyer, 1997) and reinforcing wider power relations. In order to safeguard against this the project had intended to engender a two-way learning process in which the project staff would learn systemic therapy and the organisation would learn from their cultural expertise, but despite these egalitarian intentions, the power imbalances inherent in the design could not be ignored. The appointment of six new staff who had no previous qualification in therapeutic practice into a context with mainly white senior practitioners in effect relegated these staff members to the status of trainees and 'the ethnic difference' which they embodied had fallen to the bottom of the hierarchy. Hierarchies manifested in terms of 'recognised' knowledge and experience, but also, crucially, power and pay. What is more, positive discrimination can easily feed into fantasises that BME workers are merely there by virtue of their ethnicity and not merit, and therefore should be grateful to the benevolence of their employers. This unspoken assumption can make challenging hierarchies and disparities especially difficult if it is internalised by BME staff. Thus, although the MCTC was born out of, and managed by, well intentioned, white professionals, the BME staff were nonetheless lodged at the bottom of the hierarchy, replicating wider social relations.

Pay, hierarchies and disciplines

When permanent positions were negotiated the MCTC staff did not fit into any pre-existing disciplines or job descriptions, in the then 'Whitley Scales', as we were not yet fully qualified family therapists and there was no precedent at that time for community development worker positions. We had been assigned to a junior nursing scale, with few prospects for progression, and yet assigned the complex tasks of developing the service, building links with community organisations, delivering a service to 'hard-to-reach clients' bilingually, and developing culturally competent ways of working. This trap of proposing sweeping changes to be delivered by low-paid and inexperienced staff is common amongst innovating projects. Inevitably, over the years, rumblings of discontent emerged as the staff progressed in their mainstream qualifications and grew in experience.

An opportunity for reviewing job descriptions and resolving the dispute over pay was provided by the NHS restructuring of pay in *Agenda for Change* (Department of Health, 2005a), introduced in 2005–6. By then the management of the MCTC had been transferred to the Head of Family Therapy in the Trust, as a number of us had qualified as family therapists, whilst other colleagues had in part completed the training. New job titles and a flexible pay structure with a progression route had to be negotiated. The service wanted to retain a specialist position referred to as 'family clinician', which would enable us to continue to recruit staff who, although not fully qualified in a mainstream training, could be employed with recognition of their cultural knowledge and expertise, and also to retain the potential to integrate staff who had a mainstream qualification into pay scales commensurate with other members of their discipline whilst recognising their cultural expertise. This required building and articulating a case for the similarities and distinctiveness in our work and the need for a both/and structure which took into account our mainstream qualifications as well as culture as an area of speciality. We were often met with the vexed question, 'What is it that you do that is any different to any other mainstream mental health professional working with BME clients?' Underlying this question is the assumption that a more or less standardised approach to mental health works equally well with all clients, and a negation of difference. It did not take into account the inordinate amount of community work that had been an essential feature of our work in reaching out to hard-to-reach clients, the knowledge of different cultural systems – for example kinship patterns and parenting practices – which did not fit neatly into normative ideas about family functioning, health and illness that underpin mainstream trainings, not to mention the bilingual language skills required. There seemed to be no acknowledgement of the gaps in pre-existing services and knowledge that we were constantly trying to plug, or at least clumsily raise questions about. The concerted effort and energy taken up in this knotted task of trying to bring what is marginal to the centre should not be under-estimated, and yet when the importance of knowledge of culture and communities is presented it is easily re-appropriated into dominant mainstream practices and services, thereby diluting the awareness needed to sustain something 'different'. This need to repeatedly justify the importance of such work continues to plague BME projects and services and success is highly dependent on the understanding and support of managers and commissioners. It is vital that they have some knowledge and experience of the challenges of working with discriminated groups – especially so when they themselves are from dominant white society.

This experience, however, brought to the fore for us the need for self-representation and management. Although we did not at the time have sufficient years of experience as family therapists to qualify to clinically line-manage ourselves, we felt able and were able to build a case for us to manage our own service development. This move towards autonomy and being involved in decision-making was crucial for the further development of the service and the personnel. Needless to say, it generated much conflict and was again met with some resistance as it did not fit into, and correspond with, existing discipline management structures. To break this new ground, invaluable support was provided by the MFS service director, Eia Asen, who brokered with, and persuaded, the executive head of the Trust, Peter Carter, to authorise the creation of a new post called the Cultural Service Co-ordinator. This in turn though inevitably created the potential for some competition within the service as to who should lead, and what skills, qualifications and experience were required, or should be privileged, for this job description.

Meaning of knowledge

Knowledge typically is valued or given credence by virtue of qualifications or experience, but what if mainstream mental health qualifications do not build in a sufficiently rigorous component that assesses cultural competence, or indeed knowledge of cultural systems and assumptions that underlie our normative notions of health, illness and family functioning? Years of clinical experience also cannot necessarily be taken as a reliable indicator, if that experience does not involve meaningfully and effectively engaging with those at the margins. The mainstream system thus can easily support knowledge and ways of working that can obscure the needs of cultural minorities, whilst masking the limitations of the system, which is not routinely assessed from the point of view of those in marginal positions. An understanding of the dynamics that operate around anti-discriminatory practice and a complex under-standing of culture is needed.

When culture is attended to, it is often treated as a variable – a social category, rather than a process or meaningful system (see Chapter 1) – which questions our own deep assumptions of what we know and how our own taken-for-granted notions of health, illness, agency, emotions, cognitions and relationships are culturally pat-terned. To truly appreciate culture as a meaningful system we need to understand it as a 'whole' and be aware of the deep conscious and unconscious aspects of culture, which cannot be separated from the self of the client or the presenting problem (Fateh et al., 2002). Indeed interventions need to be meaningful within the cultural system of the client to be effective. Different cultures have different orientations and worldviews that can challenge our compartmenta-lised ways of working within statutory settings. Through the research and interviews conducted with Asian clients during the project phase of the MCTC (Malik, 1988) we became aware that clients expressed a need for a more holistic approach. This included practical and social input as well as psychological and emotional, and can be linked with the indigenous holistic paradigms of the Chinese, Pakistani and Bangladeshi traditions. In these traditions notions of health, illness and healing have not been split and compartmentalised along the lines of western Cartesian mind/body dualism and so the potential for misdiagnoses of symptoms and mismatch in expectations for treatment in professionals and clients working across cultures greatly increases (see Chapter 1 for discussion of these issues). As Walker (2005) stresses, failure to understand the cultural background of families can lead to unhelpful assessments, non-compliance, poor use of services and alienation of clients from the welfare system. However, in order to build a bridge between mainstream mental health services and BME communities by engaging with cultural differences, workers who are comfortable navigating different systems are required.

People and relationships

Identity politics

Occupying the middle ground between mainstream settings and BME communities can be precarious. It has required us to develop strong identities and work through issues of potential contradiction. Working in pairs and with the back-up of a BME team, as well as supervision that addresses these challenges, has facilitated this process of 'self making'. A vital component of this was a 'reflections group' that was run during the initial project phase of the service by a senior Asian psychiatrist and analyst. This was a closed group, which provided a safe space for us to talk as a team about the challenges we were facing and group dynamics and conflict within and without the service. Although this was not a comfortable space (as these spaces rarely are), looking back now it was a forum where we could voice our anxieties and ambivalence about working in the mainstream, as well as with our communities and our own cultural identities, in an often un-articulated way.

Many BME workers get jostled into the position of working with their clients by virtue of their ethnicity, but may themselves have highly ambivalent feelings about their personal identity, their professional identity in the mainstream and their position within their communities. These at times competing and contradictory multiple identities need to be worked through if clinicians are going to be able to develop the skills to be able to hold multiple views with regard to both dominant and minority cultures, which can often seem polarised and rigidified, in order to allow alternative new possibilities to emerge. Simply being from an minority ethnic background oneself is not sufficient, although it may provide some experiential knowledge of these tensions.

On the one hand, we have had to think carefully about our own relationship with culture and how we integrate our beliefs and practices into the British and professional cultural contexts in a way that upholds and does justice to the 'differences' that are important to us and/or our clients – especially when these appear to be at odds with the dominant culture of the mainstream system, such as arranged marriages, parenting practices or the role of religion and spirituality in people's lives. Voicing these differences can be uncomfortable and feel risky in terms of how one is perceived by colleagues. Of course, the assumptions made by colleagues are themselves culturally rooted, but it is the force of the assumption of universality in Eurocentric notions that can silence. The danger of this silence is that it can lead to withdrawal or the construction of boundaries, so that cultural systems do not truly engage with one another and culture becomes reified as static and polarised as opposed to dynamic and changing. This is especially dangerous in the arena of child protection, where differences in cultural practices need to be acknowledged in order to engage with clients, but also not left unchallenged if they are harmful to members of the family.

On the other hand, we have also had to think carefully about how we integrate our professional knowledge and knowledge of mental well-being more generally to raise awareness in our communities about taboo issues such as sexual abuse, domestic violence, forced marriages, etc. Again this position, this time at the margins of one's own community, can be a difficult place to occupy. Trust needs to be built by joining with the logic of the cultural system as an 'insider', before challenging issues can be raised or meaningful interventions made. This has often required attending meetings and doing presentations in evenings and weekends in community settings. We see our role as agents of change who are not just limited to individual clients and families but also essentially to communities, so that broader contexts can be created in which families can feel supported.

Thus, although our work has been mainly intra-cultural, it is simultaneously and inevitably inter-cultural as it often involves thinking about the multiple agencies and cultural contexts in which families operate. It has required us to be flexible and holistic in our approach, engaging with practical as well as social, psychological and emotional issues and addressing both child and adult needs. At times, community-based work can feel like work on the front-line and so it becomes imperative for workers to have 'back-up' and feel supported.

Staff relations

BME workers require support in the 'front-line' work that they are doing. Not only does this work often require dealing with socio-economic hardships, such as housing and issues of immigration, but also, as our work uncovered, histories of acute unmet mental health needs in multiple members of the family, where families have not sought help because of fear of misunderstandings by mental health professionals or stigma in the community. In order to deal with the complexity of cases it has been invaluable to be able to co-work with a colleague who also shares language skills and knowledge of the culture, be it from different points of view. In fact, having a team of six staff also enables other markers of differences within communities – for example, gender, age and class – to be represented and affords us a community of practice through which we can develop and share ideas. What is more, having a number of diverse staff has enabled culture to be foregrounded and made highly 'visible' within the organisation, in a way that is difficult, if not impossible, to achieve with the tokenistic appointment of one individual member of staff, who is often set the impossible task of representing 'difference' and being the catalyst for institutional change.

However, to fully break down the boundaries of mainstream services and to sustain and mainstream changes in practice the co-operation of non-BME staff is vital. Co-working and collaborating on cases with colleagues in the wider organisation has enabled the embedding of culture into the ethos of the organisation beyond the MCTC. In order for the MCTC to feel integrated into the organisation, culture needed to be integrated into the service as a whole, and the more we have worked jointly with colleagues the more confident we have become of this and our sense of 'belonging' in the organisation. We have thus resisted taking a purely 'ethnic matching' approach to our work, in order to ensure that cultural competence remained the responsibility of the staff team as a whole. Cases are allocated on the basis of cultural needs and expertise as well as multi-disciplinary needs and expertise. This not only raises the issue of culture but creates the potential for dialogue about culture across disciplines.

Community relations

Apart from building a collaborative partnership and integrating within the organisation and mainstream mental health settings, it has

been equally, if not more, important for the MCTC to work colla-
boratively and gain legitimacy with community organisations and
the voluntary sector. We know that despite community organisations doing crucial work and being important knowledge-bearers
and gateways for referrals, they often find it hard to access and make
referrals to statutory services (Malek and Joughin, 1998). They can
also be reluctant to make referrals if they lack confidence in the
cultural sensitivity of statutory services and feel that the methods of
working are not holistic and culturally or religiously appropriate.
Consequently they can be left with highly complex cases to deal with
without sufficient back-up. Overcoming such concerns and developing trusting relationships with community organisations has
required us to make a concerted effort, either through raising
awareness of mental health issues and services at community meetings, gatherings and conferences, or through establishing outreach
clinics and bases. We consider ourselves to be accountable to our
communities and have engaged in dialogue with them, through
which we have learnt immensely from them and have in return tried
to share and demystify our methods of working. As a result a significant proportion of referrals to the MCTC come through community organisations or self-referrals instigated through community
settings. Working with small tight-knit communities, though, has
made us acutely aware of the need for confidentiality. Clients can be
anxious, and rightly so, about engaging with practitioners from their
own communities, as they fear breach of confidentiality or being
judged. We have been told by clients of some terrible examples and
consequences of this over the years. We have therefore had to
carefully think through how we position ourselves as community
members and professionals at the same time, whilst adhering to a
strict code of confidentiality.

Conclusions

In order to address the disparities and inequalities in service experience between BME groups and the majority white population, we
have had to develop ways of working that engage with cultural
differences. This in turn has only been made possible through
creating an organisational context in which cultural differences can
be accepted and the self-development of professionals who are
comfortable navigating different cultural contexts can be fostered.
We have highlighted some of the ways in which we in the MCTC in

conjunction with the MFS have attempted to achieve this. Any achievements we have made have reminded us that race and ethnic relations are essentially about social relationships and power relationships, and so our task has been not just to engage with BME peoples but also with non-BME peoples. Redressing imbalances in power and providing anti-discriminatory practice has to be a joint task which requires a committed top–down and bottom–up approach. The changes in structures that have been requisite to enable the service to keep developing and to retain staff and sustain learning have only been possible with the commitment and support of management at the MFS and the Chief Executive of Central and North West London (CNWL) Mental Health Trust. This is not to skim over the resistances that we have also met along the way. Change is never easy, and inevitably involves some conflict, which we have alluded to but not dwelled on in detail for the purposes of this chapter. However, from our point of view, whilst the presence of a specialist service for BME clients has raised questions and tensions in numerous ways, it has been invaluable for us to be located within a mainstream setting.

Although the MCTC is now regarded as an integral part of the MFS, we still maintain the need to draw a boundary and to regard cross-cultural work as a 'specialism', at least for the time being, as minority differences are all too easily diluted and subsumed by the dominant culture. We therefore espouse an ethic of 'accepting' and 'recognising' 'otherness' (Treacher, 2006), rather than an assimilationist or segregationist 'ethnically matched' model. In our experience, integration only happens through real, and often tense, encounters and over time, and is cheated if differences are glossed over too quickly. It is this ethos that we also carry over into our clinical work, which we hope creates a safe space for BME clients to feel understood and accepted for the whole of who they are, rather than feel that their lives become further fragmented in the hands of the mental health system when they are at their most vulnerable.

Chapter 14

Mental health services for Chinese people

Shun Au and Rebecca Tang

The statutory sector mental health services seldom address the needs of Chinese people adequately (Li *et al.*, 1999). Yet when the community attempts to provide them it is beset by many problems. One of the major challenges for both the statutory and voluntary sectors is the dispersed nature of Chinese people across the UK (Census, 2001c): there are over 88,000 in London (mainly in the boroughs of Barnet and Westminster). In the rest of England, over 33,000 live in the southeast (mainly around Oxford and Milton Keynes) and nearly 27,000 in the northwest (around the cities of Manchester and Liverpool). There are about 16,000 Chinese people in Scotland (mainly in Glasgow and Edinburgh), around 6,000 in Wales and just over 4,000 in Northern Ireland.

Mental health problems – whether interpreted as 'mental illness' or not – affect a relatively small portion of any population. In the UK, planning, co-ordination and provision of social and health services are almost exclusively carried out at a local level. Chinese people in the UK are widely dispersed; the (Chinese) population in any given area, be it a city borough or county, never amounts to being a very significant proportion of the population. Therefore, responsibility for arranging services for people with problems who form such a small minority, even when they are recognised as needing mental health services, may not be anyone's business. This problem is accentuated in a system, such as currently being planned, where statutory health services are located at the primary care level, organised either by primary care trusts (PCTs) or by local authorities in partnership with PCTs.

Community mental health projects developed outside the statutory sector have generally sprung up within generic Chinese community centres in big cities such as London, Manchester and

Glasgow. Many of these projects have faced, and still do face, many constraints:

(a) The funding tends to be small and time-limited. Most projects tend to be supported by charity foundations rather than by the statutory sector. This means that projects have to constantly seek further funding in order to continue at all. By and large, charity foundations provide no more than the first tranche of funding to kickstart a project and expect the project to seek statutory sector funding after that. This poses a significant problem in an age where the statutory sector is facing a funding crisis at the same time. It is very rare for projects funded by charity foundations to be picked up by the statutory sector. The result is that good projects fall by the wayside.

(b) Mental health is a field where a high level of professional training and expertise is required. The capacity to provide good quality mental health care in the Chinese community is somewhat limited. Some Chinese community centres may struggle to find the right personnel even though funding is secured. As pointed out earlier, the critical mass for developing services beyond the basic ones of interpreting and emotional support does not exist at local level. Since the number of clients/patients even in big cities is not large, the funding is limited and the capacity is weak. So, few community centres are able to develop a comprehensive range of mental health services serving the Chinese populations. This explains the relatively small number of mental health projects nationally, the relatively low level of support they can provide, and the transient nature of many of these projects.

The Chinese Mental Health Association (UK) (CMHA) was set up to tackle the unresponsive nature of statutory mental health sector services in relation to the Chinese community. Despite the difficulties highlighted above, CMHA has been extremely successful in its aims; since its inception in 1992, it has gone from strength to strength. It is now a sizeable registered charity with an equivalent of ten full-time staff and a budget of £400,000 a year. We attribute the success of CMHA to several factors – a strong client base, a strong infrastructure, and working in partnership with other organisations.

CMHA is fortunate to be based in London, where nearly 40 per cent of ethnic Chinese live (Cowan, 2001). This provides the critical mass for a solid client base to be built. Over the years, CMHA has rolled out a number of services, which include counselling, home support, research into supported housing, befriending, support for carers, and a user group. Although some of these were not sustainable in the long term, they have all been well regarded. The result is that CMHA itself has now got a good reputation in the eyes of the funding bodies and in the Chinese community. Another way in which CMHA has built up a strong client base is through the use of the media. Since 2001, it has been using a range of media to tap into the Chinese community. The multimedia mental health promotion project, using a range of media including satellite TV, weekly columns in a national newspaper and a half-yearly newsletter to promote mental health awareness, has been extremely successful. This project, as well as some other projects developed by CMHA, is described below.

Practical problems

Project-based organisations often struggle to attract enough resources to be able to build an infrastructure to maintain existing services or allow further growth. The problem is acute in the voluntary sector as core funding (i.e. funding for management and administration) is notoriously difficult to attract. One way around this problem is to generate a good number of projects with built-in overhead costs so that as projects come in, they bring along with them money to fund core management and administration. CMHA used a two-prong attack with some success. This was largely due to its long-standing track record of delivering well regarded projects on time and on budget. Its good reputation also allowed CMHA to attract a certain degree of core funding.

Financial support for core management is crucial to any voluntary sector project since this gives the organisation the stability to act strategically. In other words, it is able to implement actions that lead to the achievement of long-term goals. For example, the supported housing research and development took CMHA seven years to complete. This, however, allowed it to develop a supported housing scheme that managed to attract statutory funding. CMHA now has a sound financial control system, an excellent IT system and a strong senior management team, all vital in strategic planning and fundraising.

Partnership is a buzz word. It is, however, easier said than done. At CMHA, it is axiomatic that we work with partners in all major projects we undertake. For example, the multimedia mental health promotion project involved partners from a mental health trust, a TV company and newspapers. We developed our mental health helpline by working with Saneline (http://www.sane.org.uk) and other partners. We ran a highly successful youth counselling and parenting project, working with a generic Chinese organisation in London with support from Parentline Plus (http://www.parentline plus.org.uk), a leading parenting organisation in the UK. Strategic partnerships have enabled us to call on skills and expertise that CMHA, on its own, would not have at hand. Of course, partnerships have to work both ways. It has got to be win–win for all involved.

Projects

The following are some of the projects successfully developed by CMHA over the years.

Multimedia mental health promotion project

Inspired by its mental health promotional campaigns in the West Midlands at the end of 2001, CMHA developed a partnership with the Birmingham and Solihull Mental Health Trust (BSMHT), formerly North Birmingham Mental Health Trust. Following a project to facilitate public education and raise mental health awareness for South Asian communities, CMHA adopted a multimedia mental health promotional approach to try to reach the Chinese community nationwide. Grants were secured in 2002 from the Lloyds TSB Foundation and the Big Lottery Fund (formerly the Community Fund). With these, CMHA began to run a multimedia mental health promotion project to address the lack of material being used to promote and raise awareness of mental health issues for the Chinese community. The plan was to develop a multi-faceted project using a range of media channels, encompassing television, a website (http://cmha.org.uk), a service directory, newspaper columns, user-led newsletters and translated information booklets. The main aims of the project were to encourage people to look at mental illness in a positive way, to encourage people with mental health needs as well as their carers to voice their concerns, and to help them to access quality treatment and services through greater information dissemination.

The magazine column, the mental health seminars and our service user-led newsletter were found to be very effective ways by which to convey messages to the Chinese community about positive mental health. In addition, service user involvement in producing newsletters was found to be therapeutic for the people involved, as well as empowering them. As a result of this project, bilingual mental health information resources, such as a website, a service directory and translated booklets, were developed, serving the purpose of providing mental health information in an accessible language for the Chinese community in this country. Articles from the Chinese magazine column and other multiple resources were placed on the CMHA website.

The multimedia mental health promotion project achieved its aims and objectives throughout the project span of 2002 to 2005. CMHA is looking forward to developing another mental health promotion and well-being strategy in the near future. We have learned several valuable lessons in carrying out this project. We realise that regular updates of our website are necessary and that the content of the website should be richer and contain more details on mental health, services and information from the Chinese perspective. We have decided that an electronic service directory on the website could be helpful; and the inclusion of contact details related to Chinese community organisations and organisations in other parts of the world is something we shall pursue. The magazine column is an effective channel for health promotion and should be maintained and further expanded upon in the future. A framework of user involvement should be developed as a guide in working with service users. We intend to develop training and support for facilitators and workers. Although the mental health seminar we held had a useful impact in terms of raising mental health awareness, a more effective publicity strategy should be planned in the future. Topics could also be broadened and expanded upon. CMHA could work more closely with other organisations to figure out a plan on how to attract more people to attend – for example, presentations could be arranged outside office hours to accommodate more people's schedules. Previous feedback from seminar attendees could be used in publicity leaflets to attract more people and clarify the purpose of the seminar.

Wah Sum *helpline*

Research has shown that helplines contribute to maintaining the mental health of service users (National Institute for Mental Health in England, 2002). A national mental health helpline, called the *Wah Sum* helpline, was launched by CMHA in November 2004 with the support of the Big Lottery Fund in order to provide information, advice and emotional support to Chinese communities. The service developed a range of policies and procedures, and a comprehensive in-house training manual and programme in its first nine months of operation. The workers receive ongoing supervision and support. Since its launch the service has been broken down into geographical areas in order to better serve Chinese people outside London. Between November 2004 and July 2006, the helpline received calls from 172 locations throughout England, Wales and Scotland. This is good evidence that the helpline has helped Chinese communities all over the UK. In March 2005, the helpline was awarded the Quality Standard accredited by the Telephone Helpline Association (http://www.helplines.org.uk).

The *Wah Sum* helpline has assisted people who are in need of mental health services, especially elderly Chinese people who are more vulnerable and need language support. It has helped Chinese people to overcome the difficulties involved when seeking help, and increased their chances of accessing mental health services. Also, it plays an important role in providing support to health professionals from the statutory sector and mainstream voluntary organisations, and people in the wider community, who are concerned about Chinese mental health issues.

Since the launch of the helpline, several psychosocial issues which cause mental distress amongst people in the Chinese community have been identified. Our statistics show that issues concerning marital problems, parenting, and gambling are amongst the major causes of mental distress such as depression and anxiety. In order to address these problems, CMHA has been making an effort to fundraise for new services, such as gambling rehabilitation and a parenting project, to meet the expressed needs of the callers.

User social group

The *Yao Yao* user social group began operation in 2002 with the support of a small grant from the Bridge House Trust. The idea of the social group is to create a friendly environment where CMHA service users can meet people with similar life experiences and enjoy group activities together. The group also empowers participants, as they can learn new skills useful for everyday life in a relaxed and informal setting. Here, participants also experience a close-knit social network and a sense of purpose in all the tasks that they perform. The activities that the social group organises are both diverse and fun. They include gardening, computer classes, card and badge making, origami, ceramic classes and multimedia projects such as social group radio. To highlight the achievements of the user social group, the badge-making project in 2005 was the first creative project designed specifically to fundraise for the group. The badge sales successfully raised over £100 during the Chinese New Year festival held in Chinatown in London.

Many of the service users have made great improvements in terms of their quality of life since taking part in the user social group. The fact that all the people in the social group are of Chinese origin helps the users to adapt easily; there are no language and cultural barriers to navigate, the main languages used being Cantonese and Mandarin. The user group constantly plans a diverse and wide-ranging set of activities to enable the social group members to learn as many life and educational skills as possible. The social group has regularly high attendance levels and many of the attendees have built good genuine relationships with both fellow group members and the CMHA co-ordinators. From observation, the confidence of the people who attend the *Yao Yao* group has grown over time and many are more outwardly confident and more sociable as a result.

CMHA befriending project

A befriending project run by CMHA began in June 2005, to focus on a variety of different Chinese ethnic groups which can potentially fall under a variety of Chinese categories – 'British Chinese', 'Vietnamese Chinese', 'Mainland Chinese', etc. The service targets people suffering from mental health problems and also people over the age of 60 years. A majority of the people seen within the befriending project suffer from problems such as isolation, apathetic attitude towards life, and self-neglect, either because they are old and/or because they suffer from mental health problems. The befrienders have two main aims: to improve the quality of life of the users of the service, and to reduce social stigma in the wider community.

The befriending volunteers offer a flexible range of services with an overall holistic approach. Service users are visited in their own homes, residential care homes or hospital wards by volunteers trained in mental health work and risk assessment. The befrienders offer respect, care and concern, psychological intervention and emotional support to users of the services, who are encouraged to communicate and interact with others, to leave their home and access community facilities. Users who are ready to do so are encouraged to join a range of social and rehabilitative activities and training programmes. They are taught social skills in order to maximise independent living. When appropriate, support services are offered to vulnerable users who are impaired physically and/or mentally. Befrienders also offer supervision with regard to medication intake, physical health awareness, mobility issues and environment awareness. When necessary and agreed to by service users, befrienders contact community psychiatric teams, key worker(s) and/or social worker(s) and liaise with these professionals – for example, over compliance with medication.

An important function of the befrienders is to reduce social stigma by raising community awareness about mental health problems. Thus, the user social group was featured in an article in the *Hackney Gazette*, a local newspaper. It showed our clients in a positive light; for example it showed them as being able to produce exquisite and beautiful products although suffering from mental health problems.

Chinese Oral History Project

The Chinese Oral History Project is a ground-breaking venture which started in October 2005. It aims to document the lives of the current British Chinese population and highlight the progress and development of the Chinese community in the UK since the late nineteenth century. The focus of the project is to bring the older and younger Chinese generations together by having the younger generation interview the older generation in order to extract their life stories. The sharing of life experiences is rewarding and can help the next generation gain a greater appreciation and understanding of Chinese culture; this will enable them to discover their heritage even though China is geographically thousands of miles away.

The interviews carried out so far have been enlightening, educational and, in some cases, both funny and moving. Participants have very willingly shared their fascinating life stories, which have covered a wide range of topics, including the Cultural Revolution, the Sino–Japanese war, migration, the Hong Kong and China of their youth, adapting to life in the UK, inter-generational issues, education, Chinese chess – the number of topics covered is endless. This sharing of experiences has been the starting point for a whole range of volunteer activities, including videotaping interviews, video-editing, transcribing, research and writing of articles on aspects of Chinese culture and life, and much more. The project has involved contributions from many talented and creative individuals and the final result will be the culmination of their hard work.

The future

In November 2006, CMHA launched and published three major products throughout the UK: (1) an oral history documentary on DVD; (2) an educational resource booklet; and (3) a multimedia oral history project website. All three products have been very professionally produced and are available free of charge to the public. In this way, we hope to foster an understanding of the origins of the Chinese community within the UK, to provide the Chinese population in the UK with greater exposure and to build bridges between the Chinese community and the wider population.

Chapter 15

Counselling and day care for South Asian people

Yasmin Choudhry and Qadir Bakhsh

A centre to provide counselling for Asian people living in the London Borough of Waltham Forest (LBWF) was set up in 1993 by a group of local professionals, including social workers, counsellors and psychiatrists, who felt that mainstream services were not fully meeting the needs of minority ethnic communities in spite of a documented increase in mental health problems within these communities. The Qalb Centre was successful almost from the word go. It was reported on in the journal *Openmind* (Gorman, 1995) and was soon recognised nationally – and later internationally when the staff were invited to present their work at a conference in Copenhagen in 1997. Four years after it started, we managed to get funding to establish a day centre for Asian clients who have enduring mental health problems. And in 1998 we were funded to provide 'specialist' counselling for people with problems of substance abuse, from Asian, African and Caribbean backgrounds. This chapter describes the current (September 2007) services provided by the Qalb Centre and its work with communities, set against a brief outline of the London borough in which it functions and the philosophy underlying its approach.

Background

At the last census (2001c) LBWF had 218,341 people, of whom 35.5 per cent were from black and minority ethnic (BME) groups – higher than the national average in England and Wales (8.7 per cent) and the average for London overall (28.8 per cent). The total Asian population was 14.8 per cent, encompassing within it the second largest population of people with roots in Pakistan in all the London boroughs; black people, mainly from African and

Caribbean backgrounds, made up 15.4 per cent of the population; and Chinese and other minority ethnic groups total a further 1.8 per cent. Breaking the numbers down rather differently, the three largest BME groups in LBWF were Black Caribbean (8.2 per cent), Pakistani (7.9 per cent) and Black African (5.8 per cent).

The age profile of the BME population in the borough was younger than that of the white population. Over half (51.6 per cent) of all the children under the age of 5 were from BME groups. Some 56.8 per cent of respondents in the borough gave their religion as Christianity, similar to the London average of 58.2 per cent. The next largest religious affiliation was Muslim, which accounted for 15.1 per cent of the population. At 32,902 people, this was the third largest Muslim population in London. Twenty-five per cent of the population of the borough were born outside the UK. The proportions were lower among those aged 0–15 and those of pensionable age, and higher among those of working age.

Many languages are spoken in LBWF. The ten languages most frequently requested from the local council's interpretation and translation service are Turkish, Albanian, Somali, Urdu, French, Polish, Portuguese, Arabic, Romanian and Spanish. The inhabitants in most of the wards located in the south of the borough experience a high level of deprivation, poverty, unemployment and poor housing – experienced by all the residents, but proportionately more by BME communities. The overall unemployment rate in the borough in January 2002 was 5.2 per cent of the economically active population aged 16–74, but the rate for people of Black African origin was 13.06 per cent and for those of Pakistani origin 13.7 per cent (Waltham Forest Economic Profile, 2004).

Philosophy and practice

The treatment of mental health problems in National Health Service (NHS) facilities is based largely on the use of drugs and counselling or some type of 'talking therapy'. Both approaches are seen as traditionally 'western' in their approach, focusing on symptomatic, superficial relief of distress and largely ignoring many aspects of the human condition, such as spirituality, social pressures and so on. Consequently, many Asian people with mental health problems who access NHS services are left dissatisfied and frustrated; therapy is experienced as unsuitable and culturally inappropriate because it fails to address the person as a whole in the context of their family and community. Since Qalb was set up to provide services for people whose cultural roots are in South Asia, we tried to address this problem from the very start.

We feel that our therapists maintain an innovative approach that is 'holistic' – where individuals are not seen as being divided in any fundamental sense into 'outer worlds' and 'inner worlds', into physical beings and social beings, into bodies and minds, and so on. Generally speaking, therapists at the Qalb Centre focus primarily on innate potential (in both individuals and their families and communities) for growth and development; clients are encouraged and helped to turn to their inner resources and strengths and the strengths that there are in their families and communities. From this, the client is encouraged to move on to interact positively with the wider world. In other words, our approach is to consider the outside world as secondary to the inner world. This ethos is reflected (or 'veiled') in its name *Qalb* referring to the spiritual heart of Sufi philosophy (Frager, 1999).

Qalb is a main provider of Asian mental health services in the non-statutory ('voluntary') sector in LBWF. Our services are based at two different sites in the borough – one for counselling and complementary therapies, and the other for day-care services. The former offers one-to-one counselling, reflexology, therapeutic body-works, Reiki therapy (a gentle form of healing and stress release), and support groups. The latter offers a therapeutic centre for people with severe mental health problems, nearly always carrying a diagnosis implying serious 'mental illness' (in terms of western psychiatry) in the statutory sector. Since 1998, we have been able to provide counselling and complementary therapies for people from Asian, African, and African-Caribbean backgrounds identified as suffering from alcohol and other substance abuse. At first our focus (in this specialised area) was on alcohol abuse but now our services encompass addictions to other substances, including cannabis, crack cocaine and prescription drugs. Our alcohol and drug abuse services have expanded due to a grant from the Neighbourhood Renewal Fund. The services are much valued by clients and the demand for our services in this field is growing rapidly, as a result of word-of-mouth recommendation. The following comments from users of the service are worth noting:

> 'All in all, I have felt welcomed, cared for as a person and understood.'

'A valuable service that provided me the space/time to reflect and develop myself.'

'Just that it has been invaluable. I would not have coped as well as I have done and made as much progress so quickly without A—'s help. She has also opened my eyes to the holistic approach of therapy – especially the physical aspect.'

'Talking through my feelings. Realising I am not on my own and others have been through the same.'

Counselling

Our 'holistic' services are directed at both men and women experiencing mental health problems, but we make a point of offering gender-segregated services. The languages most frequently used by the therapists are Urdu, English, French, Gujarati and Punjabi, but therapists who are able to communicate in other languages too are available if required.

At the first appointment, the client is seen by a qualified counsellor and given a comprehensive assessment. An individually tailored package of interventions and support is then planned: this may include counselling in conjunction with complementary therapies and educational sessions on diet, exercise and stress management. A loop system is available for people with hearing problems.

Counselling is provided four days a week from 9.00 a.m. to 5.00 p.m. for fifty-one weeks a year. At present we are funded to provide thirty-six hours of counselling and nine hours of complementary therapy per week covering both general counselling and alcohol counselling. Currently forty-eight people (on average) attend the Qalb counselling service each week. Asian men and women from all walks of life attend the centre; some have suffered abuse all their lives but had not sought help until they heard about our service which is specifically for Asian people. Nearly 90 per cent of women who use our services have self-harmed or attempted self-harm behaviours at some point in their lives and often they have never discussed this with anyone until they reach the centre. Many clients have lived in violent relationships, experiencing racism and also having to cope with immigration problems, child-rearing difficulties, and physical, sexual and emotional abuse. Approximately one-third of our clients are men. The problems they present include depression, perpetrating domestic violence, unemployment, stress, and awareness of the destructive role they play in their relationships, which they are now ready and willing to address. Many of the problems are ongoing and so the centre provides a telephone counselling service (via ringback) for current clients.

A client who attends the Qalb Centre receives counselling in their preferred language for six weeks, after which a review is undertaken by the centre manager. At that point a decision is made as to whether the client requires a further six sessions or is ready to complete their programme of support. In most cases, clients end counselling after six weeks, but a few continue to twelve, and very rarely some clients stay on for eighteen weeks, at which point there is compulsory completion. When the service for a client ends, a service evaluation questionnaire is completed, on which the client is able to make comments not only on the quality of the service but also on the ways the service could be changed and improved.

The types of problems and issues that clients have raised in the counselling sessions include dysfunctional relationships, marital issues, domestic violence, sexual abuse/incest, depression, alcohol/ drug issues, bereavement, racial/cultural issues, Islamophobia and other forms of racism, divorce, family conflicts, work issues/ unemployment, identity crisis, need to manage their anger, personal crises, eating disorder, sleeping problems, lack of self-esteem/ confidence/personal development, and phobias.

There are currently nine members of staff: one director, one administrator, three counsellors, one chartered counselling psychologist, two aroma therapists and a reflexologist. All the staff at the centre network with other professional services in LBWF, including general practitioners (GPs), health visitors, community psychiatric nurses, social workers and psychologists. Thus we aim to maintain close links with other voluntary organisations and the statutory sector.

Day-care services

People who attend the service are regarded as having long-term (mental) health problems. Nearly all have been or are currently attending statutory mental health services. Therefore, while struggling with personal problems of various sorts, they are contending with the stigma of having a diagnosis. The day services are currently located on the lower ground floor of a building housing various offices, centrally placed near a train and underground station. There are eight members of staff: three project workers, one art therapist, one reflexologist, a cook and two volunteers.

Referrals to the centre are taken from various professionals in voluntary and statutory organisations, families, friends or self-referral. Referrals can be made by telephone or by writing to the centre. People often find it easier to talk to us direct. Our staff team is fluent in a number of community languages, which means that we are able to reach a wide range of people and offer services in a language of their choice. Once the client makes contact, their details are entered onto a referral form and into the Qalb database.

Assessments are made initially by the centre manager and each client is given an individually tailored package of help/treatment, which may include counselling in conjunction with complementary therapies. The language used during the assessment is the one preferred by the client.

Supervision of counsellors and complementary therapists is undertaken on a regular basis by a qualified supervisor who has extensive knowledge of counselling within various settings. The supervisor may be on the staff of Qalb or an outsider.

Confidentiality is a major issue for clients using our service. Our policy on this states:

> The confidentiality of information and its sources will be respected and disclosed only to those who necessarily require it and after agreement with individuals concerned. Workers will be told to what extent information they have provided to the organisation will be made available to the client. The privacy of clients will be upheld at all times. Individual clients must not be discussed between workers and other clients.

We are commissioned (and funded) to provide a service to fifteen service users at any given time – five to have planned and struc-tured activities, five to have drop-in facilities only and five to get support and outreach help (i.e. contact outside the centre itself). However, the service is usually over-subscribed and we have well over that number, managing as best we can. Currently (September 2007), seventy-six people are clients of the service, attending at least once a week, except during the winter months, the Christmas holidays and the holy month of Ramadan. The majority of the clients are Muslims of Pakistani origin. Of a total of forty-six people who use the service daily, twenty-seven are women and nineteen men.

Although we are funded for specific numbers for each of our three types of 'care', namely structured activities, drop-in and outreach, in reality the activities at the centre and the drop-in facilities are highly sought after and so most of the clients on the register attend the centre physically. Thus there is little scope for outreach work, except when there is a genuine need for a home visit due to illness or some family crisis. The day centre services incorporate information and advice to clients, and indeed the wider Asian community with whom they may be in contact, gender-specific services – for example women-only groups – transport, help for carers to get respite, a carers' support group, counselling for individuals and/or families, relaxation therapies and the provision of (Asian) meals (at a small charge to cover costs).

During its existence, the day centre has successfully provided various structured activities (depending on demand, the weather conditions, etc.), including horticulture, arts and craft work, computer training, group discussions, women-only group work, anxiety management, cookery classes, social skills development, social support, English language development, carers' support, day trips, board games and other leisure activities including sessions watching selected videos, and exercises for both men and women. Outings to various places have proved extremely popular. During 2003 and 2004, we have been able to arrange visits to Chessington World of Adventures, the British Museum, Lakeside Shopping Centre, Southall (where there are many Asian shops and other facilities), Kew Gardens, Lloyds Park in Walthamstow, Valentine Park in Ilford, Southend-on-Sea, and Madame Tussauds. During that time, we have dined at a fashionable restaurant, and visited Walthamstow high street and local parks on at least thirty occasions.

The staff at the day centre have been involved in promoting a variety of projects apart from the activities mentioned above. For example, a support group for Asian women ex-users (of Qalb activities) has been in existence for over eleven years, incorporating up to forty-five women meeting for two hours each week. The women in this group have arranged many day trips – for example to the seaside, theme parks, museums and even a short break to Holland, and a seven-day trip to Dubai.

Client (service user) views

User feedback is obtained on a regular basis and used to improve our services and ensure user engagement in developing and delivering services that are appropriate. We keep careful records of what users tell us both informally and in formal consultations. As mentioned earlier, our staff are multi-lingual and we are confident that our ability to communicate effectively with service users is satisfactory. All the users have access to video and TV and they regularly watch films in the languages they speak. Suggestions from the users of our services indicate the need for the centre to acquire its own transport, the need for greater consultation on the food that is provided, the need for more single-sex activities for women, particularly, and the need for greater access to English language development classes.

Working with communities

In addition to the counselling and day services, Qalb is also involved in a number of community projects. For example, in the wake of the September 11 attacks, a need was identified for counselling and advice in dealing with racism directed at Muslims and generally higher levels of anxiety within the Muslim community. As a result Qalb worked jointly with the 'Asian Health Agency' and the 'Commission on British Muslims and Islamophobia' to host a seminar and training session for counsellors and case workers dealing with this problem in Waltham Forest.

A year-long research project, commissioned by the Waltham Forest Drug and Alcohol Action Team (DAAT) and the University of Central Lancashire (UCLAN) and part funded by the Department of Health, was undertaken by Qalb recently (Bakhsh *et al.*, 2004). This community-led project explored perceptions, experiences and attitudes of drug use amongst the Pakistani community in Waltham Forest. It was launched at a seminar, 'Breaking Taboos', aimed at highlighting the need to tackle substance abuse within the Pakistani community and the need for culturally sensitive approaches to help in this field. The main purpose of the meeting was to educate stakeholders by dispelling myths and breaking taboos through honest discussion and a shared understanding.

The Qalb Centre undertook a year-long community engagement programme during 2006 (Bakhsh and Sparks, 2006). Five service users and two key workers at the Qalb day-care centre formed the research team and the report is currently (April 2007) being prepared for publication (Bakhsh, 2007). This project is part of the five-year programme, *Delivering Race Equality* (Department of Health, 2005b), set up by the government to improve mental health care for BME communities (see Chapter 1).

Waltham Forest is one of eleven pilot local authorities in the country to attract funding to develop a Capital Volunteering and Befriending scheme to support users of mental health services (Waltham Forest, 2005). This scheme is aimed at increasing the number of supported volunteering opportunities, helping service users to volunteer in a range of settings, increasing confidence, skills, social networks and employability, and supporting volunteers to act as befrienders. The Qalb Centre in partnership with 'Waltham Forest Crest' has undertaken one of two major projects in delivering this programme in Waltham Forest. A full-time project worker has been allocated to work exclusively with the Asian communities to develop these initiatives.

The future

Our aims for the future are clearly to meet the expectations of current service users but we also hope to extend services to meet what we have identified as unmet needs of the communities we serve, predominantly Asian people of Waltham Forest. First, we hope to develop projects for users of our services who wish to seek employment. These would aim to build self-esteem and confidence and develop interview skills. Many of our current clients face considerable degrees of social exclusion. We believe that individual mentoring may help them to become more integrated in the local community and that we should develop a service to provide this. Some of our clients clearly need long-term support and so we hope to develop a special project for them. Another proposal we are pursuing is to develop a respite care unit for clients receiving a considerable degree of care but living in their own home, so that their carers can have a break. Finally we aim to expand our services to neighbouring boroughs.

Chapter 16

African and Caribbean Mental Health Services in Manchester

Jeanette Stanley

Many publications have highlighted the fact that statutory mental health services in the UK do not address adequately the needs of Black communities – the most recent being the *National Service Framework for Mental Health* (Department of Health, 1999a), *Inside Outside* (National Institute for Mental Health in England, 2003), *Breaking the Circles of Fear* (Keating *et al.*, 2002), *Delivering Race Equality: A Framework for Action* (Department of Health, 2003) and *Mental Health and Social Exclusion* (Social Exclusion Unit, 2003). In fact, this state of affairs was noted in an official report way back in 1994 – *Black Mental Health – A Dialogue for Change* (Mental Health Task Force, 1994):

> African Caribbeans, including large numbers of women, continue to be over-represented in psychiatric institutions at all levels. Predominant psychiatric treatment does not take account of the impact of race and racism. Likewise, there is no widespread acceptance of the importance of culturally diverse methods in working with Black mental health service users and carers.
>
> (1994: 19)

The problems faced by Black people from African and Caribbean communities when they access – or are forced to access – statutory mental health services stem from many sources, generally subsumed under the headings 'cultural insensitivity' and 'racism' (for discussions see Bhui, 2002; Fernando, 2002, 2003; and Chapters 5 and 8). In short, cultural misunderstandings compounded by negative perceptions by the public regarding mental health, exacerbated by the media's image of 'big, black and dangerous' with reference to Black men, appear to pervade the services (Special Hospitals Service Authority, 1993). As a result (but not because of it) alternative services for Black people are necessary, due in no small measure to the individual and institutional racism that Black people continue to experience within the mental health system. The services described in this chapter arose out of a recognition and acknowledgement that African and Caribbean people have been experiencing, and continue to experience, inappropriate treatment through misdiagnosis, misunderstanding and forced hospitalisation exacerbated by prejudice, discrimination and institutional racism.

Racism within service provision affects policy, service delivery, practice and attitudes of individuals, which in turn has an effect on Black service users. Research has indicated that perceptions and attitudes of health care professionals about the causes, consequences and appropriateness of responses to mental health problems differ in significant ways depending upon the ethnicity of the patient in their care (see Chapter 3). The tendency of health care professionals to misinterpret differences in cultural and racial expression and experiences of mental health and illness has serious implications for Black people. The understanding of ethnicity including race and culture has positive outcomes on diagnosis, treatment and the potential for recovery and rehabilitation.

African and Caribbean Mental Health Services (ACMHS) is a community-led service embodying a range of disciplines. ACMHS aims to provide free, confidential, holistic and culturally appropriate services across socially and economically disadvantaged areas of Salford, Trafford, Manchester and surrounding areas, such as Ashworth Hospital in Merseyside. The approach of ACMHS is to be pragmatic, recognising the realities of life for Black people in Manchester. Apart from being culturally sensitive (see Chapter 1 for a discussion of 'cultural sensitivity'), ACMHS aims to address, in whatever ways are possible, the debilitating effects of racism upon the mental health of Black people and their communities, and the problems faced by Black people when they encounter statutory mental health services.

At ACMHS, decisions regarding care packages are made within a framework that acknowledges that behaviour and experiences that are appropriate, acceptable and 'normal' to individual people of African and Caribbean descent may often be culture-specific. For example, they may place high value on recognising the key role of the elderly within the extended family; or such a framework may place great emphasis on the importance of cultural matching between users and volunteer befrienders. But more importantly, ACMHS recognises that societal and environmental factors associated with racism, such as high levels of unemployment, social exclusion, poor housing and alienation, have a significant impact upon the way a community feels, and how it is perceived by mainstream society. As a consequence, ACMHS strives to address social issues that disproportionately affect African and Caribbean people.

Staff and volunteers who work at ACMHS reflect the cultural and bilingual characteristics of those who use the services. They are acutely aware of cultural norms from a Black perspective, and strive to ensure that the services they provide are culturally sensitive, appropriate to the needs of Black people in Manchester, and that the services, including the types of treatment available, are locally based, flexible, accessible and sensitive to the social environment in which Black people in Manchester live and work.

Background

From as early as 1970, the Black community in Manchester, through its local organisations based in the Moss Side district of Manchester, highlighted their concerns about the frequency with which increasing numbers of local Black people, particularly second-generation African and Caribbean young men, were being inappropriately diagnosed as 'schizophrenic' or 'mad' (see Chapter 3). In response to these concerns, a small group of local Black professional workers, with considerable experience, knowledge and skills in youth, community and probation work, mobilised the Black community by establishing support structures for individuals (and their families) who were experiencing inappropriate labelling and incarceration in mental health institutions. This group became known as CHEL, an acronym formed by their first names, Charles (Moore), Hartley (Hanley), Elouise (Edwards) and Les (Chambers).

In 1985, Dr Phil Thomas, a consultant psychiatrist then based at Manchester Royal Infirmary's St Mary's site, advised of the availability of Home Office funds through its 'After Care Grants Scheme'. The Afro-Caribbean Mental Health Project (ACMHP) with a steering group comprising CHEL, other local people and representatives from Manchester City Council's Social Services Department was formed in October 1989. Dr Thomas was invited to join the steering group. ACMHP secured funding to appoint a development worker, while Dr Thomas undertook research (unpublished) which confirmed misdiagnosis and over-representation of Black people held in mental health secure units.

Between 1990 and 1992, funding from Joint Finance, the Mental Health Foundation, the King's Fund and the government's Mental Illness Specific Grant enabled ACMHP to appoint staff to posts in Development, Project Support and Communications, Self-Help Development and Outreach, Research and Education, Casework, Project Management, and (temporary part-time) secretarial duties. During this period ACMHP provided services in hospitals, secure units, service users' homes and community settings, as well as operating an Afternoon Club and a Thursday Evening Drop-in and providing casework support to African and Caribbean people and their families experiencing mental health problems. Funding from North West Arts enabled the production of a video, 'Quiet Strength', which involved service users and carers presenting their perspective on mental illness. Service users' participation in the video helped to empower them and assisted practitioners during training sessions to learn more about mental health from an African Caribbean perspective.

In 1994, funding from Trafford Metropolitan Borough's Social Services Department was obtained to support the ever increasing numbers of residents from Trafford, in using ACMHP services. A caseworker was appointed to provide a culturally sensitive programme to heighten awareness of mental health issues amongst the African and Caribbean communities in Trafford. Also, ACMHP became engaged in a dialogue with Oldham Social Services regarding the development of a 'drop-in' for African and Caribbean residents in Oldham who were experiencing mental ill health. The partnership with Oldham Social Services evolved in 1996 with the three-year funding of a caseworker, working with their mental health team to deliver a culturally sensitive service to African and Caribbean people living in Oldham. In 1996 ACMHP became a registered charity and changed its name to 'African and Caribbean Mental Health Services'. Today (March 2008) a Board of Trustees consisting of fifteen members governs ACMHS. The make-up of the Board includes service users, carers and volunteer representatives, interested individuals and local organisations. Specific sub-groups are mandated to plan and review particular areas of work such as Executive, Finance, and Personnel.

ACMHS is now (March 2008) one of the largest community-based organisations in Greater Manchester, providing a unique mental health service to Black communities. Currently, the organisation receives funding from Manchester and Trafford Social Services Department, Manchester Joint Commissioning Executive, the Department of Health, Voluntary Action Manchester, the Llankelly Chase Foundation, Age Concern, Greater Manchester Probation, South Manchester Healthy Living Network, and the Centre for Ethnicity and Health.

In addition to providing services, ACMHS encourages, facilitates and assists other voluntary and statutory agencies to develop culturally appropriate and sensitive services, by the production and distribution of information, advice and training. ACMHS is committed to positively influencing and raising awareness of cultural issues and mental health to bring about changes in policy and practice, as well as raising awareness of mental health issues within the Black community and, more importantly, empowering individuals to make informed decisions about their care, diagnosis, medication and treatment.

Staff and services

With a complement of thirteen staff and an active volunteer programme, ACMHS provides the full spectrum of support, from the presentation of illness, through to diagnosis, treatment and eventual rehabilitation in the community. The staff provide individual advocacy; attend ward rounds and mental health review tribunals to support Black patients in hospital; carry out casework; run drop-ins; provide advice on employment, education and training; support Black people in prison; and provide advice and counselling to both users of statutory services (in secure units, hospitals and community settings) and their carers and families.

Referrals to ACMHS services are received from a variety of sources (friends, family, social workers, general practitioners, psychiatrists, probation officers, etc.) as well as self-referrals. In cases where ACMHS is unable to meet the needs of a client, they are referred to other appropriate agencies. ACMHS has adopted a specific methodology for monitoring its work. This comprises questionnaires at the first point of contact, user satisfaction questionnaires, one-to-one interviews and focus group discussions.

Services fall into four main categories: Primary Care Services (PCS), Secondary Care Services (SCS), Support Services (SS) and Trafford Services (TS).

Primary Care Services (PCS)

This service is aimed at African and Caribbean people, aged 16–65 years, experiencing common mental health problems, such as mild to moderate depression or anxiety disorders, with complex needs. The service excludes people with psychotic illnesses such as schizophrenia and bipolar disorder.

The service provides an initial screening and triage by a member of the Primary Care Mental Health Team within five working days of referral, followed by allocation to an appropriate worker within ten working days for one of the following types of service provision:

- Assessment
- Guided self-help
- Telephone support
- Public health information and development
- Group work
- Brief interventions of six to eight sessions (which may consist of counselling, cognitive behavioural therapy, etc.)
- Psychosocial support (for people with complex needs)
- Referral to and liaison with other appropriate services

The team providing PCS currently consists of appropriately qualified and experienced staff, i.e. a clinical manager, two mental health practitioners and one mental health worker.

Secondary Care Services (SCS)

This is a short-, medium- or long-term service for people experiencing severe and enduring mental health problems. SCS provides service users with access to a designated named worker, who is either a qualified social worker or a psychiatric nurse, and is responsible for the service users' case management. Provisions include:

- Assessment
- Joint planning, implemention and evaluation of care in conjunction with other mental health practitioners
- Ensuring medication compliance

- Emotional and practical support to aid independent living
- Hospital visits
- Referrals to internal and external services, according to service users' needs
- Psychiatric reports

SCS support work

This service supports service users with various aspects of daily living. It encourages them to develop their personal and life skills, enabling them to attain greater independence and self-esteem, by:

- Supplying practical and emotional support such as assistance with shopping and cooking
- Accompanying service users to GP and hospital appointments
- Assisting service users in accessing community resources and social activities
- Liaising with internal and external practitioners regarding service users' needs

Support Services (SS)

Services in this section involve a variety of activities that are crucial to a holistic approach to help people; therefore, the approach is one of reaching out to clients. This may be the only provision that a service user may access and can be short- or long-term depending on the individual's need. Several of the activities in this section are organised and run by volunteers who are trained, supported and supervised. Support is user-led and so the nature of what staff actually do depends on what service users ask for. So support may include advocacy, help in seeking education, training or employment, prison liaison, access to sport and recreation, participation in music, and getting together in groups. The following account covers the work so far undertaken.

Advocacy

Users of mental health services may be disadvantaged by the nature of their illness, including the social stigma of their mental health, as well as by the controlling nature of many psychiatric interventions. An independent and impartial advocacy service provides support, representation and information to service users in order to begin the process of self-advocacy, redressing the imbalance of power within the system through constructive and challenging dialogue, to improve provision within mental health services. Clients of this service may be helped with housing matters, obtaining benefits, debt management, legal rights under the Mental Health Act 1983 and the Human Rights Act 1998, mental health review tribunals and problems with the criminal justice system. Additionally, ACMHS provides advocacy support to service users who are inpatients across numerous hospitals and institutions.

Education, training and employment

A partnership was established in 2001 with Manchester Mental Health and Social Care Trust (the Moving on Project) funded by the European Social Fund (ESF) to provide service users with opportunities to access education, training and employment. From January 2005 to December 2006, the service was funded by the Neighbourhood Renewal Fund through Job Centre Plus, and thereafter by the Llankelly Chase Foundation. This provision enables service users to engage with the world of work as part of central government's agenda to promote mental health, social inclusion and sustainable communities. Other benefits include addressing and reducing many of the barriers facing service users in respect of social isolation, poverty, low self-esteem, and discrimination.

Prison liaison

This provision commenced in October 2003 and was funded by the Department of Health to employ a Prison Liaison Officer to deliver high quality counselling and advocacy to African and Caribbean inmates with common mental health problems, on issues such as deportation/immigration appeals, legal representation, resettlement, housing, education, training, employment and family contacts. Funding for this post expired in March 2006, but such is the commitment of the worker concerned that the service continues to be provided on a voluntary basis, until future funding, which is actively being sought, is eventually secured.

Drop-ins

Drop-ins are held each Thursday evening and offer group discussions, health initiatives, educational/cultural activities, excursions, outings to the theatre or cinema and presentations from external facilitators, as well as African or Caribbean meals. Drop-ins provide meaningful opportunities for service users to interact and socialise whilst participating in activities such as group discussions, art, sport, health, education and confidence-building programmes, as well as accessing other services within ACMHS.

Sport and recreation

ACMHS advocates the commonly held view that a healthy body contributes to a healthy mind, and enables service users to monitor and control their weight, especially since some medications that service users have been prescribed cause weight gain. Sports sessions are held weekly at the local leisure centre, and jointly facilitated with Manchester Mental Health and Social Care Trust. Sessions for crafts, painting and drawing are held weekly at the Zion Community Resource Centre, facilitated by an art under-graduate on a voluntary basis.

Music

Music sessions were established in July 2004, with funding from Voluntary Action Manchester. These provide a valuable space for service users who do not wish to engage in other mainstream mental health services. Users of this service learn various aspects of music, music technology, disc jockeying and rapping skills, in an enjoyable, active, exciting and relaxing environment. The benefits of this programme are incalculable. Participation reduces isolation, promotes social inclusion and improves understanding and con-centration, as well as bringing pleasure to both performers and audiences.

Other activities/support

A carers group funded by the Joint Commissioning Executive, and facilitated by a sessional worker each Thursday, provides practical and emotional support to people caring for those who suffer mental ill health. Carers are able to meet and support each other in a relaxed and non-threatening atmosphere, share issues of common interest and concern, and access information on other relevant services and short respite breaks.

A women's group (run by women) enables women to meet in a safe and mutually supportive environment to share experiences and information, as well as organising social activities such as shopping, theatre, cinema and other excursions. The benefits of support and capacity-building for individual women are evidenced by the confidence gained by women taking responsibility for facilitating the group.

Trafford Services (TS)

ACMHS services located in the Trafford district of Manchester involve a caseworker, a social worker and a support worker, providing culturally sensitive and appropriate services to African and Caribbean people with mental ill health residing in Trafford. Here, staff work in partnership with other voluntary sector organisations and the statutory mental health services to provide emotional and practical support, as well as monitor mental health and medication compliance of users of statutory services. In addition, ACMHS runs a weekly carers group funded by Trafford Social Services Department and facilitated by a sessional worker. This enables carers to meet and support each other, share experience, minimise isolation, and access relevant information, services and short respite breaks.

Achievements

Since its establishment in 1989, ACMHS has developed relevant partnerships, and steadfastly provided culturally sensitive and appropriate services to African and Caribbean people, carers and families who directly or indirectly suffer mental health problems. The Trafford Caring for Carers Partnership was established in December 2001 comprising Age Concern, Trafford Carers Centre, Trafford South Asian Mental Health Project and ACMHS. The group successfully tendered for the contract to provide assessment and casework for carers in Trafford following the push from government to ensure that carers are supported appropriately. Consequently the South Asian, African and Caribbean communities of carers, who historically did not access services in the same way as their white counterparts, were able to access culturally sensitive and appropriate services. The partnership eliminated the need for all four organisations to compete separately for the same funds. As a result, each organisation's strengths were encompassed, and their skills, practices and policies were adopted or strengthened.

In April 2006, another key partnership was developed between ACMHS and the Pakistani Resource Centre, to deliver consultancy services for Black and Asian offenders. The contract with the National Probation Service enables Asian, African and Caribbean staff to work with and advise offender managers on cultural issues when working with Asian, African and Caribbean offenders.

Awards

In 1996, ACMHS received an award in recognition of services to the community from the Moss Side and Hulme Youth Challenge. In 1998, ACMHS was invited to become a member of the Independent Reference Group (IRG) initiated by the (then) Parliamentary Under-Secretary of State for Health to address re-provision and improvements to mental health services.

ACMHS achieved the Community Legal Services (CLS) Quality Mark in 'General Help with Casework', enabling the organisation to give advice to a nationally recognised standard. In February 2000, ACMHS negotiated with Trafford General Hospital short-term secondments of its ward staff and social workers, to raise cultural awareness amongst staff, exchange good practice and strengthen partnerships. ACMHS received a 'Highly Commended' award in the Whitbread Volunteer Action Award 2000, in recognition of outstanding service to the community. In February 2001, ACMHS was awarded a 'Community Health Impact Award' of £25,000 from GlaxoSmithKline, for excellence in community health work. In November 2004, ACMHS was the recipient of an award for 'Valuing the Voluntary Contribution' – an award given to organisations that make a positive and successful contribution in developing, and valuing, the skills, experience and talents of local people.

Conclusion

The bulk of mental health care in the UK is provided within the National Health Service (NHS) by statutory services. Services within the NHS that are regarded as 'appropriate' for African and Caribbean people are still scarce and far between. Despite the many initiatives in the voluntary sector – ACMHS being one of several –

the UK has a long way to go before these problems are adequately addressed. Clearly, the voluntary sector cannot hope to redress all the problems, but it has an important role to play. At ACMHS we intend to do our bit in making progress in the Manchester area.

However, in common with many other organisations in the voluntary sector, we face many problems. The main difficulties centre on sustaining funding to continue vital services. Without a strong infrastructure to underpin its programmes, ACMHS finds it very difficult to produce funding bids at the required rate to ensure necessary funding is secured. Our plans for the future include seeking alternative premises; seeking adequate funding to establish an appropriate infrastructure; establishing partners in various avenues that are related to mental health, such as housing; developing a resettlement housing post within ACMHS; extending therapeutic services to include reiki, massage, acupuncture and other 'complementary therapies'; and developing a wider basis for counselling.

Chapter 17

The Sanctuary Practice in Hackney

Angela Burnett

The service described in this chapter began in March 2002 in the London Borough of Hackney. In 2001, the government had established a system called Personal Medical Services (PMS) within the National Health Service (NHS) general practice (primary care) sector (Farrar, 2000). The Sanctuary Practice (the Practice) was the first nurse-led PMS pilot within City and Hackney Primary Care Trust (CHPCT). It was funded through a bid submitted by CHPCT to the Regional Health Authority (that part of the NHS that serves a geographical 'region') outlining the need for a primary care service catering for newly arrived asylum seekers living in an accommodation centre in Hackney called the Pembury Hotel, prior to their dispersal throughout the UK. The bid was accepted in July 2001. The aim of the Practice was to provide primary health care for asylum seekers and refugees, particularly those living in temporary accommodation within the borough. We hoped to provide a model of health care provision especially geared to maximise accessibility and different in quality and approach from the usual general practice models used in the NHS.

Health workers in Hackney have a long and proud history of providing health care for asylum seekers and refugees. However, newly arrived people are hyper-mobile; their length of stay in any one place is indeterminate and unpredictable, ranging from two weeks to over a year – a situation described in Chapter 9. This posed particular challenges for health care providers. Individual health care plans were constantly thwarted by clients being suddenly removed with no warning, discussion or notification of their destination, which could be anywhere in the UK. If a secondary care referral was made, the person was likely to have left the area by the time of the appointment. In addition, the majority of people were recent arrivals in the UK and spoke little English. An added challenge was that consultations involving an interpreter took twice as long as 'ordinary' consultations. As a result of all this, providing health care for asylum seekers was more challenging and chaotic than could be reasonably expected within a standard general practice.

Launch and structure

A manager with a nursing background was appointed to manage the project, and premises were identified in a 'portacabin' temporary building in the car park of a health centre. The author, a general practitioner (GP), was recruited in January 2002. Developments were finalised for the reception of patients over the next few months and the Practice opened in March 2002. Initially, it was staffed by a nurse practitioner/pilot lead, a GP and a receptionist. The first person seen was a woman from Afghanistan living in a hostel (as temporary accommodation) who had miscarried earlier that morning. She was due to be dispersed to Wales the following day, yet refused to postpone her journey in order to recover from the miscarriage. Her response was that she had endured far worse journeys in her escape from Afghanistan and she prioritised settling her family in permanent accommodation and her older children being able to attend school, which they were unable to do whilst living in the hostel.

The official launch of the Practice in July 2002 by the local Member of Parliament, Diane Abbott, was attended by approximately 200 guests, including residents of the Pembury Hotel with their children, and colleagues from the CHPCT and a wide range of statutory and voluntary organisations. The launch reflected the rich and varied contribution that refugees and asylum seekers make to the culture and economy of host countries. Delicious food was provided by the Rwandan catering group Umubano based at Praxis (a refugee voluntary organisation) in Bethnal Green (London) and by the Greek-Cypriot Centre in Barnet, a borough of London. The guests were entertained by Rwandan dancers and a Columbian musical trio playing Salsa and Columbian folk music.

Soon after its launch, staffing was expanded to include an additional GP, making a total GP time of 1.5 whole-time equivalents, a part-time practice nurse, an additional receptionist, a practice administrator and two counsellors. Some posts were filled by temporary staff until permanent staff were recruited. The practice placed a high priority on developing a team which was culturally diverse, and staff were of African, Asian and European heritage. We have also placed significant importance on developing a service that is culturally appropriate for our patients. A Zimbabwean woman, trained as both a nurse and a doctor, joined the practice in its early days as an agency nurse. Registered to practice in the UK as a nurse, she was facing tough barriers to obtaining a job as a GP, despite having successfully passed the exams required to revalidate her Zimbabwean medical qualifications. After six months of working at the Practice she successfully gained a place on a 'Vocational Training Rotation' (to train as a GP) and has recently qualified as a GP. A specialist health visitor with responsibility for refugee and homeless families provided support for families with young children, and district nurse support was derived from existing services. Unfortunately no midwife was allocated to the Practice, which meant that pregnant women had to attend the local hospital in order to receive ante-natal care and experienced little continuity.

Partnership working

Since its inception, the Practice has worked in partnership with other voluntary and statutory organisations – an important asset for expanding access to a wider range of services. As well as those mentioned above, the Practice has worked with other organisations including the Medical Foundation for the Care of Victims of Torture in London (where the author also works), the Refugee Council (a government agency), Finsbury Park Homeless Families (Finsbury Park being an area of London near Hackney), the Black and Ethnic Minority Working Group, and Imece and Derman, both organisations for Turkish-Kurdish women in Hackney.

Staff support

Since it was recognised at the Practice that the work we do is challenging and emotionally demanding, we set up a monthly support group for staff, with an external facilitator. Interestingly, the majority of issues which are discussed at its meetings are not those concerning individuals' situations or stories, but ones that reflect the frustrations with the system which are faced by staff. We have also organised two 'away days' for staff, in order to enable the whole team to discuss the challenges of broadening our services and practice population to include homeless people.

Service offered

The Practice aims to provide holistic health and social care to people who are extremely marginalised, with little control over their lives, but who have great difficulty in accessing statutory health services. The receptionists at the Practice have a crucial role in welcoming people and explaining a health system that is unfamiliar to the clients. Reflecting the mobility of our patients, the Practice has a wider catchment area than most others. We offer twenty-minute appointments, thus allowing more time to unravel complex stories. Interpreters are used extensively – either face-to-face for pre-booked appointments or arranged through telephone calls for emergencies. While offering as flexible a service as possible, we try to raise awareness of how to use health services, so that if clients move on to another practice they may know better what to expect.

Since it first opened, the Practice has registered nearly 3,500 people, with a very high turnover. The Pembury Hotel, where most of the clients resided when the service first opened, provided accommodation predominantly for women and children – single men were a minority. The age range was skewed towards the younger age group, with only a small number of people aged over 65. Their countries of origin were from various parts of the world, and 70 to 80 per cent of consultations required interpreters (speaking sixty-four different languages).

Health checks are offered to everyone who registers, the nurse being the first point of contact in the majority of cases. Practice information has been translated into twelve languages and is given to people on registration, along with relevant translated information from the Refugee Council and local voluntary services. People living in temporary accommodation are given a copy of their records as hand-held notes, to aid continuity of care should they be dispersed.

Psychological needs

Many people who attend the Practice show signs of anxiety and depression, with poor sleep patterns being almost universal. Many of the female refugees, and a smaller proportion of men, registered with the Practice are survivors of sexual violence and rape, which throughout history have been used as weapons of warfare to degrade and humiliate people. Deep shame remains with people who have experienced sexual violence and they may also have been put at risk of HIV and other sexually transmitted infections. Survivors of torture may experience ongoing psychological difficulties resulting from both their past and present experiences. In addition, as asylum seekers and refugees, they face poverty, hostility, isolation and detention in the UK, which can trigger or exacerbate mental health problems. Asylum seekers and refugees are amongst the highest risk groups for suicide in the UK (Medical Foundation, 2003).

The Sanctuary Practice places great importance on offering accessible psychological support. We recognise that if people need to be referred to other services with waiting lists and have difficulty accessing interpreters, they are unlikely to be able to access the support they need. Therefore we applied for extra funding in order that psychological support could be offered within the practice by two part-time counsellors. The counsellors we have appointed are bilingual and experienced in working with refugees, although with such a range of clients' languages, many of their sessions are conducted with interpreters.

A recent meta-analysis of the literature on the mental health of refugees has shown that refugee status confers an overall increase in psychological ill health (Porter and Haslam, 2005), which is not an inevitable consequence of conflict and trauma but reflects the socio-political conditions which they face in host countries. The authors conclude that improving these conditions could improve mental health outcomes. Reducing isolation and dependence, having suitable accommodation and spending time more creatively can often do much to relieve depression and anxiety (Burnett and Fassil, 2002).

In addition to providing health care and counselling, the Practice has attempted to address some of the problems which many people face in other ways. People can receive legal advice for their asylum claim, welfare advice (although asylum seekers have extremely limited access to welfare benefits), assistance with housing, and help with completing official forms. This service is provided by staff of the Hoxton Legal Advice Service.

Funding from the Neighbourhood Renewal Fund in 2002 enabled us to develop a women's group and crèche. The purpose was to bring isolated women together, and to teach them how to perform the basics of Shiatsu massage (chosen as being more widely acceptable culturally, since no clothing needs be removed). When this funding expired, the group continued as a friendship group. Subsequently the group metamorphosed into an English as a Second Language (ESOL) group, run by Diaspora, a local voluntary refugee organisation. Participants in this group had the opportunity during the summer of 2004 of working with a theatre group. The ESOL group is now (October 2006) run by Hackney Learning Trust.

User satisfaction

The Practice has invited people to register their impressions of the service, by giving their honest feedback anonymously. This was done through a standard questionnaire, given by a receptionist to English speakers to self-complete after their consultation, while an interpreter translated the questionnaire for those who needed translation. The questions covered issues of convenience, accessibility, the quality of care and communication given by clinicians, information, and whether a person feels respected by different members of the team.

The results of the questionnaire showed that people registered with the practice had a high level of satisfaction, with most responses being 'good' or 'excellent'. However, a few people had some difficulty with contacting the Practice by telephone and a few wanted extended opening hours. [The Practice is part of a telephone network which covers the whole Primary Care Trust, and this (along with the computer) has failed on several occasions.] Comments from clients included:

'You get a warm and friendly welcome'

'Excellent doctors, nurses and receptionists'

'We need more female doctors because they are kind' (the practice currently has one permanent female doctor and one long-term female locum doctor)

'Excellent care'

'Clean'

Since October 2006 the Practice has offered a late surgery, with both doctor and nurse appointments, once a week, and this appears to be satisfying the need for late appointments.

A woman from Rwanda, who registered with the practice in its first few months, has been attending the 'Patients' Forum', a body that draws membership from all four GP practices based at the health centre within which the Practice is located. Having been granted 'Exceptional Leave to Remain (ELR)' (see Chapter 9), she has been determined to rebuild her life, and is keen to participate in community initiatives. Since she is fluent in English and in settled accommodation it has been easier for her to participate than for others. However she has now trained as a welfare benefits adviser and her work commitments restrict the time she has available to attend meetings. Her story exemplifies how refugees and asylum seekers are able to contribute a great deal to their host country, if they are given the opportunity. We need to place more emphasis on facilitating the involvement of marginalised and excluded people in the planning and implementation of services.

Challenges

With its different structure, the Practice has faced many administrative challenges. The Practice administrator expends a great deal of time liaising with the Primary Care Trust (PCT) within which the Practice operates administratively, in order to ensure that information is updated. Our practice computer system has proved insufficient for our needs and much useful data have been inaccessible. After four and a half years we are still awaiting an upgrade to a new system.

We have found that our practice demographics and needs are not fully reflected within the Quality and Outcome Framework (QOF) introduced for GP practices in 2005 (Health and Social Care Information Centre, 2005), and on which practice income and incentives depend. We have relatively low numbers of people with chronic illnesses, such as asthma and coronary heart disease (contained within the QOF), but much of the supportive work that we do in the area of psychological health and practical problems is unrecognised. The author is currently involved in developing alternative QOF measurements for practices working with refugees. The local PCT recognises this problem and has agreed an alternative set of key performance indicators.

We have also faced difficulties in providing a comprehensive interpreting service reflecting the wide range of languages spoken by our patients. When we first opened we used the local PCT interpreting service, but found that the range of languages was too limited for our needs. Despite our initial annual contribution of £30,000, only approximately 25 per cent of our needs were met. Since 2005 we have retained that money ourselves and book interpreters independently. This has proved more flexible and, with less reliance on telephone interpreters, more cost-efficient. Our current annual allowance for interpreting services (September 2007) is £12,000, and we are succeeding in remaining within budget.

Many people who have failed in their asylum claim are destitute, with restricted access to secondary health care. We provide additional support in the form of advocacy and welfare advice, but trying to remain healthy whilst sleeping rough remains a significant problem for many asylum seekers.

The future

Due to the reduction in new asylum applications and the emphasis on moving new arrivals away from London, the Pembury Hotel ceased housing asylum seekers in January 2004. Since then the practice has continued to look after asylum seekers and refugees, but has also expanded and diversified to look after the list of a retired local GP and to register local residents. In April 2006, the practice took on responsibility for homeless people in Hackney. An additional site in the south of the borough is planned, to provide health care for single homeless and vulnerable people within an integrated partnership including housing and voluntary agencies. The plan to expand the practice to two sites will bring with it challenges of communication and continuity, and the team have had an opportunity to discuss these issues at the 'away days'. More time will be needed for discussion as plans develop.

The Practice has developed a structure and skills to provide specialised health care to asylum seekers and refugees, who represent the majority of people registering. These skills will also be useful in providing care for other vulnerable groups. However, we value the fact that our practice population reflects the local community, since it reduces the potential for marginalisation and enables health workers to maintain their general skills. The team have faced many challenges in developing the practice, but have learnt a great deal from each other and from the patients. We have hosted many visitors from the UK and other countries and welcome further discussion about new developments and ways (new and old) of facing and overcoming challenges.

Chapter 18

A movement led by Black service users in south London

Robert Jones

A number of mental health service user/survivor groups have emerged across England in recent years. Yet, there still exists only a handful of such groups that are 'visibly' composed of people from Black or minority ethnic (BME) communities. This handful is reduced even further if we exclude groups that are run by statutory organisations or workers from those organisations.

What we have instead are BME groups that operate on the margins – the 'invisible to the system groups' who often meet informally, arrange social events, provide support for one another, and whose members often make impromptu visits to support people on hospital wards, taking home-cooked food, cigarettes, hair and skin care products, magazines, papers, books, etc. and, more importantly, giving people a sense of community, helping in reducing isolation and providing people in hospital with the most basic of human needs – the need to talk, be listened to, and feel valued and cared for. In this chapter I trace the achievements, problems and difficulties encountered by one of those groups, namely SIMBA, a Black-led mental health service user/survivor group operating at the Maudsley Hospital in south London. SIMBA means 'strength' in Swahili, and the symbol chosen by the group was that of a roaring tiger (Trivedi and members of SIMBA, 2002). In this chapter the term 'Black' is used to refer to people of African, African-Caribbean and Asian descent and people who identify as 'Black British'.

This is essentially the story of a group of individuals who identify as 'Black', who have experienced life with a mental health label, people who have had periods of ill health and who have spent time as inpatients in a mental health hospital. These individuals, driven by the desire to make things better for others who experience the mental health system, could not sit back and do nothing; their story embraces frustration, anger, disappointment, periods of re-admission, joy and great sadness but their determination has taken SIMBA from the edges of involvement to today's position where the organisation is well known, respected and retains a strong and active membership base.

Barriers to user involvement

Barriers exist for service user groups, particularly if groups need to raise funds to support their activities. Most funders require the group to develop formal structures such as a constitution, a board of trustees, and accounts systems in order to satisfy funding requirements. Although some groups welcome the opportunity to formalise their structures in this way the vast majority don't, particularly groups from BME communities where people often view these formal structures as layers of bureaucracy that get in the way of the group's reason for being. SIMBA did not have these structures; instead it used the financial and management structures of another group to employ workers and to provide the necessary financial systems.

User groups who receive funding from statutory bodies such as Primary Care or Mental Health Trusts are often funded so that they are able to meet the needs of statutory services, i.e. having members who sit and contribute on committees, working groups, etc.; the idea is that involvement at this level will help to create a service that has been influenced and shaped by service users. Statutory bodies are pleased with this arrangement because they are able to satisfy the requirements of user involvement, and user groups that contribute in this manner are somewhat pleased, because they receive funding for this role, either directly in the form of a grant for the organisation or in the form of payment for members.

It is becoming recognised that this approach is not representative – that the majority of people who have used or are using mental health services do not engage in such a process, and that the situation creates an environment where a few service users become 'service user experts' and dominate user involvement. There is also an ever-increasing body of evidence which shows that groups who focus on the needs of statutory organisations rather than the needs of their members are unable to sustain a healthy or diverse membership. Despite such evidence this model of service user involvement remains the most dominant.

Creating a Black user group

SIMBA was established to raise awareness of the issues facing Black people within the South London and Maudsley (SLAM) NHS Trust. Members were clear from the outset that they did not want the traditional user involvement model of meetings, formal committees and paperwork; they found their own creative ways to engage – ways which kept the issues at the forefront but did not leave members feeling frustrated or emotionally drained.

Resisting pressure to conform

As soon as word got around that Black people were coming together, even before SIMBA was officially launched in 1999, members were inundated with requests to go to meetings and to sit on various committees from staff across SLAM. In their eyes SIMBA members were a resource that they could use and SLAM, like some other mental health trusts, were desperate to show that they were involving Black people in the decisions that they were taking. Staff at SLAM got the message early on that SIMBA did not go about its business in the 'usual' way (see above). Apart from attending the cultural competence committee, where members of SIMBA felt they needed to know what was going on, SIMBA set down conditions before responding to requests for participation on committees – conditions that were often ignored by the authorities. SIMBA refused to provide responses to consultation documents unless assured that their views would be taken on board.

Although requests to attend meetings trickled to a virtual stand-still, SLAM did not ignore SIMBA. Before long, a request came for SIMBA to do a five-minute 'talk' to the SLAM board. SIMBA used this opportunity to put on a performance of poetry and prose accompanied by African drumming. This included the SIMBA anthem written by members of the group, 'Free again', 'Dr SIMBA', 'Medication', Control and restraint', 'The side effect', 'Images of me', 'I often sit' and 'Is there a doctor in the house'. The performance concluded with a take on Martin Luther King's 'I have a dream' speech and ended with Bob Marley's 'Redemption song', with its haunting lines, 'Emancipate yourselves from mental slavery, none but ourselves can free our minds' – a finale which was applauded by workers from the trust, particularly its Black workers who joined in the 'Redemption song'.

SIMBA was on the map; mental health professionals knew that its remit was to address race and cultural issues from a BME perspective; they knew that SIMBA members did not 'do' committees or other formal meetings, merely for the sake of being 'involved'. Staff had to start considering alternative ways to work with members – they knew that if they wanted SIMBA's involvement then they had to work with SIMBA, on SIMBA's terms. SIMBA became a respected force that could not be ignored. SIMBA members picked and chose the events that they wanted and worked with other Black groups, sharing knowledge and skills and using the contacts that were made to support their cause. In particular, SIMBA worked closely with the Transcultural Psychiatry Society (TCPS) which enabled SIMBA to gain access to professionals involved in pursuing issues that SIMBA felt strongly about and gain credibility as a user group to be reckoned with. All of this happened without any substantial funding and helped to create an organisation that could pursue its own agenda.

Progress

Once SIMBA obtained funding (see below) and an office base, it was able to use the latter as a social space for people to meet. The group attracted artists, poets, singers and musicians who in turn helped to draw out the talents of non-artists. As a development worker at the time, I recall the wide-ranging discussions that were held, which focused on world events, not just the day-to-day life of mental illness. Mental health talk focused on recovery, people sharing their experiences and survival strategies often through poetry or people breaking out into song or just via often lengthy but always-supported discussions.

Over the years, SIMBA diversified its activities and was soon providing a barbering service and a regular supply of free hair and skin care products to service users on wards, running a book library service, and ensuring regular support to people on the wards. On the social side, SIMBA held barbecues in the hospital grounds and in local parks and organised a series of trips around the country. As its work became known and its members made contacts and participated in joint work, SIMBA emerged from the

shadows of SLAM and was invited to address conferences, participate in staff training events and support the development of other
such groups.

The impact of funding

About two years after its founding, SIMBA applied for funding
from SLAM's charitable trust fund. The application was successful, and the funding enabled SIMBA to appoint a full-time co-
ordinator and purchase office equipment. Also, the trust provided
SIMBA with an office within the hospital for the worker to use as a
base, and enabled SIMBA to access a shared meeting room with
the another user group. Although access to funding enabled
SIMBA to widen its activities, paradoxically, funding seemed to
stifle the freedom of SIMBA members, stifle their desire to do as
they wished, their creativity and their independence. Members
became mindful of the huge responsibility that having such funding
brought and of their accountability to other BME users. Tensions
started to emerge between SIMBA and another user group based
within the same hospital, as this group had applied for funding at
the same time as SIMBA but had been refused. But, despite these
difficulties, SIMBA's practical approach to doing things and its
reluctance to be drawn into endless meetings allowed SIMBA to
maintain its commitment to make a practical difference to the lives
of Black service users in the hospital and develop its campaigning
role in the wider mental health field.

Conclusions

SIMBA began as a result of Black people who were using mental
health services at the Maudsley Hospital realising the need to get
together as a group that was separate from the main service user
organisation in the hospital. It has developed into an established
organisation that is recognised by the hospital authorities and by
Black people who have used (or are currently using) the services of
Maudsley Hospital. Indeed SIMBA is now recognised across BME
communities as an important organisation for service users and one
that is able to voice their needs. Despite the difficulties encountered
as a consequence of funding, SIMBA has been able to maintain its
independent position of focusing on the needs of its members, not
the needs of the mental health trust. Admittedly, this situation does

lead to a degree of tension. SIMBA's strength and survival are a real testimony to its founding members.

SIMBA seems on the face of things a unique venture; it functions effectively as a service user/survivor group which is run by and for Black mental health survivors, providing individuals with support on the wards, operating as peer advocates when necessary, and providing self-awareness and identity-building activities through music, poetry and creative writing. Yet, in an important way SIMBA is not that unique; the reality is that up and down the country informal groups such as SIMBA exist, but the fact that they operate differently from the dominant model of service user involvement means that they are invisible to the system, not supported and invariably not funded or recognised outside of the area where they operate.

Part 4

Lessons for the future

The future is never certain but today uncertainties seem magnified in the case of both the mental health scene and the issues around racism and cultural diversity in Britain. In these circumstances, the one chapter in this part of the book looks at the way ahead by drawing on important lessons from contributions in the previous eighteen chapters and making suggestions on how, in spite of likely increasing uncertainty in the political and social context, people of good will could strive for a better future in mental health service provision for a multi-ethnic society.

Chapter 19

The way ahead

Suman Fernando and Frank Keating

In this final chapter we draw from the previous eighteen chapters those themes that could provide pointers for what the future may hold, adding our own observations and suggestions whenever appropriate. Naturally, the themes reflect issues around cultural diversity and the persistence of racism, mainly in its institutional form, and keep referring back to the need for change in statutory sector service provision.

Being mindful that mental health service provision must always be seen in its socio-political context, we begin by considering what this context may look like in the next few years, at least as far as the UK is concerned. From time to time there have been policy initiatives to deliver race equality; the most recent was the government plan *Delivering Race Equality* (Department of Health, 2005b) – and DRE is mentioned several times throughout the book. The failure to make much progress in mainstream service provision for black and minority ethnic (BME) communities is disconcerting and worrying. So we ask why the statutory sector seems so impervious to the sort of changes needed to enable it to be equitable. From there we consider how things may be done differently in the statutory sector, which, after all, should be servicing the mental health needs of everyone who lives in this country, whatever their ethnic origin, 'race' or cultural background. After this, we try to see what we can learn from successes in the voluntary sector and we consider how the profile of service users may be raised. We discuss briefly the role of training in bringing about change, suggest changes in the Mental Health Act that may help by setting a framework within which change could take place, and consider the place of management in driving through the culture-change that is needed. We then have a section on the role of families and carers seen from a BME perspective – a matter often overlooked in the literature. Finally, this chapter attempts to draw some general conclusions on mental health services, proposing strategies for change in statutory sector provision and practice at least in the short term.

Emerging socio-political context

As this final chapter was being written (September 2007), a pioneering 'atlas of identity' in Britain was published (Thomas and Dorling, 2007). The division between the 'haves' and 'have-nots' in Britain is similar now to that in the 1930s. Stark social contrasts across the country show that, 'where once the chart [of advantage and disadvantage] showed a bell curve, with rich and poor places at each end but always more in between, the chart now shows two curves – one of advantage and one of disadvantage' (Ward, 2007: 17). Then, there is the issue of civil liberties. In the introduction to this book we point out a 'serious retreat [recently] from civil liberties, mimicking what is taking place in the United States' (Kennedy, 2004: 184). And we point to a shift in political pronouncements (from all major political parties) away from focusing on racism as an impediment to social inclusion of BME communities in mainstream society, to an emphasis on BME communities being responsible for integrating into 'British' society; *away* from emphasising systemic injustices, to focusing on the *nature* of minority ethnic communities – what the various BME communities are *like*, how well they have taken on 'British values' and so on. The description in Chapter 2 of the way the government pushed through legislation that widened the scope of compulsory detention ('sectioning') under the Mental Health Act, ignoring opposition by every professional group involved in mental health, including the Royal College of Psychiatrists *and* Mind (the National Association for Mental Health) which speaks for service users, illustrates a worrying undemocratic tendency. Chapter 9 points to discrimination experienced by most BME groups being exacerbated in the case of asylum seekers through legal restrictions on (for example) their access to free health care. And the situation for refugees and asylum seekers may well get worse since their predicament has become a political football with different parties vying with each other to appear as being 'against' what is called 'unfettered immigration' (Telegraph, 2007). In such a situation, racial inequalities in the mental health system, which Chapter 3 notes as resonating with similar themes in the criminal justice system and education, are only likely to get worse – *unless something specific is done about them.*

In the mental health field, the shift in emphasis from institutional to community care during the 1980s and 1990s has resulted in the closure of nearly all big mental hospitals in England and Wales. But recent research across Europe (Priebe *et al.*, 2005) finds that, 'although acute psychiatric beds have been reduced in the UK, forensic beds have increased and more people are being placed in supported housing' (Moncrieff, 2007: 23). This seemingly 'invisible' re-institutionalisation is ominous for BME communities because it is they who have, up to now, been over-represented in such facilities. And Chapter 2 points out that this situation is likely to worsen after changes in the Mental Health Act come into force in October 2008. Not surprisingly, as *Delivering Race Equality* (Department of Health, 2003, 2005b) nears its crunch point in 2010 for being judged by the criteria set down at its launch (see Chapter 3), the general expectation is that most or all of the targets will be missed. Our view is that the mental health system will continue to be experienced as racist by BME service users for quite some time if not the foreseeable future.

The emerging socio-political context seems bleak. But the struggle to lift the burden of injustice and neglect within the statutory mental health system that falls heavily on BME communities could be strengthened if there was a political will to do so; that will only occur in our view if BME communities demand that it be done. However, the lessons of the past ten years must be taken on board. One lesson is that, on the whole, BME service users cannot look to BME professionals to bring about or even participate in leading campaigns for change – although admittedly there are significant exceptions. So developing a BME service user movement for change, for speaking out, for campaigning, is a must if the next few years are to show change for the better, not just for BME people but for everyone.

Why is the statutory sector stuck?

The chapters in Part 1 of this book address in their own ways the shortcomings of the statutory sector. Part 2 explores some ways and means through which attempts have been made to confront issues that result in those shortcomings. Part 3 reports on projects and services, mostly within the voluntary sector, that demonstrate meeting some of the needs of BME communities. The message that comes through in all parts of the book is that very little progress has been made in the mainstream statutory sector over the past twenty or so years. The statutory sector seems stuck in a culture that is impervious to much change.

Failure of government plans

First let us consider why government plans seem to fail, taking *Delivering Race Equality* (DRE) (Department of Health, 2005b) as an example. We believe that it was flawed from the start. While claiming to be based on an earlier document, *Inside Outside* (National Institute for Mental Health in England, 2003), DRE was far removed from it in many ways. The first DRE document (Department of Health, 2003), DRE 2003, was produced without any consultation with people who had experience on the ground – in effect it emanated from an ivory tower of a university department. Then, when DRE 2003 was criticised, some attempts were made to consult with BME organisations and individuals (mainly the latter), but these did not result in substantial change before the final document (Department of Health, 2005b), DRE 2005, was brought out. The emphasis remained on the need for information gathering, although there was a great deal of information already available, especially about racism within mental health services; and the document talked of training without specifying who should be trained and how. Although called a plan to deliver 'racial equality' there was no strategy within the document to address racism. But more importantly, DRE 2005 looked to medical research to formulate ways of bringing about (what was called) 'whole systems change'. In Chapter 3, we see that, by 2006, DRE was failing to deliver the sort of results it had promised. Then, the Department of Health (DH) proceeded to develop the idea that racism may not be a problem after all! The DH commissioned work and produced publications that promoted this theme – for example in articles by Singh and Burns (2006) and Singh *et al.* (2007). The former met with serious criticism including a joint statement by the President of the Royal College of Psychiatrists and the Chairperson of its special committee on ethnic issues that this publication had set psychiatry back twenty years, by denying the impact of racism within psychiatric settings (Hollins and

Moodley, 2006). The political dimension of all this seems obvious; the lesson is that the movement to obtain racial equality in mental health service provision is more political than it is medical.

In our view, one reason for the inadequacy of attempts by government to meet the challenges in the mental health system posed by cultural diversity in society and the strength of institutional racism has been the tendency to look for answers in the wrong places. First, they seem to turn to academics, who can be relied on not to be too outspoken on issues of racism. Then, the tendency is to accept uncritically the concept of mental health developed in the medical framework of nineteenth-century western culture; thence naturally, the government turns to medical research to examine what are seen as 'psychiatric' problems such as over-representation of black people in mental institutions and excessive vulnerability of black people to being compulsorily detained ('sectioned') under the Mental Health Act. In our view, meaningful help for BME people with mental health problems is inseparable in many instances from social, economic and political problems they face in society; medical research cannot provide explanations or indeed remedies for these social ills. Further, as suspected and claimed by black service users (see Chapters 1, 3, 8 and 10), institutional racism within the (medical) psychiatric system itself, especially its decision-making based on diagnosed 'illness' constructed socially in a racist and culture-specific context (see Chapter 3), cannot be explored by *medical* research alone. It is essentially a social and political problem which requires exploration and remedies that are basically social and political.

Chapter 3 of this book shows that the underlying themes that have to be confronted in mental health systems are similar to those in the judicial and educational systems. If the government is serious in wanting to bring about 'racial equality' in mental health service provision, a much broader view than the purely medical one of what 'mental health' actually means has to be taken on board; in-depth approaches are required on how systemic change can be brought about in service provision; and, most importantly, the processes of diagnosis, management and suchlike have to be examined as *social* processes. A result of doing all this should be a fairly radical revision of current assessment procedures applicable for 'diagnosing' mental health and ill health, for making risk-assessments, and for decision-making on therapy. But for such changes to be made, powerful forces have to confronted, not least the power of institutional psychiatry and to a lesser extent clinical psychology, and the racism within these disciplines.

Lessons from history

In our view, far too often governments look to academic medical research to provide answers to social questions; they look to medical psychiatry for answers to institutional problems and to doctors to diagnose racism. In our view, once racism is found to be a problem in a system such as psychiatry or a system for delivering mental health care, looking to medical research based on identifying illness is not the way forward. This approach is both unrealistic and misleading. A very different approach to researching racism and cultural diversity in mental health service provision would occur if we looked at the history of (western) psychiatry over the past 150 years, during which service provision for people deemed 'mentally ill' has undoubtedly improved in countries such as the UK. In the nineteenth century, by and large 'the mentally ill' were incarcerated in asylums where they were often physically maltreated; then, laws were brought in to regulate 'care' in asylums, and gradually forms of physical restraint of 'the mentally ill' were largely abolished (Shorter, 1997). All these improvements were carried out, not because of medical research but because of the realisation by the general public – and hence the pressure of public opinion – that 'the insane' were human beings like the rest of us; a realisation that human rights applied to them as much as to the 'sane'. In the 1940s, vast numbers of people were subjected to psychosurgery of a most brutal and destructive type, endorsed by leading academics and clinicians because it was claimed to 'work' (Eisenberg, 2000). These operations, if they can be called that, were abandoned when power-ful psychotropic drugs which had prolonged actions became available in the 1950s and 1960s. In fact, the discovery that particular chemicals 'controlled' certain symptoms of 'illness' was a chance finding and not something that came out of medical research.

A major change in mental health service provision came about after the 1939–1945 war. In the 1950s and 1960s mental hospitals developed 'therapeutic community' approaches to inpatient care, led by Claybury Hospital in Woodford (Essex) (Shoenberg, 1972) and Mapperley Hospital in Nottingham (M. Jones, 1968). And the emptying of mental hospitals – de-institutionalisation (Scull, 1977) – which started in the 1960s accelerated rapidly in the 1980s and

1990s when the era of community care came into being. As Eisenberg (2000) points out, drug therapy had little to do with de-institutionalisation, the impetus for this coming from economic considerations coupled with humanitarian arguments.

The remarkable point is that none of the changes in mental health service provision (and hence in psychiatric practice) noted above occurred as a result of medical research. Admittedly, refinement of drug therapy over the past fifty years has been promoted by research – mainly the method of random controlled trials (RCTs) – and research has added to information on the effectiveness (or otherwise) of drugs, judged on the basis of symptom relief as observed by psychiatrists. But, on the whole, what may be accurately described as improvement in mental health service provision, judged from the point of view of improved quality of care for people who use services, has never happened because of medical-type research but on general principles of humanity, appeal to human rights and the enforcement of laws designed to promote the rights of all people to liberty and equality. The tragedy appears to be that when it comes to equity around 'race', cultural background or religious belief, the powers that be appear to turn to medical research for ways forward (see above). The suspicion is that, in reality, the political will to confront inequality is lacking and it is convenient for government, and indeed society at large, to hide behind a 'medical' shield, implying that 'science' will provide the answers.

How can things be different?

The chapters in Part 1 set the scene; those in Part 2 show that changes require a variety of strategies and approaches; and in Part 3 we see clear indications that change is indeed possible, although so far very piecemeal, difficult to sustain, and largely confined to the voluntary sector. The previous section of this chapter discussed the fallacy of looking to medical-type research for answers to questions about racism and cultural issues. So the question arises as to how we can approach these problems.

Perhaps the struggle to bring about change is not unlike that of tackling issues of liberty and justice in Asia and Africa during the nineteenth and twentieth centuries. Then this meant facing up to the power of colonial imperialism in Asia and Africa, and before that to slavery of black Africans by the white establishment. Just as in the British empire black and brown people colluded, often unwittingly, in keeping the system going, what has become obvious over the past ten years in the UK is that having black and brown faces in positions of visibility in mental health systems and indeed even in government – sometimes people who seem to be carrying power and influence – has not made much difference to progress towards redressing racial inequalities. Indeed, high profile plans such as *Delivering Race Equality* seem to have helped personal careers more than the lot of ordinary people from BME communities – or rather BME people caught up in the mental health system. However, one positive and encouraging sign in the mental health field is the emergence of BME networks (see http://www.bmementalhealth.org.uk) and possibly the voice of BME service users emerging at last from the shadows.

Although bringing about systemic change is ultimately a political matter, the discussions in Part 3 show that efforts of individuals or groups of people working at the coal face can indeed help people from BME communities caught up in the mental health system to survive the system and/or use the system to their advantage in spite of its limitations. It is unwise to assume that psychotherapy/ counselling provided by therapists trained in narrow western models is always helpful to people from BME communities because the models are often imbued with culture-bound stereotypes of health, 'self' and so on (see Fernando, 2002). Yet, the sort of personal interaction that takes place during counselling may well be helpful irrespective of the particular model used by the therapist. Indeed many services for BME communities provided in the voluntary sector, such as those described in Chapters 15 and 16, depend to a greater or lesser extent on some form of counselling, although practitioners at these centres often claim that their approach to clients is 'different' from that provided by statutory services (Fernando, 2005). Ways of adapting psychotherapy/ counselling to suit BME communities have been described in several books – for example those by Lago (1996), d'Ardenne and Mahtani (1999) and Eleftheriadou (1994). And, as Chapter 13 demonstrates, systemic family therapy may well be adapted quite easily to suit BME communities. So, providing the opportunity for service users from BME communities to interact with counsellors should be encouraged.

It is not often that psychotherapy or counselling is seen as a way of coping with racism in society. Chapter 12, however, shows how a particular way of analysing the effects of racism as a 'grinding down experience' can enable a psychotherapist trained in a traditional psychoanalytic setting to help people at an individual level to find their way through complex issues subsumed under the heading 'race relations' in western society. If a school of individual counselling or psychotherapy can be built on this, we may indeed have a powerful weapon – or rather shield – in the struggle against racism.

Learning from the black-led voluntary sector (BVS)

It is often stated that a feature of the BME mental health scene in the UK during the past twenty years has been the activities in the (non-governmental) voluntary sector. Part 3 of this book describes some examples of the initiatives taken by this sector, but includes two that are essentially within the statutory sector although resembling voluntary sector initiatives in terms of being very different in approach from the general run of statutory sector services. These are the Marlborough Cultural Therapy Centre, described in Chapter 13, where systemic family therapy models are used, and the Sanctuary Practice, described in Chapter 17, where the complex mixture of psychological, social and medical needs of refugees and asylum seekers is addressed by a unique general ('medical') practice which emphasises partnership and liaison with a range of services in both the voluntary and statutory sectors.

Chapter 7 discusses the specific nature of the contribution of the voluntary sector, which we call here the black-led voluntary sector (BVS). Apart from programmes and projects that are overtly concerned with 'mental health', the BVS makes its contribution to mental health through programmes that are ostensibly concerned with 'housing', social enterprise and training. Indeed the BVS appears to be giving the lead in innovation in mental health care, where 'mental health' is not seen in a narrow person-centred 'western' sense but as something that emanates from a range of policies and activities in the social and political fields, an outcome of community involvement, of people working together and learning to do so in harmony.

In the case of services that have been developed in the BVS that are more specifically concerned with 'mental health' (in a narrow sense of the term), many of these too are often innovative and sensitive to political and social aspects of mental health, as well as to the particular pressures that BME communities face in society. Generalisation about innovation is always fraught, especially since there has been no systematic research into the variety of BME mental health projects in the voluntary sector. Hence the statements here must be viewed as a mere indication of what has happened in the voluntary sector over the past twenty years, based largely on hearsay and anecdotal reports. The main characteristics of innovations in mental health provision that have worked include:

- adapting traditional psychotherapy/counselling by learning from clients;
- using skills of therapists derived from their cultural backgrounds and community links;
- using alternative therapies derived from Asian cultural traditions;
- supportive therapies linked to housing and social integration;
- advocacy in dealing with statutory services;
- therapies aimed at community integration;
- guidance to clients on strategies to deal with racism.

(Fernando, 2005: 431)

It is evident from many of the chapters in Part 3 that BVS agencies provide meaningful sources of help to alleviate mental distress, but more importantly they seem to work from a conceptual understanding of mental illness that embraces the whole person. This means addressing lived experiences both as individuals and communities in a context of pressures that include racism. It means understanding people's mental distress in their social, economic and political contexts. So a key conclusion must be that services that speak to the 'whole person' are valued by BME communities, and that the replication of such approaches across the board, especially in the statutory sector, may be a crucial ingredient of the mixture of changes that could well result in mental health services becoming equitable and culturally appropriate for all sections of British society. Indeed this is because a 'whole person approach' is likely to benefit everyone, whatever their cultural background, 'race' or ethnicity, emphasising that bringing about services that meet the needs of BME communities will benefit all sections of society.

Black-led initiatives make critical observations about psychiatry and offer a perspective that involves an understanding of the political reality of black people's experiences and the hardships that they endure. Such initiatives are conducive to meeting black people's cultural and racial identity needs as voiced by writers from a range of backgrounds, from service users (e.g. Gray, 1999) to professionals (e.g. Bhui, 2002). It is clear to us from the evidence in the chapters in Parts 2 and 3 of this book that the BVS is making a significant contribution to promoting mental health in BME communities, but they continue to do this in the face of serious challenges. The problems faced by the BVS have been explored elsewhere (Fernando, 2003: 78–83; Keating, 2002) and may be summarised as comprising the following themes:

- Short-term contracts
- Continuous struggle for survival
- Limited opportunities for developing robust infrastructures
- Lack of resources resulting in limited opportunities to evaluate effectiveness
- Inadequate research into ways of working and consequently effective training

Clearly, the BVS will continue to play an important role in the future scheme of things and we must strive to support it in every way. However, it should be noted that in terms of what is required, voluntary sector services are only a drop in the ocean. As a start, we believe that (a) funding should be on a long-term basis and include core activities such as administration, staff development, and evaluation; (b) support should be available without pro-gramme leaders having to 'prove' their worth; and (c) evaluation should be done on criteria set by BME communities.

Raising the profile of black service user involvement

Chapter 3 ends by pointing to the need for a strong service user voice and input into service development from BME communities. Chapter 10 makes it clear that, although current government policy puts service users at the heart of services, this does not seem to be happening for service users from BME communities. But Chapter 18 provides a different slant on this situation: although there are clearly tremendous obstacles to be overcome, black service users do come together and get involved with each other in a distinctive way; but the support they give to each other is ignored and almost hidden from view of mainstream service providers. In general, black service users continue to be marginalised in the mainstream service user movement and to date we have no documented history of service user development in BME communities (Begum, 2006). But, even more importantly, unless the experiences and outcomes for BME service users in terms of *what services do to them* change from *their* (the service users') perspective, government attempts to get black service user involvement will remain an empty exercise. In other words, service users want a service that meets their needs as defined by themselves – and it is only when that happens that we can ask service users to become 'involved'.

So what is the lesson to be learned? Is there a chicken and egg situation? On one side, service providers may think that if BME service users do not get involved, services will not change; on the other side, black service users see no joy in being involved – in fact the very opposite – while services seem so hostile to them and their needs. In situations where there is such an impasse, the usual practice is to try arbitration of some sort. Unfortunately the people who, on the face of it, may be in the best position to arbitrate – primarily by voicing the views of black service users and bringing about the first traces of positive change – namely black professionals, seem relatively inactive; either they are disempowered in power structures within the professional and statutory sectors in which many hold positions of apparent influence, or they are unwilling to take up the challenge. In the view of the authors, the failure of black professionals to make a difference has been a major disappointment. Possible reasons for this have been explored elsewhere (Fernando, 2003: 83–86) and touched on in the introduction to this book.

Training, legal framework, and management

Training is a word that is bandied about *ad nauseam* as a panacea for delivering race equality. Chapter 5 points to a long history of failure to bring about national standards for training. Chapter 8 shows that, as a single strategy for change, training is not merely insufficient but often a cover-up for inaction. Clearly a new approach is needed to the whole question of training. In Chapter 8 we see the challenges for training in a context where institutional racism in psychiatry itself is not being confronted adequately; there is a lack of co-ordination between administrative structures in the National Health Service (NHS) and the bodies that are responsible for training mental health professionals; the government tends to prioritise public safety over help for people with mental health problems; and a medical approach, as opposed to a social one, appears to be getting stronger over recent years. It may be that training is being aimed at the wrong points or levels in the hierarchy of the power structure in the mental health system. Maybe it is not training and education that are primarily required but changes in the way power is exercised, and training can have little effect unless there are major changes in society at large, including the law. And this brings us to the question of a legal framework for mental health practice.

Chapter 2 explores how the current legal framework for mental health services fails to support anti-discriminatory practice adequately – at least in the way the relevant laws are interpreted and the way changes in law are being worked through. The chapter outlines how, far from improving matters, legal changes pushed through by the government have worsened the inequalities suffered by BME communities. In fact, powerful forces appear to be afoot making it very difficult to shift the status quo.

In our view, the chances of bringing about change in psychiatric practice – and hence in the inequalities suffered by BME communities – would be facilitated by a legal framework that promotes a shift away from the narrow medical model of 'illness' towards social perspectives in understanding the complex nature of what constitutes mental health problems. We see in Chapter 2 how recently (2007) amended mental health legislation allows mental disorder to be diagnosed in broad terms. We believe that in this case there should be a series of exclusions incorporated into the Act so that diagnosis may not be made solely on the grounds of what may be construed as religious or cultural beliefs or sexuality. Further, the Mental Health Act should make it obligatory for psychiatrists to take into consideration cultural diversity and the reality of racism implemented through stereotypes and assumptions about people. Treatment should be defined as that which is culturally and socially acceptable to patients, taking into consideration their background. Finally, the Mental Health Act should have clear principles of non-discrimination and equity applicable to all sections of the Act. Indeed these very points were put to government ministers in 2006 when the changes to mental health legislation were being considered (see Chapter 2). We believe that such a legal framework would set a standard for psychiatric practice and would, sooner or later, result in changes in the training of psychiatrists and thence the training of other professionals involved in mental health practice, especially at the hard end of service provision. Race equality training would then be taken seriously and, if imaginative management played its part, real change in statutory services would result.

Chapter 6 outlines fundamental approaches that are needed in developing a coherent framework for implementing change, delivering race equality. These include proper performance management, consultation, and attention to employment practices, all within an overall drive from the top towards culture change of the organisation. But one of the greatest problems encountered in such a drive is in the form of entrenched staff attitudes. Chapter 11 shows how this may be approached. Merely saying that people should behave differently or just providing training courses is insufficient. Also, attitude change at the top seldom filters down to grass roots level staff. Yet, together with attitude change there needs to be strategies to empower staff, to equip them with the personal attributes that are needed to make change, and to support them in enacting change where it really matters at the point of delivery of services.

Families and carers

Family members play an important role in providing mental health care. It has been estimated that as many as 1.5 million people in the UK may be involved in caring for a relative or a friend with mental health problems (Arksey et al., 2002). They are often the ones to instigate calls for professional help. There is well-documented evidence about the needs of caregivers in general, but little is known about the experience of BME carers of adults with mental health problems in the UK. Evidence shows that black carers remain one of the most neglected and invisible groups in the country (Atkin and Rollings, 1996; Keating et al., 2002). This further adds to the invisibility of their needs. Black carers tend to have negative views about mental health services and are therefore not eager to engage with them. Stereotypical views of these communities – for example, that 'they look after their own' – have influenced the paucity of mainstream responses to black carers (Social Services Inspectorate, 1998).

The interest in black carers is a recent development, an agenda that is not driven by mainstream mental health services but has its origins in black self-organisation. The Black Carers Network, for example, published a good practice guide in which the plight of black carers is highlighted (Powell, 2002). Black carers share many of the basic needs of other carers, but in addition they have more specific needs that arise out of cultural difference, stereotypical views and racism. It has been suggested that 'race' and culture are known to affect the experience of caregiving, but research on the caregiving experience of BME communities has been neglected (Milne and Chryssanthopoulus, 2005).

Recent policy developments regarding families and carers, reflected for example in the *National Service Framework for Mental Health* (Department of Health, 1999a), Carers (Recognition and Services) Act 1995 and Carers (Equal Opportunities) Act 2004, have pushed their needs and interests onto the service agenda (Gall *et al.*, 2003). However, it is surprising that the Department of Health's DRE framework (Department of Health, 2005b) does not make specific reference to the needs of this group despite the fact that the needs of carers from these communities have been highlighted in the *National Service Framework for Mental Health* (Department of Health, 1999a). In instances where the needs of black carers are mentioned they are often referred to in relation to the needs of service users. For example, DRE states that there should be 'training for new Support Time and Recovery Workers on the effects of racism and the cultural needs of service users and carers' (Department of Health, 2005b: 62). Gall *et al.* (2003) argue that contact with carers is largely determined by priorities that are set in a user-centred context. This is particularly pertinent for caregivers from BME communities because of differing family traditions and different conceptualisations of what family means. Clements (2004) suggests that carers are often viewed as people in need rather than a group who have particular rights in relation to their caregiving role.

The Sainsbury Centre for Mental Health (Keating *et al.*, 2002) carried out a study to examine the nature of the relationship between mental health services and African and Caribbean communities and found that carers reported negative experiences in their contact with mental health services. For example, they reported their struggles to obtain help for their relative; their exclusion from the care process; stereotypical views about them as black carers; and perceptions about them as being 'a nuisance' or as part of the problem. This study found that there is a lack of carer support organisations specifically designed to meet the needs of carers and families from African-Caribbean and Asian backgrounds.

It is clear that the needs of families and carers from BME communities have been overlooked. We therefore do not know the nature and extent of caring for people with mental health problems in these communities. We also do not know how caring is under-stood in these communities and therefore need a greater knowledge of how caring is conceptualised in these communities. There is a need to acknowledge the contributions carers make to providing mental health care and they should be provided with adequate support.

General conclusions

The reading of the initial eighteen chapters suggests to us that we can learn important lessons from examining closely the issues underlying the failures in the statutory sector to grapple with issues around cultural diversity in the population and institutional racism in service provision. Similarly, we should be devising ways of learning from (often successful) innovation in the black-led volun-tary sector. In addition, we believe that the following fields of activity should be looked at: (a) raising the profile of black service users; (b) instituting proper training for mental health profes-sionals; (c) changing the legal framework for service provision (especially compulsory detention); and (d) instituting imaginative management geared to promoting liberty and justice. But overriding all this there are important issues to be faced in society at large and in professional practice if mental health services are to draw towards equity and fairness.

Mental health can never be seen apart from all that goes on in society – especially discrimination and social inequality. It is clear from the thrust of this book, especially Chapters 1 and 3, that the dominance of mainstream discourses on mental health and dis-courses on ethnicity has resulted in a narrow focus on culture, seen as a fixed entity that calls for control rather than understanding;

and an equally narrow view of diversity, obscuring the more critical aspects of racism, powerlessness and inequality. It seems that the 'bureaucratisation' of an agenda to bring about 'race equality' has resulted in services paying lip service to 'race equality' without challenging racism. In some ways, 'institutional racism' is talked about so much that the need to enact changes on the ground is discounted; the paradigm around institutional racism does not inform service development and delivery, and so institutional reform does not take place. 'Change' is talked about until the cows come home but no one does anything about re-designing the cowsheds. The meaning of 'culture', and what the term cultural sensitivity may mean in practical terms, is often not appreciated. In practice, policies abound but practical action that carries meaning on the ground is negligible.

Reducing inequality

A major lesson that needs to be drawn is that the aim of changes in the mental health scene should be geared to reducing inequalities rather than the possibly unrealistic goal of 'race equality'. The struggle against racism in wider society – indeed in a universal context – must of course continue, and people of goodwill in all sections of society should be involved in this, but until that struggle is successful, it is unrealistic to think of 'race equality' within one part of society – the mental health field. We believe that within the narrow mental health field, our endeavours should be directed towards bringing about a more just and rights-conscious system of mental health care and service provision for everyone, irrespective of cultural background, 'race', etc., and not just improving services for BME communities. The primary – perhaps crucial – challenge for mental health services is not to reinforce the racism that BME communities experience.

Having said that, we propose that critical reflection on how inequalities in the provision of services in mental health can be alleviated, reduced in intensity and circumvented should be vigorously pursued and action devised that takes on board all the barriers to implementing change. But *at the same time*, attention should be given to the numerous other sources of injustice in society around 'race' – in education, housing, employment, criminal justice, leisure, etc. In other words the purpose of our endeavours should be broader than just geared to 'mental health' as understood in terms of service provision; it should encompass all aspects of social and political injustice arising from what is broadly called 'institutional racism', taking on board the changing pattern of how this type of oppression is being implemented – through reference to religion, nationality, ethnicity, culture and so forth.

Changing individual professional practice

An important impediment to change appears to be the structure and ethos of psychiatry itself, which seems to dominate many aspects of mental health service provision, affecting the way all mental health professionals go about their business. In spite of the change in discourse – 'the talk' – over the past ten years within mental health circles, what actually happens on the ground seems to reflect an unwarranted domination by an inflexible traditional psychiatry based on an outdated approach claimed incorrectly to be 'scientific'; this is so across the board in the statutory sector, but especially so in forensic services. The resistance to a paradigm shift in psychiatry (Mezzina, 2005) which is required for the 'talk' to be reflected in 'walk' – action – comes from several quarters and social forces (Pilgrim, 2005). As things stand at present, talk is likely to continue and the most we can hope for in terms of action is a 'biopsycho-social' approach (Double, 2005; White, 2005), where the dominant power of psychiatry will accede to some power sharing. But there is no guarantee that any significant change will result for service user experience if some power shifts to clinical psychology or social work or any other professional group involved in mental health service provision. Systemic change accompanied by a paradigm shift is (in our view) the only way of ensuring sustainable change for the better as far as race and culture issues are concerned. In the face of the realities of power within mental health, it would seem that strategies for changes that confront issues of racism and cultural diversity must begin by tackling the discourse within psychiatry in such a way that talk leads to walk. Meanwhile BME communities can do little else but continue chipping away at the edges, developing the BVS and campaigning for, and striving to achieve, systemic change within mental health services. So the question – admittedly limited in scope – for us here is how this chipping can best be pursued over the next ten years.

Clearly lobbying and pressurising at various levels is important. At the level of professional practice individual efforts have very limited scope because of the 'team-work' structure of service provision and the domination of these teams by what is euphemistically called 'normal practice' – practices that all professionals have to adhere to at the risk of being excluded and even punished. In our view, some short-term change in the way people who access – or are forced to access – statutory services are assessed and generally cared for may well result from training that is about to be put in place following work under DRE (see Chapter 8). Professionals should support this as much as possible, ensuring that lessons are not just learned but result in changes on the ground. The topic of training is pursued above. Be that as it may, we believe that there is mileage in professionals making determined efforts in other ways. We suggest these should cover (a) alleviating the negative effects of the mental health system, while (b) providing where possible individual help through negotiating alternative (so-called) complementary therapies.

Since the main sources of stress within the mental health system come from racism it behoves all professionals to deal effectively with obvious (direct) racism while not ignoring the systemic or institutional racism that many chapters in this book have referred to, and which Chapters 1 and 3 go some way in exploring. Yet, whatever problems service users encounter in services, what ultimately matters in an immediate way is the issues around 'treatment'. In our view, one short-term remedy is to promote alternative therapies which can be introduced without rocking the boat of traditional psychiatry too much. These may be brought into play in the mental health system via government initiatives that seek – or say they seek – to promote therapies that are acceptable to service users and consistent with their wishes – i.e. the drive to provide choice [Care Services Improvement Partnership (CSIP) and National Institute for Mental Health in England (NIMHE), 2005]. It may be possible for professionals to make accessible to service users forms of 'talking therapies' that are provided through the BVS, and even therapies derived from Asian and African cultures, as part of implementing user-choice (see below). Another way for professionals to have some effect in helping BME service users in the short term is to put them in touch with the BVS whenever possible and/or arrange for the BVS to provide services on contract to BME users of the NHS. This means making sure that information on BVS services is available to both service users and service providers in the NHS.

Clearly, the 'short-term change' that professionals can undertake is very limited and may be almost impossible to achieve in the case of secure forensic services – the very locations where BME service users are most significantly over-represented. That is why systemic change is what should be aimed at in spite of all the barriers discussed in many parts of this book.

Advocacy

The negative relationships between BME communities and mainstream mental health services have been highlighted throughout this book. The challenge remains to find lasting solutions to reduce the inequalities experienced by BME communities. Chapter 2 noted that one of the few benefits of the contentious Mental Health Act 2007 is that service users are given the right to advocacy in certain limited situations. How this change is implemented in practice is not clear at present (September 2007). It may well be the case that advocacy schemes put in place during 2008 to satisfy the Mental Health Act 2007 are directly or indirectly controlled by the statutory services. There must be strong pressure to prevent this happening.

In a review of best practice in mental health, Goering (1997) found that advocacy decreased the duration of inpatient stays, reduced the frequency of contacts with mental health professionals, built self-esteem, strengthened support networks and ultimately challenged stigma and discrimination. It has been suggested that advocacy could be a potential way of securing access to the most appropriate forms of support, securing basic rights and challenging racism and discrimination (Newbigging et al., 2007). While offering opportunities at the individual level of empowerment, advocacy could also work at a structural level to challenge discrimination and inequality. In a review of advocacy for African and Caribbean men, Newbigging et al. (2007) found that advocacy services are mainly offered by BME mental health services, not by statutory services. The significance of this is that these services are rooted in the community, they embrace cultural, religious and spiritual beliefs and work for empowerment. In our view, advocacy services that are responsible to the statutory sector are unlikely to do this. Therefore, although the evidence on the impact of advocacy for BME communities is sparse, we propose that advocacy could serve as an important tool to reduce the persistent inequalities that BME communities face in mental health. The BVS should be supported to develop and provide advocacy services to promote individual empowerment, but also to challenge racist practices in services.

Psychological therapies

Just before this chapter was written (September 2007), the DH announced a drive towards providing therapies under what it calls an 'Improving Access to Psychological Therapies (IAPT)' programme (Care Services Improvement Partnership, 2007). Although psychological therapies are being promoted for 'mental health problems such as anxiety and depression' (2007: 1) and are aimed at improving well-being, this emphasis may be a way for BME communities to seek redress for their relative exclusion from therapy such as 'psychotherapy' (see Box 3.2, p. 55). Chapter 12 presents a unique approach to helping people who may be adversely affected by subtle forms of racism at a very personal level. Chapter 13 shows that systemic family therapy is conducive to being helpful (if adapted properly) to people from non-western cultural backgrounds. Chapter 16 reports cognitive behaviour therapy (CBT) being available at a centre for African-Caribbean service users. According to Chapter 15, Asian people clearly find so-called 'complementary therapies', such as reiki, helpful. Indeed there are anecdotal reports of CBT being adapted – for instance as 'mindfulness-based cognitive therapy' (MBCT) provided at the London Buddhist Centre in London (Clay, 2007). The Acupuncture Research Resource Centre (2002) has collected evidence on the effectiveness of acupuncture in depression and anxiety. A major problem in BME communities accessing psychological therapies, especially those that are based on non-western psychologies – namely therapies such as yoga, meditation, reiki, acupuncture and forms of healing – is that the current structure of mental health service provision is, by and large, geared to diagnosis. Chapter 3, as well as many other chapters in this book, shows how misleading diagnosis based on western illness models can be in pointing to mental health needs of BME people.

Recovery frameworks

The discourse around the theme of 'recovery', developed in the US (see Deegan, 1988; Young and Ensing, 1999), has been promoted in the UK recently and supported by the DH (2001) – in theory at any rate. As expounded by Repper and Perkins (2003) and Kloos (2005), the approach of recovery subsumes the pursuit of personal goals of hope, making sense of experiences, understanding and empowerment as a sort of journey undertaken after life-disruptive effects of mental health problems. To judge from Chapters 10 and 18, it is possible that some of these non-medicalised responses connect with feelings about resisting the oppressive psychiatric system, voiced by black service users and supported by approaches in the BVS (see above). However, there seems little evidence that the meaning of 'recovery' as applicable to the statutory mental health system is being explored in a transcultural perspective; moreover, the place of this approach in dealing with racism in service provision, especially racism in psychiatry, is unclear. Another problem is that there are still serious debates about the concept itself, such as whether symptom reduction, firmly within the medical model, is central or not (see Schrank and Slade, 2007). A multicultural view that addresses racism could well find that the word 'recovery' is not right anyway and that (for example) 'liberation', presented in Chapter 1 as a non-western approach that is opposed to 'control', which psychiatry favours, may be better suited to herald a movement that is service user-centred including BME service users. In our view, it is very doubtful at present (September 2007) that 'recovery' – an approach that is currently being pursued with little reference to the issues that service users from BME communities are mainly concerned with – has sig- nificant meaning at the grass roots level of service provision in mainstream, especially forensic, services – and Chapter 3 noted that forensic services are the areas in which black people are particularly over-represented. There is a possibility that if the current recovery approach is popularised and applied extensively in determining the style of mental health service provision, this may form another focus for social exclusion of BME communities.

Spirituality

Lack of spirituality in clinical practice – both in assessments and in a therapeutic approach based on western psychology and psy- chiatry – is a criticism often heard in the UK, especially from people from Asian and African backgrounds. So recent discourse on promotion of 'spirituality' in mental health services (e.g.

Cornah, 2006; Sperry, 2001; Swinton, 2001) and the adoption by NIMHE of a 'Spirituality and Mental Health Project' (http://www. nimhe.csip.org) may provide an opening for developing mental health services that reach out to some of the needs of BME communities. However, we believe that it is far too early to be sure. It is very unclear at present (September 2007) what 'spirituality' in the context of mental health actually means; and its interpretations across cultures are variable (Fernando, 2003, 2007b). How it can be brought into mental health work is even less clear. At present the tendency in Britain is to assume that spirituality is equivalent to 'religion' and to imply that reaching out to so-called 'faith communities' – i.e. established religious institutions – is the way forward in practice. If, on the one hand, the spirituality discourse progresses towards encouraging professionals to give some credence to explanations of (mental) distress and 'illness' as being 'spiritual' as opposed to being biological, and if this leads to looking to religious models of helping people in distress or in the throes of so-called 'psychosis', such a discourse may shift mainstream services away from the narrow western medical approach to mental health that Chapter 1 is so critical of. However, if all that the spirituality discourse does is to encourage professionals to work with religious leaders or organise services that include 'faith communities' – i.e. religious leaders becoming part of the 'team' providing for service users – BME service users, and indeed service users in general, may have little to gain eventually from mental health services dabbling in 'spirituality'.

Summary

So looking to the next ten years, it is our view that BME communities must continue to strive towards changes in service provision that focus on reducing inequalities all round and bringing about changes in professional practice. There is little mileage for BME communities in pursuing the discourse on recovery but the implementation of advocacy may be beneficial if it comes out of BME community groups and does not just involve top–down advocacy services under control of statutory bodies. Although recent discourses on recovery and spirituality may offer some ways for improving services generally, the main thrust from a BME viewpoint should be toward raising the profile of black service users, instituting proper training for mental health professionals, changing the legal framework for service provision (especially compulsory detention), and developing imaginative management geared to promoting liberty and justice in mental health services. And all this while supporting at all levels the BVS, enabling, where possible, approaches developed in this sector to infiltrate statutory mental health services.

References

The 1990 Trust (2005) *London NHS Organisations Race Equality Schemes – Headline Review 2005*, London: The 1990 Trust.

Aakster, C.W. (1986) 'Concepts in alternative medicine', *Social Science and Medicine*, 22: 265–273.

Abel, K., Buscewicz, M., Davison, S., Johnson, S. and Staples, E. (eds) (1996) *Planning Community Mental Health Services for Women*, London: Routledge.

Acupuncture Research Resource Centre (2002) *Depression, Anxiety and Acupuncture. The Evidence for Effectiveness*, London: British Acupuncture Council (BacC). Available: http://www.acupuncture.org.uk (accessed 20 September 2007).

Akbar, N. (1996) *Breaking the Chains of Psychological Slavery*, Tallahassee, FL: Mind Productions.

Ali, S. (2003) *Mixed-race, Post-race: Gender, New Ethnicities and Cultural Practices*, Oxford and New York: Berg.

Alleyne, A. (2004a) 'Race-specific workplace stress', *Counselling and Psychotherapy Journal*, 15(8): 30–33.

Alleyne, A. (2004b) 'The internal oppressor and black identity wounding', *Counselling and Psychotherapy Journal*, 15(10): 48–50.

Alleyne, A. (2005) 'The internal oppressor – the veiled companion of external racial oppression', *The Psychotherapist*, 26: 10–13.

Allport, G. (1954) *The Nature of Prejudice*, New York: Doubleday.

Amin, K., Drew, D., Fosam, B., Gillborn, D. and Demack, S. (1999) *Black and Ethnic Minority Young People and Educational Disadvantage*, London: Runnymede Trust.

Amnesty International (2006) *Amnesty International Report 2006: The State of the World's Human Rights*, London: Amnesty International.

Anonymous (1999) 'Unanswered questions – a user's perspective', in K. Bhui and D. Olajide (eds) *Mental Health Service Provision in a Multi-Ethnic Society*, London: Saunders, pp. 11–20.

Aponte, J.E., Rivers, R.Y. and Wohl, J. (1995) *Psychological Interventions and Cultural Diversity*, Boston and London: Allyn and Bacon.

Appiah, L. and Chunilal, N. (1999) *Examining School Exclusions. Runnymede Trust Briefing Paper December 1999*, London: Runnymede Trust.

Arskey, H., O'Malley, L., Baldwin, S., Harris, J., Newbronner, E., Hare, P. and Mason, A. (2002) *Services to Support Carers of People with Mental Health Problems: Overview Report*, York: Social Policy Research Unit, University of York.

Ash, B. (2003) *Working with Women Prisoners*, London: HM Prison Services.

Atkin, K. and Rollings, J. (1996) 'Informal care in Asian and Afro/Caribbean communities: a literature review', *British Journal of Social Work*, 22: 405–418.

Audit Commission (2003) *Journey to Race Equality: Delivering Improved Services to Local Communities*, London: Audit Commission.

Bach, G.R. (1985) *The Inner Enemy: How to Fight Fair with Yourself*, New York: Berkley Publishing Group.

Bagley, C. and Coard, B. (1975) 'Cultural knowledge and rejection of ethnic identity in West Indian children in London', in G. Verma and C. Bagley (eds) *Race and Education across Cultures*, London: Heinemann, pp. 322–331.

Bakhsh, Q. (2007) *Delivering Race Equality in Mental Health Care: Implications for South Asians in Waltham Forest*, London: Qalb Centre.

Bakhsh, Q., Ahmed, Y., Yunus, S. and Mir, S. (2004) *Breaking Taboos: A Community Led Research Project Exploring Perceptions, Experiences and Attitudes of Drug Use among the Pakistani Community in Waltham Forest*, London: Qalb Centre and Community Safety Team, London Borough of Waltham Forest.

Bakhsh, Q. and Sparks, D. (2006) *Delivering Race Equality in Mental Health – A Seminar Report*, London: Qalb Centre and London Borough of Waltham Forest.

Banton, M. and Harwood, J. (1975) *The Race Concept*, London: David and Charles.

Barclay, G., Munley, A. and Munton, T. (2005) *Race and the Criminal Justice System. An Overview to the Complete Statistics 2003–4*, London: Criminal Justice System Race Unit. Available: http://www.homeoffice.gov.uk (accessed 20 September 2007).

Barker, P. and Stevenson, C. (2000) *The Construction of Power and Authority in Psychiatry*, Oxford: Butterworth Heinemann.

Begum, N. (2006) *Doing it for Themselves: Participation and Black and Minority Ethnic Service Users*, London: Social Care Institute for Excellence (SCIE).

Bernal, M. (1987) *Black Athena. The Afroasiatic Roots of Classical Civilisation*, vol. 1, London: Free Association.

Berthoud, R. and Beishon, S. (1997) 'People, families and households', in T. Modood, R. Berthoud, J. Lakey, P. Smith, V. Satnam and S. Beishon (eds) *Ethnic Minorities in Britain. Diversity and Disadvantage*, London: Policy Studies Institute, pp. 18–59.

Bertram, M. (2002) '"User involvement" and MH: critical reflections on critical issues'. Available: http://www.psychminded.co.uk (accessed 15 December 2002).

Bhabha, H. (1994) *The Location of Culture*, New York and London: Routledge.

Bhavnani, R., Mirza, H.S. and Meetoo, V. (2005) *Tackling the Roots of Racism: Lessons for Success*, Bristol: Policy Press.

Bhugra, D. and Desai, M. (2003) 'Attempted suicide in South Asian women', *Advances in Psychiatric Treatment*, 8: 418–423.

Bhui, K. (1997) 'London's ethnic minorities and the provision of mental health services', in S. Johnson, R. Ramsay, G. Thornicroft, L. Brooks, P. Leliott, E. Peck, H. Smith, D. Chisholm, B. Audinini, M. Knapp and D. Goldberg (eds) *London's Mental Health: The Report to the King's Fund London Commission*, London: King's Fund, pp. 143–166.

Bhui, K. (2002) *Racism and Mental Health: Prejudice and Suffering*, London: Jessica Kingsley.

Biehal, N., Clayden, J., Stein, M. and Wade, J. (1995) *Moving On: Young People and Leaving Care Schemes*, London: Her Majesty's Stationery Office (HMSO).

Bion, W. (1967) 'Attacks on linking', *International Journal of Psycho-Analysis*, 30: 308–315.

Bird, L. (1999) *The Fundamental Facts: All the Latest Facts and Figures on Mental Illness*, London: Mental Health Foundation.

Birtwistle, T. (2002) *Modernising Mental Health Services: Inspection of Mental Health Services*, London: Department of Health.

Black, K. and Shillitoe, R. (1997) 'Developing mental health services sensitive to women's needs', *British Journal of Health Care Management*, 3(10): 27–29.

Black Women's Mental Health Project (BWMHP) (1999) *National Newsletter*, London: WMHP.

Bohm, D. (1990) 'On meaning, purpose and exploration in dialogue' (edited with permission from tapes of an August 1990 conversation). Available: http://www.david-bohm.net/dialogue/dialogue_exploration. html (accessed 2 September 2007).

Bojer, M., Knuth, M., Magner, C., McKay, E. and Roehl, H. (2006) *Mapping Dialogue: A Research Project Profiling Dialogue Tools and Processes for Social Change. A Report Commissioned by German Technical Co-operation*, Johannesburg, South Africa: Pioneers of Change Associates. Available: http://pioneersofchange.net (accessed 2 September 2007).

Brown, C. and Lawton, J. (1992) *Training for Equality: A Study of Race Relations and Equal Opportunities Training*, London: Policy Studies Institute.

Browne, D. (1997) *Black People and Sectioning. The Black Experience of Detention under the Civil Sections of the Mental Health Act*, London: Little Rock Publishing.

Burnett, A. and Fassil, Y. (2002) *Meeting the Health Needs of Refugees and Asylum Seekers in the UK: An Information and Resource Pack for Health Workers*, London: London Directorate for Health and Social Care/ Department of Health.

Burnett, A. and Rhys Jones, D. (2006) 'Health care for asylum seekers. Rapid response', *British Medical Journal online*, 4 August. Available: http://www.bmj.com (accessed 6 August 2006).

Butler, P. and Kousoulou, D. (2006) *Women at Risk: The Mental Health of Women in Contact with the Judicial System*, London: London Development Centre (LDC) and Care Services Improvement Partnership (CSIP).

Campbell, D. (2006) 'Low IQs are Africa's curse, says lecturer', *Observer*, 5 November. Available: http://observer.guardian.co.uk (accessed 29 January 2007).

Campbell, P. (2001) 'The role of users in psychiatric services in service development – influence not power', *Psychiatric Bulletin*, 25: 87–88.

Cantle, T. (2005) *Community Cohesion. A New Framework for Race and Diversity*, Basingstoke: Palgrave Macmillan.

Care Services Improvement Partnership (CSIP) (2005) *Count Me In*, London: Commission for Health Care Audit and Inspection.

Care Services Improvement Partnership (CSIP) (2007) Available: http// www.mhchoice.csip.org.uk (accessed 20 September 2007).

Care Services Improvement Partnership (CSIP) and National Institute for Mental Health in England (NIMHE) (2005) *Choices in Mental Health. National Service Framework Autumn Assessment 2005*, London: Department of Health.

Carers (Equal Opportunities) Act 2004, London: The Stationery Office.

Carers (Recognition and Services) Act 1995, London: Her Majesty's Stationery Office (HMSO).

Carmichael, S. and Hamilton, C. (1967) *Black Power*, Harmondsworth: Penguin Books.

Carothers, J.C. (1951) 'Frontal lobe function and the African', *Journal of Mental Science*, 97: 12–48.

Carothers, J.C. (1953) *The African Mind in Health and Disease. A Study in Ethnopsychiatry*, WHO Monograph Series No. 17, Geneva: World Health Organization.

Cartwright, S.A. (1851) 'Report on the diseases and physical peculiarities of the Negro race', *New Orleans Medical and Surgical Journal*, May,

691–715. Reprinted in A.C. Caplan, H.T. Engelhardt and J.J. McCartney (eds) (1981) *Concepts of Health and Disease*, Reading, MA: Addison-Wesley.

Casciani, D. (2004) 'Islamophobia pervades UK – report', *BBC News, 2 June*. Available: http://news.bbc.co.uk (accessed 29 January 2007).

Castel, R. (1988) *The Regulation of Madness*, Berkeley: University of California Press.

Census (2001a) *Resident Population Estimates for Local Authorities, All Persons, June 2003 (for total population)*. London: Office for National Statistics. Available: http://www.statistics.gov.uk/census2001 (accessed 15 October 2006).

Census (2001b) *Ethnicity: Population Size*. London: Office for National Statistics. Available: http://www.statistics.gov.uk/census2001 (accessed 22 August 2006).

Census (2001c) *Supplement to the National Report for England and Wales and Key Statistics for Local Authorities in England and Wales*, London: Office for National Statistics. Available: http://www.statistics.gov.uk/census2001 (accessed 10 July 2007).

Chand, A. (2000) 'Over representation of black children in child protection system: possible causes, consequences and solutions', *Child and Family Social Work*, 5(1): 67–77.

Chantler, K. (2002) 'The invisibility of black women in mental health services', *Mental Health Review*, 7(1): 22.

Chantler, K., Bashir, C., Chew-Graham, C., Burman, E. and Batsleer, J. (2002) 'South Asian women, psychological distress and self harm: lessons for primary care trusts', *Health and Social Care in the Community*, 10(5): 339–347.

Charities Bill (2004). Available: http://www.publications.parliament.uk (accessed 15 September 2007).

Clay, L. (2007) 'Breaking the moods that can fuel depression,' *East End Life*, 16–22 April, p. 6.

Clements, L. (2004) 'Keynote Review: Carers – the sympathy and services stereotype', *British Journal of Learning Disabilities*, 32(1): 6–8.

Cobbs, P. and Grier, W. (1968) *Black Rage*, New York: Basic Books.

Coid, J., Kahtan, N., Gault, S. and Jarman, B. (2000) 'Ethnic differences in admission to secure forensic psychiatric services', *British Journal of Psychiatry*, 181: 473–480.

Collett, P. and Cook, T. (2000) *Diversity UK: A Study on Managing Diversity in the UK*, Oxford: Department of Experimental Psychology, University of Oxford.

Commission for Racial Equality (2000) *Strengthening the Race Relations Act*. CRE general guidance document, London: Commission for Racial Equality.

Commission for Racial Equality (CRE) (2002) *Code of Practice on the*

Duty to Promote Racial Equality, London: Commission for Racial Equality.

Commission for Racial Equality (CRE) (2006) *The Race Equality Duty. Specific Duties – Public Authorities: Selecting Trainers.* Available: http://www.cre.gov.uk/duty/training_select.html (accessed May 2006).

Cook, D. (2002) 'Consultation for a process for change? Engaging users and communities in the process', *Social Policy and Administration*, 36(5): 516–531.

Cornah, D. (2006) *Impact of Spirituality on Mental Health*, London: Mental Health Foundation.

Cowan, C. (2001) 'The mental health of Chinese people in Britain: an update on current literature', *Journal of Mental Health*, 10(5): 501–511.

Cowan, R. (2004) 'Young Muslims "made scapegoats" in stop and search. Figures soar under new anti-terror laws', *Guardian*, 3 July, p. 8.

Cox, J. (2001) 'Commentary: Institutional racism in British psychiatry', *Psychiatric Bulletin*, 25: 248–249.

Crawford, M. (2001) 'Involving service users in the development of psychiatric services – no longer an option', *Psychiatric Bulletin*, 25: 84–86.

Crawford, M.J., Rutter, D., Manley, C., Weaver, T., Bhui, K., Fulop, N. and Tyrer, P. (2002) 'Systematic review of involving patients in the planning and development of health care', *British Medical Journal*, 325: 1263–1265.

Cross, T., Brazen, B., Dennis, K. and Isaacs, M. (1989) *Towards a Culturally Competent System of Care*, vol. 1, Washington, DC: Georgetown University Child Development Center.

Culley, L. (1996) 'A critique of multiculturalism in health care: the challenge for nurse education', *Journal of Advanced Nursing*, 23: 564–570.

Dalal, F. (2004) *Race, Colour and the Process of Racialization – New Perspectives from Group Analysis, Psychoanalysis and Sociology*, London: Jessica Kingsley.

d'Ardenne, P. and Mahtani, A. (1999) *Transcultural Counselling in Action*, 2nd edn, London: Sage Publications.

Darwin, C. (1871) *The Descent of Man and Selection in Relation to Sex*, vol. 1, London: John Murray.

Davis, M., Erel, U. and Gumbrell, R. (2003) *RITU Project Work Package 1: National Report on the UK*, London: London Metropolitan University, Working Lives Institute.

Day, L.E. (1995) 'The pitfalls of diversity training', *Training and Development*, 49(12): 25–29.

Deegan, P.E. (1988) 'Recovery: the lived experience of rehabilitation', *Psychosocial Rehabilitation Journal*, 11(4): 11–19.

Department for Education and Skills (DfES) (2005) *Ethnicity and Educa-*

tion. The Evidence on Minority Ethnic Pupils. Research Topic Paper: RTP01-05, Nottingham: DfES Publications.

Department of Health (1997) *Saving Lives: Our Healthier Nation*, London: Department of Health.

Department of Health (1998) 'Frank Dobson outlines Third Way for mental health', press release, 29 July (reference no. 98/311). Available: http://www.dh.gov.uk (accessed 10 April 2006).

Department of Health (1999a) *National Service Framework for Mental Health. Modern Standards and Service Models*, London: Department of Health.

Department of Health (1999b) *Reform of the Mental Health Act 1983. Proposals for Consultation*, London: The Stationery Office.

Department of Health (1999c) *Review of Mental Health Act 1983. Report of Expert Committee* (Chair: Genevra Richardson), London: Department of Health.

Department of Health (2000a) *The NHS Plan*, London: Department of Health.

Department of Health (2000b) *Reform of the Mental Health Act 1983. Summary of Consultation Responses*, London: Department of Health.

Department of Health (2001) *The Journey to Recovery – the Government's Vision for Mental Health Care*, London: Department of Health.

Department of Health (2002a) *Draft Mental Health Bill*. London: The Stationery Office. Available: http://www.dh.gov.uk (accessed 10 August 2007).

Department of Health (2002b) *National Suicide Prevention Strategy for England*, London: Department of Health.

Department of Health (2002c) *Women's Mental Health: Into the Mainstream*, London: Department of Health.

Department of Health (2003) *Delivering Race Equality: A Framework for Action*, London: Department of Health.

Department of Health (2004a) *Choosing Health: Making Healthy Choices Easier*, Public Health White Paper. Cm 6374. Available: http://www.dh.gov.uk (accessed 7 February 2007).

Department of Health (2004b) *Draft Mental Health Bill*, London: The Stationery Office. Available: http://www.dh.gov.uk (accessed 10 August 2007).

Department of Health (2005a) *Agenda for Change: NHS Terms and Conditions of Service Handbook*, London: Department of Health.

Department of Health (2005b) *Delivering Race Equality in Mental Health Care: An Action Plan for Reform Inside and Outside Services and The Government's Response to the Independent Inquiry into the Death of David Bennett*, London: Department of Health.

Department of Health (2005c) *Government Response to the Report of the*

Joint Committee on the Draft Mental Health Bill 2004, London: The Stationery Office.

Department of Health (2006a) The Mental Health Bill 2006: Briefing sheets on key policy areas. Available: http://www.dh.gov.uk (accessed 31 March 2007).

Department of Health (2006b) 'Mental Health Bill and related documents'. Available: http://www.dh.gov.uk (accessed 2 July 2007).

Department of Health (2006c) *Our Health, Our Care, Our Say: A New Direction for Community Services*, London: Department of Health. http://www.library.nhs.uk/healthmanagement (accessed 27 January 2007).

Department of Health and Home Office (1994) *Review of Health and Social Services for Mentally Disordered Offenders and Others Requiring Similar Services* (Chairman: Dr John Reed), vol. 6, *Race, Gender and Equal Opportunities*, London: Her Majesty's Stationery Office (HMSO).

DeRosa, P. (2001) *Social Change or Status Quo? Approaches to Diversity Training*, Randolph, MA: Change Works Consulting. Available: http://www.changeworksconsulting.org (accessed 25 September 2005).

Dobzhansky, T. (1971) 'Race equality', in R.H. Osborne (ed.) *The Biological and Social Meaning of Race*, San Francisco: Freeman, pp. 13–24.

Double, D. (2005) 'Paradigm shift in psychiatry', in S. Ramon and J.E. Williams (eds) *Mental Health at the Crossroads. The Promise of the Psychosocial Approach*, Aldershot: Ashgate, pp. 65–79.

Down, J.L.M. (1866) 'Observations on an ethnic classification of idiots', *Lectures and Reports from the London Hospital for 1866*, reprinted in C. Thompson (ed.) *The Origins of Modern Psychiatry*, Chichester: Wiley, 1987, pp. 15–18.

Duffy, D., Ryan, T. and Purdy, R. (2003) *Preventing Suicide: A Toolkit for Mental Health Services*, London: National Institute for Mental Health in England (NIMHE).

Dyer, R. (1997) *White: Essays on Race and Culture*, London: Routledge.

Edge, D., Baker, D. and Rogers, A. (2004) 'Perinatal depression among black Caribbean women', *Health and Social Care in the Community*, 12(5): 430–438.

Editorial (2001) 'Inside our changing land', in *Race in Britain*, Special Edition, *Observer*, 25 November, p. 1.

Eisenberg, L. (2000) 'Is psychiatry more mindful or brainier than it was a decade ago?', *British Journal of Psychiatry*, 176: 1–5.

Eleftheriadou, Z. (1994) *Transcultural Counselling*, London: Central Book Publishing.

Ellis, J. and Latif, S. (2006) *Capacity Building: Lessons from a Pilot Programme with Black and Minority Ethnic Voluntary and Community Organisation*, York: Joseph Rowntree Foundation.

'Equalities for All' Best Value Review Team (2002) *'Equalities for All'*

Review Stage 3 – Final Report, London: Greater London Authority, Metropolitan Police Authority/Metropolitan Police Service, London Development Agency, Transport for London, London Fire and Emergency Planning Authority.

Ethnos Research and Consultancy (2005) *Citizenship and Belonging: What is Britishness?* A research study. London: Commission for Racial Equality. Available: http://www.cre.gov.uk/downloads/what_is_britishness.pdf (accessed July 2007).

Ethnos Research and Consultancy (2006) *The Decline of Britishness*. A research study, London: Commission for Racial Equality. Available: http://www.cre.gov.uk/downloads/decline_of_britishness.pdf (accessed July 2007).

European Convention on Human Rights (1950) Strasbourg: Council of Europe. Available: http://www.hri.org/docs/ECHR50.html (accessed 30 September 2007).

Eze, E.C. (1997) *Race and the Enlightenment. A Reader*, Cambridge, MA and Oxford: Blackwell.

Fanon, F. (1952) *Peau Noire, Masques Blancs*, Paris: Editions de Seuil. Trans. C.L. Markmann, *Black Skin, White Masks*, New York: Grove Press, 1967 (paperback edn, London: Pluto Press, 1986).

Farrar, M. (2000) *PMS Pilots under the NHS (Primary Care) Act 1997 – A Comprehensive Guide*, 3rd edn, London: NHS Primary Care Executive.

Fateh, T., Islam, N., Khan, F., Ko, C., Lee, M., Malik, R. and Krause, I-B. (2002) 'Can talking about culture be therapeutic?', in K. Dwivedi (ed.) *Meeting the Needs of Ethnic Minority Children II*, London: Routledge, pp. 130–150.

Fernando, S. (1988) *Race and Culture in Psychiatry*, London: Croom Helm (paperback edn, London: Routledge, 1989).

Fernando, S. (2002) *Mental Health, Race and Culture*, 2nd edn, Basingstoke: Palgrave.

Fernando, S. (2003) *Cultural Diversity, Mental Health and Psychiatry. The Struggle against Racism*, Hove and New York: Brunner-Routledge.

Fernando, S. (2005) 'Multicultural mental health services. Projects for minority ethnic communities in England', *Transcultural Psychiatry*, 42(3): 420–436.

Fernando, S. (2006) 'Blowing in the wind', *Openmind*, 137: 24–25.

Fernando, S. (2007a) 'From "whole systems change" to no change', *Openmind*, 143: 25.

Fernando, S. (2007b) 'Spirituality across cultures', in M.E. Coyte, P. Gilbert and V. Nicholls (eds) *Spirituality, Values and Mental Health: Jewels for the Journey*, London: Jessica Kingsley, pp. 59–66.

Fernando, S., Ndegwa, D. and Wilson, M. (1998) *Forensic Psychiatry, Race and Culture*, London: Routledge.

Ferns, P. (2005) *A Holistic Approach to Black and Minority Ethnic Mental Health. The Letting Through Light Training Pack*, Brighton: Pavilion Publishing.

Frager, R. (1999) *The Sufi Psychology of Growth, Balance and Harmony*, Wheaton, IL: Quest Books.

Frazer, S. (2005) *The Government Agenda on Engagement and Innovation*, London: Community Links. Available: http//www.community-links.org (accessed 5 September 2007).

Freire, P. (1970) *Pedagogy of the Oppressed*, New York: Continuum.

Freud, S. (1915) 'Thoughts for the times on war and death', *Imago*, 4(1): 1–21. Trans. J. Strachey, in *The Standard Edition of the Complete Psychological Works of Sigmund Freud*, vol. 14, London: Hogarth, pp. 273–300.

Freud, S. (1930) 'Civilization and its discontents'. Trans. J. Riviere, 1961, in J. Strachey (ed.) *The Standard Edition of the Complete Psychological Works of Sigmund Freud*, vol. 21, London: Hogarth, pp. 57–145.

Furedi, F. (2001) 'How sociology imagined "mixed race"', in D. Parker and M. Song (eds) *Rethinking 'Mixed Race'*, London: Pluto Press, pp. 23–41.

Gall, S.H., Atkinson, J., Elliot, L. and Johansen, R. (2003) 'Supporting carers of people diagnosed with schizophrenia: evaluating nurse practice following training', *Journal of Advanced Nursing*, 41(3): 295–305.

Gillborn, D. and Mirza, H. (2000) *Educational Inequality – Mapping Race, Class and Gender – Synthesis of Research Evidence*, London: Ofsted.

Gilman, S.L. (1985) *Difference and Pathology. Stereotypes of Sexuality, Race and Madness*, Ithaca, NY and London: Cornell University Press.

Goering, P. (1997) *Review of Best Practices in Mental Health Reform*, Ottawa: Health Canada.

Gorman, G. (1995) 'Qalb', *Openmind*, 76: 19.

Gottesman, I.I. (1991) *Schizophrenia Genesis: The Origins of Madness*, New York: Freeman.

Granville-Chapman, C. (2004) *Harm on Removal*, London: Medical Foundation.

Gray, P. (1999) 'Voluntary organisations' perspective on mental health needs', in D. Bhugra and V. Bahl (eds) *Ethnicity: An Agenda for Mental Health*, London: Gaskell, pp. 202–210.

Greater London Authority (2003) *Into the Mainstream. Equalities within the Greater London Authority*, London: Greater London Authority.

Green, E.M. (1914) 'Psychoses among Negroes – a comparative study', *Journal of Nervous and Mental Disorder*, 41: 697–708.

Gregg, J. (2004) 'Letter to the editor', *Journal of General Internal Medicine*, 19(900): 36 (para. 5).

Griffith, J., Jochum, V. and Wilding, K. (2006) *Voluntary Sector Strategic*

Analysis 2006/7, London: National Council for Voluntary Organisations (NCVO).

Griggs, I. (2006) 'Institutionally racist', *The Independent on Sunday*, 10 December, pp. 8–11.

Grimston, J. (2007) 'Mixed-race Britons to become biggest minority', *The Sunday Times*, 21 January. Available: http://www.timesonline.co.uk (accessed 28 January 2007).

Grotberg, E. (1995) 'The international resilience project: research and application', in Emily Miao (ed.) *Proceedings of the 53rd Annual Convention of ICP: Cross-cultural Encounters*, Taipei, Taiwan: General Innovation Service (GIS).

Hall, G.S. (1904) *Adolescence: Its Psychology and its Relations to Physiology, Anthropology, Sociology, Sex, Crime, Religion and Education*, vol. II, New York: D. Appleton.

Hall, P. (2006) 'Failed asylum seekers and health care', *British Medical Journal*, 333: 109–110.

Halliday, F. (1999) 'Islamophobia reconsidered', *Ethnic and Racial Studies*, 22(5): 892–902.

Handy, C. (1993) *Understanding Organizations*, 4th edn, London: Penguin Books.

Hansen, F. (2003) 'Diversity's business case doesn't add up (Diversity on Trial)', *Workforce*, 82(4): 28.

Hanvey, C. and Philpot, T. (1996) *Sweet Charity: The Role and Workings of Voluntary Organisations*, London: Routledge.

Health and Social Care Advisory Service (2005) *Making a Real Difference: Strengthening Service User and Carer Involvement in NIMHE*, Leeds: National Institute for Mental Health in England.

Health and Social Care Information Centre (2005) *National Quality and Outcomes Framework Statistics for England 2004/05*, London: Health and Social Care Information Centre.

Healthcare Commission (2005) *Count Me In: Results of a National Census of Inpatients and Facilities in England and Wales*, London: Commission for Healthcare Audit and Inspection. Available: http://www.health carecommission.org.uk (accessed 28 June 2007).

Healthcare Commission (2007) *Count Me In: Results of a National Census of Inpatients in Mental Health Hospitals and Facilities in England and Wales*, London: Healthcare Commission, Mental Health Act Commission and Care Services Improvement Partnership/National Institute for Mental Health in England.

Hodge, J.L. and Struckmann, D.K. (1975) 'Some components of the western dualist tradition', in J.L. Hodge, D.K. Struckmann and L.D. Trost (eds) *Cultural Bases of Racism and Group Oppression*, Berkeley, CA: Two Riders Press, pp. 122–195.

Hollins, S. and Moodley, P. (2006) 'Racism and mental health'. Rapid response to paper by Singh and Burns (2006). Available: http://www.bmj.com (accessed 12 September 2007).

Home Department (1999) *The Stephen Lawrence Inquiry. Report of an Inquiry by Sir William Macpherson of Cluny*, London: The Stationery Office.

Home Office (1981) *The Brixton Disorders 10–12 April 1981. Report of an Inquiry by the Rt. Hon. The Lord Scarman*. Cmnd 8427. London: Her Majesty's Stationery Office (HMSO).

Home Office (1996) *Race and the Criminal Justice System*, London: Home Office.

Home Office (2001) *New Laws for a Successful Multi-Racial Britain: Consultation Paper on the Implementation of the Race Relations (Amendment) Act 2000*, London: Home Office.

Hood, R. (1992) *Race and Sentencing. A Study in the Crown Court*, Oxford: Clarendon Press.

hooks, b. (1989) *Talking Back: Thinking Feminist, Thinking Black*, Boston, MA: South End Press.

hooks, b. (1996) *Killing Rage: Ending Racism*, Harmondsworth: Penguin Books.

House of Lords (2005) *Joint Committee on the Draft Mental Health Bill*, London: The Stationery Office.

Howitt, D. and Owusu-Bempah, J. (eds) (1994) *The Racism of Psychology. Time for Change*, London: Harvester Wheatsheaf.

Human Rights Act (1998) London: The Stationery Office.

Husband, C. (1982) '"Race", the continuity of a concept', in C. Husband (ed.) *Race in Britain. Continuity and Change*, London: Hutchinson, pp. 11–23.

Ibrahim, F. (2003) 'Bollywood and beyond', *Openmind*, 120: 20.

Identity Cards Bill (2004) Available: http://www.publications.parliament.uk (accessed 15 September 2007).

Immigration, Asylum and Nationality Bill (2005) Available: http://www.publications.parliament.uk (accessed 15 September 2007).

Independent Review Team (2001) *Community Cohesion: A Report of the Independent Review Team Chaired by Ted Cantle*, London: Home Office.

Ingleby, D. (2004) *Critical Psychiatry. The Politics of Mental Health*, 2nd edn, London: Free Association.

International Council on Human Rights Policy (ICHRP) (2000) *The Persistence and Mutation of Racism*, Geneva: International Council of Human Rights Policy.

International Council on Human Rights Policy (ICHRP) (2002) *Human Rights after September 11*, Versoix: International Council on Human Rights Policy.

International Labour Organisation/United Nations (1999) *The Evaluation of Anti-discrimination Training Activities in the United Kingdom*, Geneva: International Labour Organisation/United Nations.

Jones, J.S. (1981) 'How different are human races?', *Nature*, 293: 188–190.

Jones, M. (1968) *Social Psychiatry in Practice*, Harmondsworth: Penguin.

Jones, R., Ramsden, N. and Tuck, S. (2003) *Reaching Multicultural Britain – The Black and Minority Ethnic Community and Fundraising in the Top Charities*, London: Development Agency.

Jung, C.G. (1930) 'Your Negroid and Indian behaviour', *Forum*, 83(4): 193–199.

Kakar, S. (1984) *Shamans, Mystics and Doctors. A Psychological Inquiry into India and its Healing Tradition*, London: Unwin Paperbacks.

Karpf, A. (1988) 'Why we get bad health by media', *Guardian*, 11 May, p. 21.

Katz, J. (1978) *White Awareness: Handbook for Anti-racist Training*, Norman: Oklahoma University Press.

Kavanagh, K., Duncan-McConnell, D., Greenwood, K., Trivedi, P. and Wykes, T. (2003) 'Educating in-patients about their medication – is it worth it?', *Journal of Mental Health*, 12(1): 71–80.

Keating, F. (2002) 'Black-led initiatives in mental health: an overview', *Research Policy and Planning*, 20(2): 9–20.

Keating, F. (2005) *4 Sight Mellow Drama: An Evaluation of Theatre as a Medium of Race Equality Training*, London: Sainsbury Centre for Mental Health.

Keating, F. (2006) 'Breaking the spiral of oppression: racism and race equality in the MH system', *Mental Health Today: A Handbook*, Brighton: Pavilion Publishing.

Keating, F., Robertson, D., McCulloch, A. and Francis, E. (2002) *Breaking the Circles of Fear. A Review of the Relationship between Mental Health Services and African and Caribbean Communities*, London: Sainsbury Centre for Mental Health.

Kennedy, H. (2004) *Just Law. The Changing Face of Justice – and Why It Matters To Us All*, London: Chatto and Windus.

Killaspy, H., Dalton, J., McNicholas, S. and Johnson, S. (2000) 'Drayton Park, an alternative to hospital admission for women in acute mental health crisis', *Psychiatric Bulletin*, 24: 101–104.

Kirmayer, L. (2006) 'Culture and psychotherapy in a Creolizing world', *Transcultural Psychiatry*, 43(2): 163–168.

Kloos, B. (2005). 'Creating new possibilities for promoting liberation, well-being, and recovery: learning from experiences of psychiatric consumers/survivors', in G. Nelson and I. Prilleltensky (eds) *Community Psychology: In Pursuit of Well-being and Liberation*, London: Macmillan, pp. 426–447.

Knowles, C. (1991) 'AfroCaribbeans and schizophrenia: how does psychiatry deal with issues of race, culture and ethnicity?' *Journal of Social Policy*, 20(2): 173–190.

Kohut, H. (1997) *The Restoration of the Self*, New York: International Universities Press.

Krause, I-B. and Miller, A.C. (1995) 'Culture and family therapy', in S. Fernando (ed.) *Mental Health in a Multi-ethnic Society: A Multi-disciplinary Handbook*, London: Routledge, pp. 148–171.

Lago, C. (1996) *Race, Culture and Counselling*, Buckingham: Open University Press.

Lambo, A. (1969) 'Traditional African cultures and Western medicine', in F.N.L. Poynter (ed.) *Medicine and Culture*, London: Wellcome Institute of the History of Medicine, pp. 201–210.

Lasch-Quinn, E. (2001) *Race Experts: How Racial Etiquette, Sensitivity Training and New Age Therapy Hijacked the Civil Rights Revolution*, New York and Oxford: Rowman & Littlefield Publishers.

Lees, S. (2002) 'Gender, ethnicity and vulnerability in young women in local authority care', *British Journal of Social Work*, 32(7): 907–922.

Leff, J. (1973) 'Culture and the differentiation of emotional states', *British Journal of Psychiatry*, 123: 299–306.

Leff, J. (1981) *Psychiatry around the Globe. A Transcultural View*, New York: Marcel Dekker.

Leighton, A.H. and Hughes, J.M. (1961) 'Culture as causative of mental disorder', *Millbank Memorial Fund Quarterly*, 39(3): 446–470.

Leppard, D. (2006) 'Race chief warns of ghetto crisis', *The Sunday Times Online*, 18 September, pp. 1–3. Available: http://www.timesonline.co.uk/article/0,,2087-1785773,00.html (accessed 29 November 2006).

Lester, H. and Gask, L. (2006) 'Delivering medical care for patients with serious mental illness or promoting a collaborative model of recovery?' *British Journal of Psychiatry*, 188: 401–402.

Li, P.L., Logan, S., Yee, L. and Ng, S. (1999) 'Barriers to meeting the mental health needs of the Chinese community', *Journal of Public Health Medicine*, 21(1): 74–80.

Linnett, P. (1999) 'Thoughts on "user involvement"', *Openmind*, 98: 18–20.

Lipsky, S. (1987) *Internalised Racism*, Seattle: Rational Island Publishers.

Little, A. (1975) 'The educational achievement of ethnic minority children in London schools', in G. Verma and C. Bagley (eds) *Race and Education across Cultures*, London: Heinemann, pp. 48–69.

Littlewood, R. and Lipsedge, M. (1989) *Aliens and Alienists. Ethnic Minorities and Psychiatry*, London: Unwin Hyman.

Lloyd, K. and Fuller, E. (2002) 'Use of services', in K. Sparton and J. Nazroo (eds) *Ethnic Minority Psychiatric Illness Rates in the Community (Empiric)*, London: Policy Studies Institute, pp. 101–115.

Local and Regional Government Research Unit (2003) *Research*

Summary. Evaluation of the Long-term Impact of the Best Value Regime, London: Office of the Deputy Prime Minister.

Lombroso, C. (1871) *L'uomo bianco e l'uomo di colore: letture sull'origine e varietá delle razze umane* (White Man and the Coloured Man: Observations on the Origin and Variety of the Human Race), Padua.

Lombroso, C. (1911) *Crime: Its Causes and Remedies*. Trans. H.P. Horton, London: Heinemann.

Lorde, A. (1984) *Sister Outsider*, Trumansburg, NY: Cross Press.

Lowe, F. (2006) 'Containing persecutory anxiety: child and adolescent mental health services and black and minority ethnic communities', *Journal of Social Work Practice*, 20(1): 5–25.

Luthra, M. and Oakley, R. (1991) *Combating Racism through Training: A Review of Approaches to Race Training in Organisations*. Policy paper in Ethnic Relations, No. 22, Coventry: Centre for Research in Ethnic Relations.

McGovern, D. and Cope, R. (1987) 'The compulsory detention of males of different ethnic groups, with special reference to offender patients', *British Journal of Psychiatry*, 150: 505–512.

McKenzie, K. (2007) 'Being black in Britain is bad for your health', *Guardian*, 2 April. Available: http://society.guardian.co.uk/socialcare/comment/0,,2048216,00.html (accessed 28 June 2007).

Mahtani, A. (2003) 'The rights of refugee clients to an appropriate and ethical psychological service', *International Journal of Human Rights*, 7(1): 40–57.

Malek, M. and Joughin, C. (1998) *Mental Health Services for Minority Ethnic Children and Adolescents*, London: Jessica Kingsley.

Malik, R. (1988) Report on service delivery of Asian counselling service. Unpublished document.

Mathes, E. (1981) 'Maslow's hierarchy of needs as a guide for living', *Journal of Humanistic Psychology*, 21: 69–72.

Maule, M., Trivedi, P., Wilson, A. and Dewan, V. (2007) 'A journey – with faith', in M.E. Coyte, P. Gilbert and V. Nicholls (eds) *Spirituality, Values and Mental Health*, London: Jessica Kingsley, pp. 89–101.

Medical Foundation (2003) *Suicide in Asylum Seekers and Refugees – Medical Foundation Response to the Department of Health's Consultation Document National Suicide Prevention Strategy for England*. Available: http://www.torturecare.org.uk (accessed 27 September 2007).

Mental Capacity Act (2005) London: The Stationery Office.

Mental Health Act (1983) London: Her Majesty's Stationery Office (HMSO).

Mental Health Act (2007) (Chapter 12) London: The Stationery Office.

Mental Health Act Commission (1987) *Second Biennial Report 1985–87*, London: HMSO.

Mental Health Act Commission (1989) *Third Biennial Report 1987–1989*, London: HMSO.

Mental Health Act Commission (1991) *Fourth Biennial Report 1989–1991*, London: HMSO.

Mental Health Act Commission (2006) *Count Me In: The National Mental Health and Ethnicity Census. 2005 Service User Survey*, Nottingham: Mental Health Act Commission.

Mental Health Task Force (1994) *Black Mental Health – A Dialogue for Change*, London: Department of Health.

Metropolitan Police Authority (2004) *Report of the MPA Scrutiny on MPS Stop and Search Practice*, London: Metropolitan Police Authority.

Metropolitan Police Authority (2007) *Borough Breakdown of Stops and Searches under the Terrorism Act between April and August 2007*, London: Metropolitan Police Authority. Available: http://www.met. police.uk (accessed 27 September 2007).

Mezzina, R. (2005) 'Paradigm shift in psychiatry', in S. Ramon and J.E. Williams (eds) *Mental Health at the Crossroads. The Promise of the Psychosocial Approach*, Aldershot: Ashgate, pp. 81–93.

Miller, P. and Rose, N. (1986) *The Power of Psychiatry*, Cambridge: Polity Press.

Milne, A. and Chryssanthopoulus, C. (2005) 'Dementia care-giving in black and Asian populations: reviewing the research agenda', *Journal of Community and Applied Psychology*, 15(5): 319–337.

Mind (2003a) *Statistics Factsheet 1: How Common is Mental Distress?*, London: Mind.

Mind (2003b) *Statistics Factsheet 3: Race, Culture and Mental Health*, London: Mind.

Mizra, M. (2005) *Ticking All the Boxes*. Available: http://news.bbc.co.uk (accessed February 2007).

Molnar, S. (1983) *Human Variation. Races, Types and Ethnic Groups*, 2nd edn, Englewood Cliffs, NJ: Prentice-Hall.

Moncrieff, J. (2007) 'The re-institutionalisation of mental health care', *Openmind*, 146: 23.

Montgommery, P., Tompkins, C., Forchuk, C. and French, S. (2006) 'Keeping close: mothering with serious mental illness', *Journal of Advanced Nursing*, 54(1): 20–28.

Moodley, P. and Thornicroft, G. (1988) 'Ethnic group and compulsory detention', *Medicine, Science and the Law*, 28: 324–328.

Morel, B-A. (1852) *Traite des Mentales*. Paris: Masson.

Muinteras (1996) *Researching Irish Mental Health: Issues and Evidence – A Study of the Mental Health of the Irish Community in Haringey*, London: Muinteras.

National BME Mental Health Network (2006) *Proposed Amendments to*

Mental Health Act 1983. Available: http://www.bmementalhealth.org.uk (accessed 10 December 2006).

National Health Service (NHS) and Commission for Racial Equality (CRE) (2004) *NHS Strategic Health Authority Race Equality Guide. A Performance Framework*, London: North Central London Strategic Health Authority. Available: http://www.cre.gov.uk (accessed 7 February 2007).

National Institute for Mental Health (2003) *Engaging and Changing: Developing Effective Policy for the Care and Treatment of Black and Minority Ethnic Detained Patients*, London: Department of Health.

National Institute for Mental Health in England (NIMHE) (2002) *First Year Strategy for Mental Health in England*, London: NIMHE.

National Institute for Mental Health in England (NIMHE) (2003) *Inside Outside. Improving Mental Health Services for Black and Minority Ethnic Communities in England*, London: Department of Health.

National Statistics (2004) *Ethnicity and Identity: Education*, London: Office for National Statistics. Available: http://www.statistics.gov.uk/cci/nugget.asp?id=461 (accessed 30 November 2006).

Newbigging, K., McKeown, M., Hunkins-Hutchinson, E.A. and French, B., with Habte-Mariam, Z., Coleman-Hill, L., Mullings, D., Stephens, A. and Holt, K. (2007) *Developing Mental Health Advocacy with African and Caribbean Men*, London: Social Care Institute for Excellence (SCIE).

Newham Innercity Multifund and Newham Asian Women's Project (1998) *Young Asian Women and Self-Harm: A Mental Health Needs Assessment of Young Asian Women in Newham, East London: A Qualitative Study*, London: Newham Innercity Multifund and Newham Asian Women's Project.

Norfolk, Suffolk and Cambridgeshire Strategic Health Authority (2003) *Independent Inquiry into the Death of David Bennett* (Chairman: Sir John Blofeld), Cambridge: Norfolk, Suffolk and Cambridgeshire Strategic Health Authority.

Oates, M. (1997) 'Patients as parents; the risk to children', *British Journal of Psychiatry*, 170: 22–27.

Office for National Statistics (2004) *Focus on Gender*, London: Office for National Statistics.

Owen, S. and Milburn, C. (2001) 'Implementing research findings into practice: improving and developing services for women with serious and enduring mental health problems', *Journal of Psychiatric and Mental Health Nursing*, 8: 221–231.

Palmer, S. (ed.) (2002) *Multicultural Counselling. A Reader*, London: Sage Publications.

Papadopoulos, R. (2003) 'The Papadopoulos, Tilki and Taylor model for the development of cultural competence in nursing', *Journal of Health, Social and Environmental Issues*, 4(1): 5–7.

Parker, D. and Song, M. (2001) 'Introduction: rethinking "mixed race"', in D. Parker and M. Song (eds) *Rethinking 'Mixed Race'*, London: Pluto Press, pp. 1–22.

Parsons, C. (2005) *Minority Ethnic Exclusions and the Race Relations (Amendment) Act 2000 Interim Summary – November 2003*. Available: http://www.dfes.gov.uk/exclusions/uploads/Minority%20Ethnic%20Exclusions%20Interim%20Findings%20Final.doc (accessed 30 November 2006).

Patel, N. (2003) 'Clinical psychology: reinforcing inequalities or facilitating empowerment?', *International Journal of Human Rights*, 7(1): 16–39.

Patel, N. and Fatimilehin, I. (1999) 'Racism and mental health', in C. Newnes, G. Holmes and C. Dunn (eds) *This is Madness: A Critical Look at Psychiatry and the Future of Mental Health Services*, Ross-on-Wye: PCCS Books, pp. 51–73.

Peay, J. (2000) 'Reform of the Mental Health Act 1983: squandering an opportunity', *Journal of Mental Health Law*, February, pp. 5–15.

Peck, E., Gulliver, P. and Towel, D. (2002) 'Information, consultation or control: "user involvement" in mental health services in England at the turn of the century', *Journal of Mental Health*, 11: 441–451.

Pedersen, P.B., Draguns, J.G., Lonner, W.J. and Trimble, J.E. (1981) *Counselling across Cultures*, revised and expanded edn, Honolulu: University Press of Hawaii.

Pegg, L.C. (1997) 'Diversity training and education in the workplace', *Journal for Vocational Special Needs Education*, 19(2): 62–66.

Peppard, N. (1981) 'Towards effective race relations training', *Journal of Intergroup Relations*, 9(3): 35–45.

Perkins, R. (ed.) (1996) *Women in Context: Good Practice in Mental Health Services for Women*, London: Good Practices in Mental Health.

Philpot, M., Collins, C., Trivedi, P., Treolar, A., Gallacher, S. and Rose, D. (2004) 'Eliciting users' views of ECT in two mental health Trusts using a user-designed questionnaire', *Journal of Mental Health*, 13(4): 403–413.

Pick, D. (1989) *Faces of Degeneration. A European Disorder, c. 1848–c. 1918*, Cambridge: Cambridge University Press.

Pieterse, J.N. (1992) *White on Black. Images of Africa and Blacks in Western Popular Culture*, New Haven and London: Yale University Press.

Pilgrim, D. (2005) 'Foreword', in S. Ramon and J.E. Williams (eds) *Mental Health at the Crossroads. The Promise of the Psychosocial Approach*, Aldershot: Ashgate, pp. xii–xiii.

Pitt, L., Kilbride, M., Nothard, S., Welford, M. and Morrison, A.P. (2007) 'Researching recovery from psychosis: a user-led project', *Psychiatric Bulletin*, 31(2): 55–64.

Porter, H. (2007) 'After a sinister year, it's down to us to protect our freedoms', *Observer*, 31 December, p. 21.

Porter, M. and Haslam, N. (2005) 'Pre-displacement and post-displacement factors associated with the mental health of refugees and internally displaced persons: a meta-analysis', *Journal of the American Medical Association*, 294: 602–612.

Porter, R. (1990) *Mind-forged Manacles. A History of Madness in England from the Restoration to the Regency*, Harmondsworth: Penguin Books (first published, London: Athlone Press, 1987).

Poulter, S. (1990) *Cultural Pluralism and its Limitations: A Legal Perspective*, London: Commission for Racial Equality. Available: http://www. catalystmagazine.org/catalyst/Cultural-Pluralism-and-its-Limits.pdf (accessed 28 November 2006).

Powell, E. (2002) *We Care Too – a Good Practice Guide for People Working with Black Carers*, London: Afiya Trust.

Powney, J. (2002) 'A decade of change', *Scottish Council Research in Education (SCRE) Newsletter*, 70: 1–5. Available: http://www.scre.ac.uk (accessed 12 December 2006).

Priebe, S., Badesconyi, A., Fioritti, A., Hansson, L., Kilian, R., Torres-Gonzales, F., Turner, T. and Weisman, D. (2005) 'Re-institutionalisation in mental health care: comparison of data on service provision from six European countries', *British Medical Journal*, 330: 123–126.

Prilleltensky, I. (1989) 'Psychology and the status quo', *American Psychologist*, 44: 795–802.

Pugh, J.F. (1983) 'Astrological counseling in contemporary India', *Culture, Medicine and Psychiatry*, 7: 279–299.

Race Relations Act (1965) London: Her Majesty's Stationery Office (HMSO).

Race Relations Act (1968) London: Her Majesty's Stationery Office (HMSO).

Race Relations Act (1976) London: Her Majesty's Stationery Office (HMSO).

Race Relations (Amendment) Act (2000) London: The Stationery Office.

Raine, R. (2000) 'Does gender bias exist in the use of specialist health care?' *Journal of Health Services Research and Policy*, 5(4): 237–249.

Repper, J. and Perkins, R. (2003) *Social Inclusion and Recovery. A Model for Mental Health Practice*, London: Baillière Tindall.

Rogers, D. (2001) 'Diversity training: good for business but insufficient for social change', *Western States Center Views*, Winter, pp. 12–13.

Roland, A. (1996) *Cultural Pluralism and Psychoanalysis. The Asian and North American Experience*, New York and London: Routledge.

Said, E.W. (1978) *Orientalism. Western Conceptions of the Orient*, London: Routledge & Kegan Paul (reprinted with a new Afterword, Harmondsworth: Penguin, 1995).

Sainsbury Centre for Mental Health (2007) *Guide to User-focused Monitoring*, London: Sainsbury Centre for Mental Health.

St John, T. (2002) *Into the Mainstream. A Review of the Women's Mental Health Strategy*, Updates, vol. 4, part 7, London: Mental Health Foundation.

Sampson, E. (1993) *Celebrating the Other. A Dialogic Account of Human Nature*, New York: Harvester Wheatsheaf.

Samuel, M. (2007) 'Commission for Racial Equality slams government over Mental Health Bill'. Available: http://www.communitycare.co.uk/Articles/2007/06/19/104841 (accessed 2 July 2007).

Sartre, J-P. (1948) *Antisemite and Jew*, New York: Schocken Books.

Sarup, M. (1996) *Identity, Culture and the Postmodern World*, Edinburgh: Edinburgh University Press.

Sashidharan, S.P. (2001) 'Institutional racism in British psychiatry', *Psychiatric Bulletin*, 25: 244–247.

Schrank, B. and Slade, M. (2007) 'Recovery in psychiatry', *Psychiatric Bulletin*, 31: 321–325.

Scull, A. (1977) *Decarceration. Community Treatment and the Deviant. A Radical View*, Englewood Cliffs, NJ: Prentice Hall (2nd edn, Cambridge: Polity Press, 1984).

Seabrook, J. (2004) 'Religion as a fig leaf for racism', *Special Report: Race in the UK, Guardian*, 23 July. Available: http://www.guardian.co.uk/race/story (accessed 29 January 2007).

Sen, A. (2006) *Identity and Violence. The Illusion of Destiny*, London: Allen Lane.

Shoenberg, E. (1972) *A Hospital Looks at Itself*, London: Bruno Casirer.

Shorter, E. (1997) *A History of Psychiatry from the Era of the Asylum to the Age of Prozac*, New York: Wiley.

Simpson, L. (2004) 'Statistics of racial segregation; measures, evidence and policy', *Urban Studies*, 41(3): 661–681.

Singh, S.P. and Burns, T. (2006) 'Race and mental health: there is more to race than racism', *British Medical Journal*, 333: 648–651.

Singh, S.P., Greenwood, N., White, S. and Churchill, R. (2007) 'Ethnicity and the Mental Health Act 1983', *British Journal of Psychiatry*, 191: 99–105

Skrivánková, K. (2006) *Trafficking for Forced Labour: UK Country Report*, London: Anti-Slavery International. Available: http://www.slavery.org (accessed 10 August 2007).

Smith, L. (2007) 'Silent minority', Society supplement, *Guardian*, 26 September, p. 15.

Social Enterprise Unit (2002) *Social Enterprise: A Strategy for Success*, London: Department of Trade and Industry (DTI). Available: http://www.dti.gov.uk (accessed 27 January 2007).

Social Exclusion Unit (2000) *Minority Ethnic Issues in Social Exclusion and Neighbourhood Renewal*, London: Cabinet Office.

Social Exclusion Unit (2003) *Mental Health and Social Exclusion*, London: Office of the Deputy Prime Minister.

Social Services Inspectorate (1998) *They Look After Their Own, Don't They? Inspection of Community Care Services for Black and Ethnic Minority Older People*, London: Department of Health.

Special Hospitals Service Authority (SHSA) (1993) *Report of the Committee of Inquiry into the Death in Broadmoor Hospital of Orville Blackwood and a Review of the Deaths of Two Other Afro-Caribbean Patients: 'Big, Black and Dangerous?'* (Chairman: Professor H. Prins), London: SHSA.

Sperry, L. (2001) *Spirituality in Clinical Practice*, Hove and Philadelphia: Brunner-Routledge.

Stevens, A. and Raftery, J. (1992) 'The purchasers' information requirements on mental health needs and contracting for mental health services', in G. Thornicroft, C.R. Brewin and J. Wing (eds) *Measuring Mental Health Needs*, London: Gaskell, pp. 42–61.

Swinton, J. (2001) *Spirituality and Mental Health Care. Rediscovering a Forgotten Dimension*, London: Jessica Kingsley.

Tait, L. and Lester, H. (2005) 'Encouraging "user involvement" in mental health services', *Advances in Psychiatric Treatment*, 11: 168–175.

Tamkin, P., Aston, J., Cummings, J., Hooker, H., Pollard, E., Rick, J., Sheppard, E. and Tackey, N.D. (2002) *A Review of Training in Racism Awareness and Valuing Cultural Diversity*, Brighton: Institute for Employment Studies.

Tedeschi, R.G. and Calhoun, L.G. (1995) *Trauma and Transformation: Growing in the Aftermath of Suffering*, Thousand Oaks, CA: Sage Publications.

Telegraph (2007) 'The negative effects of unfettered immigration', *Telegraph online*, 20 September. Available: http://www.telegraph.co.uk (accessed 20 September 2007).

Terrorism Act (Chapter 11) (2000) London: The Stationery Office.

Tew, J. (2005) 'Power relations, social order and mental health', in J. Tew (ed.) *Social Perspectives in Mental Health*, London: Jessica Kingsley, pp. 71–89.

Tew, J., Gell, C. and Foster, S. (2004) *Learning from Experience – Involving Service Users and Carers in MH Education and Training*, York: Mental Health in Higher Education/National Institute for Mental Health in England/West Midlands/Trent Workforce Development Confederation.

Thomas, A. and Sillen, S. (1972) *Racism and Psychiatry*, New York: Brunner/Mazel.

Thomas, B. and Dorling, D. (2007) *Identity in Britain. A Cradle-to-Grave Atlas*, Bristol: Policy Press.

Treacher, A. (2006) 'Something in the air: otherness, recognition and ethics', *Journal of Social Work Practice*, 20(1): 27–37.

Treasury (2002) *Cross Cutting Review of the Role of the Voluntary and Community Sector in Service Delivery*, London: HM Treasury.

Trivedi, P. (1996) 'Partners not adversaries', *Nursing Times*, 92(21): 59–60.

Trivedi, P. (1999) 'Writing the user chapter', *A Life in the Day*, 13(2): 20–24.

Trivedi, P. (2001) 'Never again', *Openmind*, 110: 19.

Trivedi, P. (2002) 'Racism, social exclusion and mental health', in K. Bhui (ed.) *Racism and Mental Health*, London: Jessica Kingsley, pp. 71–82.

Trivedi, P. (2004) 'Are we who we say we are or who you think we are?' *Asylum*, 14(4): 4–5.

Trivedi, P. (2007a) For Bhen Aum Shanti Shanti, in M.E. Coyte, P. Gilbert and V. Nicholls (eds) *Spirituality, Values and Mental Health: Jewels for the Journey*, London: Jessica Kingsley, pp. 67–69.

Trivedi, P. (2007b) 'SIMBA's diversity', in M.E. Coyte, P. Gilbert and V. Nicholls (eds) *Spirituality, Values and Mental Health: Jewels for the Journey*, London: Jessica Kingsley, pp. 243–249.

Trivedi, P. and members of SIMBA (2002) 'Let the tiger roar', *Mental Health Today*, August, pp. 30–33.

Trivedi, P. and Wykes, T. (2002) 'From passive subjects to equal partners – "user involvement" in research', *British Journal of Psychiatry*, 181: 468–472.

Ture, K. (formerly known as Stokely Carmichael) and Hamilton, C. (1992) *Black Power. The Politics of Liberation* (with new afterwords by the authors), New York: Vintage Books.

United Nations High Commissioner for Refugees (UNHCR) (1996) *Convention and Protocol Relating to the Status of Refugees. Text of the 1951 Convention Relating to the Status of Refugees and Text of the 1967 Protocol Relating to the Status of Refugees*, Geneva: Public Information Section UNHCR.

Walker, S. (2005) *Culturally Competent Therapy: Working with Children and Young People*, Basingstoke: Palgrave Macmillan.

Wallcraft, J. (2003) *On Our Own Terms. Users and Survivors of MH Services Working Together for Support and Change*, London: Sainsbury Centre for Mental Health.

Waltham Forest (2005) *Capital Volunteering Waltham Forest Strategic Plan*, London: London Borough of Waltham Forest.

Waltham Forest Economic Profile (2004) Available: http://www.waltham forest.gov.uk (accessed on 30 September 2007).

Ward, L. (2007) 'Where you live can be crucial to your future', *Guardian*, 8 September, pp. 16–17.

Warner, L. and Ford, R. (1998) 'Conditions for women in in-patient units: the Mental Health Act Commission 1996 national visit', *Mental Health Care*, 1(7): 225–228.

Webb, E. and Sergison, M. (2003) 'Evaluation of cultural competence and anti-racism training in child health services', *Archives of Disease in Childhood*, 88: 291–294.

Wellman, D. (1977) *Portraits of White Racism*, Cambridge: Cambridge University Press.

White, G.M. and Marsella, A.J. (eds) (1982) *Cultural Conceptions of Mental Health and Therapy*, Dordrecht: D. Reidal.

White, P. (ed.) (2005) *Biopsychosocial Medicine. An Integrated Approach to Understanding Illness*, Oxford: Oxford University Press.

Williams, J. and Scott, S. (2002) 'Service responses to women with mental health needs', *Mental Health Review*, 7(1): 6.

Wilson, M. (2001) 'Black women and mental health', *Feminist Review*, 68: 34–51.

Wilson, M. and Francis, J. (1997) *Raised Voices*, London: Mind.

Winnicott, D. (1965) *The Maturational Process and the Facilitating Environment*, New York: International Universities Press.

Winnicott, D. (1967) 'Mirror-role of mother and family in child development', in P. Lomas (ed.) *The Predicament of the Family: A Psychoanalytical Symposium*, London: Hogarth Press and the Institute of Psycho-Analysis, pp. 26–33.

Wrench, J. and Taylor, P. (1993) *A Research Manual on the Evaluation of Anti-discrimination Training Activities*, Geneva: International Labour Office.

Young, S.L. and Ensing, D.S. (1999) 'Exploring recovery from the perspective of people with psychiatric disabilities', *Psychosocial Rehabilitation Journal*, 22: 219–231.

Name index

Subject index